Ethics for Journalists

Richard Keeble

LONDON AND NEW YORK

On the whole human beings want to be good, but not too good, and not quite all of the time

George Orwell (*The Art of Donald McGill* 1941)

First published 2001
by Routledge
11 New Fetter Lane, London EC4P 4EE

Simultaneously published in the USA and Canada
by Routledge
29 West 35th Street, New York, NY 10001

Routledge is an imprint of the Taylor & Francis Group

© 2001 Richard Keeble

Typeset in Goudy Old Style and Syntax by Wearset, Boldon, Tyne and Wear
Printed and bound in Great Britain by MPG Books Ltd, Bodmin

British Library Cataloguing in Publication Data
A catalogue record for this book is available from the British Library

Library of Congress Cataloging in Publication Data
has been applied for

ISBN 0-415-24296-7 (hbk)
ISBN 0-415-24297-5 (pbk)

Ethics for Journalists

'Richard Keeble's book asks questions which dominate our working lives, and it is invaluable not just to working journalists and students, but to the reading and listening public on whom our work depends. There isn't a journalist who would not benefit from reading this book, especially if he or she attempts to answer some of the questions in it.' *Paul Foot*

Ethics for Journalists tackles many of the issues which journalists face in their everyday lives – from the media's supposed obsession with sex, sleaze and sensationalism, to issues of regulation and censorship. Its accessible style and question and answer approach highlight the relevance of ethical issues for everyone involved in journalism, both trainees and professionals, whether working in print, broadcast or new media.

Ethics for Journalists provides a comprehensive overview of ethical dilemmas and features interviews with a number of journalists, including the celebrated correspondent Phillip Knightley. Presenting a range of imaginative strategies for improving media standards and supported by a thorough bibliography and a wide ranging list of Websites, *Ethics for Journalists* considers many problematic subjects including:

- the representation of women, blacks, gays and lesbians, and the mentally ill
- controversial calls for a privacy law to restrain the power of the press
- journalistic techniques such as sourcing the news, doorstepping, deathknocks and the use of subterfuge
- the impact of competition, ownership and advertising on media standards
- the handling of confidential sources and the dilemmas of war reporting.

Richard Keeble is director of undergraduate studies in the Journalism Department at City University, London, and a former editor of *The Teacher*. He is the author of *The Newspapers Handbook*, now in its third edition.

Media Skills

Series Editor: Richard Keeble, City University, London
Series Advisers: Wynford Hicks and Jenny McKay, Napier University

The *Media Skills* series provides a concise and thorough introduction to a rapidly changing media landscape. Each book is written by media and journalism lecturers or experienced professionals and is a key resource for a particular industry. Offering helpful advice and information and using practical examples from print, broadcast and digital media, as well as discussing ethical and regulatory issues, *Media Skills* books are essential guides for students and media professionals.

Also in this series:

English for Journalists, 2nd edition
Wynford Hicks

Writing for Journalists
Wynford Hicks with Sally Adams and Harriett Gilbert

Interviewing for Radio
Jim Beaman

Producing for the Web
Jason Whittaker

Scriptwriting for the Screen
Charlie Moritz

Interviewing for Journalists
Sally Adams, with an introduction and additional material by Wynford Hicks

Researching for Radio and Television
Adele Emm

Reporting for Journalists
Chris Frost

Find more details of current *Media Skills* books and forthcoming titles at
www.producing.routledge.com

Contents

Preface   vii

1   Ethical controversies today: an overview   1

2   Regulating the mainstream media: dawdling in the last chance saloon?   13

3   At the root of relationships: sourcing dilemmas   26

4   The ethics of sleaze coverage: privacy, bugging, surveillance and subterfuge   47

5   Dumbing down or dumbing up? The tabloidisation controversy   61

6   Race/anti-racism matters   71

7   Getting the representation right: tackling issues over gender, mental health, disability, HIV/AIDS and gays/lesbians   84

8   Battling for news: the dilemmas of war reporting (and not just on the frontline)   97

9   Constraints on journalists   110

10   The ethical challenge: how you may respond   124

11   And finally: more useful websites   147

Bibliography   148

Index   157

Preface

The main focus of this text is on the everyday ethical challenges facing media workers. Yet I'm also also aiming to raise some of the fundamental questions about the goals of journalism, the media's relation to the state and the impact of hyper-competition on journalists' behaviour. A wide range of possible responses is identified. In the face of the complex ethical/political challenges posed by the modern media it is perhaps not surprising that many journalists settle for the easy life of quiet compromise. The questioning approach I have adopted challenges that consensus, seeking to encourage reflection – and inspire action. And, while so much of the ethical debate appears the preserve of an elite, remote from the everyday concerns of working journalists and media consumers, I hope the questioning approach helps highlight its relevance to everyone.

The bibliography contains a wide range of sources. But at times journalistic style is followed and references are omitted to avoid over-burdening the text.

Special thanks go to my colleagues in the Journalism Department of City University, London, who supported me during my sabbatical, providing me with the time to complete this work. Also belated thanks to Professor Howard Tumber, Phillip Knightley, Tessa Mayes, John Grubb, Waltraud Boxall, Nol van der Loop. Professor Thom Blair and Claude-Jean Bertrand deserve mentions, as do Christopher Cudmore, of Routledge – and Maryline Gagnère and Gabi Keeble for, once again, bearing with me as I buried myself in cuttings and books. Thanks also to Molly Keeble, Yves and Geneviève Gagnère for their love and support over the years and to whom this book is dedicated.

Great Abington, Cambridgeshire
September 2000

1
Ethical controversies today: an overview

WHY ETHICAL DILEMMAS ARE ESPECIALLY DIFFICULT TODAY

Ethical inquiry is crucial for all media workers – and managers. It encourages journalists to examine their basic moral and political principles; their responsibilities and rights; their relationship to their employer and audience; their ultimate goals. Self-criticism and the questioning approach are always required. But many factors in Britain are making ethical challenges particularly difficult today.

- The vastness of the media industry in Britain and its increasing globalisation may suggest it is impossible to apply general principles to all of them. For instance, one survey in 2000 suggested there were 20,000 stations globally broadcasting on the Web, any of them accessible with a simple click of a button (Karpf 2000).

- Along with the plethora of media outlets go the many journalistic roles: reporters, designers, sub-editors, reviewers, photographers, editors, freelances, broadcast producers, researchers, HTML experts. To complicate the situation further, rapid technological changes are impacting on journalists' jobs. The range of specific ethical dilemmas ends up being enormous. Is it possible to speak in general terms?

- The dominant journalistic culture stresses the importance of technical skills (this bias being intensified with the introduction of new technology, direct-input and multi-skilling) and 'on the job' experience. Accordingly, the reflective, analytical, ethical approach is downgraded. There is a general scepticism in the industry about 'political correctness' which is often linked with issues such as racism, sexism,

militarism and this serves to constrain further ethical debate amongst
mainstream journalists.

At a time of hyper-competition and falling circulations amongst the
media, the need for profits in an advertising/ratings-driven environment could be seen to outweigh all other considerations. Colin Sparks
(1999: 46) argues

> Newspapers in Britain are first and foremost businesses. They do not
> exist to report news, to act as watchdogs for the public, to be a check
> on the doings of government, to defend the ordinary citizens against
> abuses of power, to unearth scandals or to do any of the other fine
> and noble things that are sometimes claimed for the press. They exist
> to make money, just as any other business does. To the extent that
> they discharge any of their public functions, they do so in order to
> succeed as businesses.

Significantly, Joanna Prior, sacked as section editor at the *Sunday Telegraph* after just six months, having been director of Fourth Estate publishing company at the age of 26, said: 'One revelation was how
uninterested they are in their readers. They care about numbers, they
care about circulation.'

- Ethics implies freedom to choose. But journalists are constrained by so
  many factors – proprietors, fear, the law, time and space to name but a
  few. There is much talk about the freedom of the press but the freedom
  of the individual journalist (particularly of the young trainee) in any
  media operation is restricted by vested interests, routinised working
  practices and hierarchical, bureaucratic, organisational structures.

- Further questions complicate the issues: can, say, gender representations by journalists be considered without reference to the powerful
  stereotypes of male and female sexuality found in advertising, Hollywood films and TV soaps? Can journalistic ethics be separated from
  their broader cultural and political contexts?

- Moreover, while globalisation trends in media monopoly ownership
  increase along with the global ambitions of US/UK militarism, is it
  relevant and even possible to study media ethics in relation to one
  country, Britain, as here? Is it possible to discuss the relative cultural
  and political freedoms in the West without detailed reference to the
  suppression of such freedoms and the financial impoverishment in
  Second and Third World countries on which they are based?

THE MORAL PANIC OVER THE MEDIA

Significantly, ethical considerations have become a major preoccupation in dominant political circles since the end of the Cold War between the West and East (the North/South conflict, it is argued, continues). President Bush proclaimed the moral defence of the 'new world order' against 'evil monster' Saddam Hussein in 1991. Tory premier John Major talked of going 'back to basics', Labour PM Tony Blair preached a 'moral crusade' and boasted for a while of pursuing an 'ethical' foreign policy. The US/UK bombing of Serbia in 1999 was, according to the rhetoric, 'humanitarian'. Even Hollywood has joined in. Michael Mann's 2000 blockbuster, *The Insider*, about a *60-Minute* exposé of the tobacco industry (pulled when CBS detected a conflict with its commercial interests) was described in the *Big Issue* (6–12 March 2000) as 'that rarest of things: a story about ethical journalism'.

And while ethics dominates political discourse, a moral panic has emerged over the 'dumbing down' and 'tabloidisation' of the media – in both Britain and the United States. A typical view is expressed by Andrew Belsey and Ruth Chadwick (1992: 4): 'In the light of the problems the world faces, the typical daily content of an American television channel or a British tabloid newspaper is not just a shame but a crime.' Politicians' concerns were summed up in a Commons Early Day Motion in 1996 – signed by 46 MPs – which deplored 'the steep decline in serious reporting and analysis of politics and current affairs in the UK', and 'notes that this decline has gathered pace in recent times with the increasing emphasis on personalities rather than policies and on trivia rather than substance'.

Surveys of public opinion place journalists at the bottom of 15 groups in terms of public credibility – even below politicians. Phil Hall (2000), former editor of the *News of the World*, comments: 'One of the most frustrating parts of working on the *NoW* was the lack of trust the public has in journalists.' The British Social Attitudes survey revealed that only 15 per cent of readers trust national newspaper journalists to pursue the truth above getting a good story. According to Postman (1985: 4), entertainment has become the supra-ideology; the natural format for the representation of all experience. 'Our politics, religion, news, athletics, education and commerce have been transformed into congenial adjuncts of show business, largely without protest or even much popular notice. The result is that we are a people amusing ourselves to death.' Franklin (1997) bewails the spread of trashy 'newzak'. And Ian Jack (1999) condemns the media's 'fickle, orgasmic sensationalism. Every branch is infected'.

During the 1990s major controversies emerged over invasions of privacy by the media, particularly of celebrities, male Tory MPs, a certain US President and various randy royals. And calls grew, supported by some prominent journalists, for the introduction of privacy laws such as in Germany where politicians' private lives (marriage problems, sexual inclinations and so on) are protected. The media in general, and not just the red-top tabloids, were accused of promoting 'bonk journalism', being obsessed with sex, sleaze and 'human interest'. Interestingly, Tessa Hilton, editor of the *Sunday Mirror*, when asked what her perfect story was, replied: 'A cabinet minister who is married and having an illicit affair with some very big name actress who is very glamorous . . . and we have got pictures' (the *Guardian*, 11 March 1996). Kelvin MacKenzie, former editor of the *Sun* and chairman and chief executive of TalkSport radio, made clear his own priorities: 'I wish there was more sex in the *News of the World*. I look to it for a good dollop of shagging and if I don't get it I feel robbed' (*The Times*, 17 March 2000). Right-wing commentators such as Mark Steyn (1998) blame the human interest obsessions of the media on the 'sentimentalisation' of the broader culture.

Even a central theme of 1999 Booker prize-winning novel, *Amsterdam* (London: Vintage), by Ian McEwan, had as its central theme the growth of chequebook journalism according to which news and information becomes a commodity to sell to the highest bidder. Serious political analysis and coverage is said to be giving way to 'attack journalism' with politicians (within a corrupted civil society) trading good-sounding but essentially simplistic 'sound-bites' at each other. In 1996, the publication in the US of James Fallows' *Breaking the News: How the Media Undermine American Democracy* drew claims that a similar process was at work in Britain. Andrew Marr (1999), for instance, commented on the media's 'culture of abuse': 'It is acid. It is eating away at the thoughtful culture of public discourse, burning out nuance, gobbling up detail, dissolving mere facts. And that, in turn, cannot help a struggling democracy.'

Alongside these criticisms go concerns over a decline in straight reporting and the arrival on the media scene of a New Punditocracy with their often under-researched comment pieces mixing extremist views, speculation, gossip, innuendo and abuse (Glover 1999; Heller 1999). As Nick Cohen argues (1999: 125): 'Those who believe in the information revolution should measure the space in newspapers filled with consumer and show-business journalism, trite features and opinion from the same pundits who – the best fat can be chewed for ever – will be back on television later in the day to read out their columns.' Political coverage is said to be coming under the growing dominance of 'spin-doctors' – a clique of unelected, though immensely powerful officials. Even the mainstream media began to demonise Alastair Campbell, Tony Blair's personal spin-doctor (Oborne 1999). As publicists such as Max Clifford came to outnumber journalists, PR-manufactured pseudo-events won increasing media space (Boorstin 1962).

The depoliticisation of the media and their obsessions with sport, lifestyles, sex, health and single events (such as the O.J. Simpson trial, the Gulf War, the death of Princess Diana) are said to be transforming citizens into indifferent consumers. Some critics even argue that media saturation of the cultural space is leading to political apathy (Bourdieu 1998). Critics have also focused on the rundown of foreign news coverage (with the media becoming paradoxically more parochial while communications systems are increasingly globalised) and the narrowing of range of debate permitted. Journalists are also accused of being too close to the political establishment. As Franklin (op. cit.: 30) argues

> The spheres of journalism and government increasingly overlap as journalists and politicians have grown mutually reliant, with each pursuing goals which can only be achieved with some degree of co-operation from the other. Contra the image of journalists as independent of government, many observers consider it more accurate to describe their relationship as collusive.

At the same time, the dissenting voices of feminists, peace campaigners, environmental activists, anarchists, lesbians and gays, it is claimed, have been marginalised or even demonised – in ways so acutely dissected in Heinrich Böll's *The Lost Honour of Katarina Blum* (Harmondsworth: Penguin 1978). In May 2000, concerns over the impact of distorted media representations of women culminated with a British Medical Association report claiming that the promotion of rake thin models (such as Kate Moss and Jodie Kidd) was contributing to the rise in the number of people suffering from eating disorders.

Journalists themselves have highlighted failures of management ethics with the increasing stresses of the job, particularly with the launch of 24-hour news services and the information overload accompanying the spread of the Internet. Multi-skilling is seen as threatening the very future of journalistic professionalism. As Michael Bromley argues (Bromley and O'Malley 1997: 350):

> Multi-skilling contains the potential for the final fragmentation of journalism, enskilling some as 'entrepreneurial editors' but deskilling others to the status of machine hands and extensions of the computer.

In between there may develop several levels of employment as media-technicians-with-words (and pictures). None, however, will be journalists, as such.

Alongside the growth of union derecognition and the decentralisation of collective bargaining came management assaults on journalists' jobs, wages and conditions leading to fear, obsequiousness and conformism within newsrooms (Foot 1991). As American media theorist John C. Merrill argues (1996): 'The journalist finds that he has less and less incentive, encouragement or chance to exert his own creativity; he knows that his organisation demands more and more of his time and effort. He conforms or he suffers. So generally he conforms.'

BROADCASTING: PUBLIC SERVICE ETHOS UNDER THREAT?

Most people claim TV is their main source of national and international news. Every UK household has at least one radio and research undertaken by the Henley Centre for Forecasting suggests radio's popularity will grow still further in the future, particulary with the increase in car usage. More than 43.4 million people tuned into an average of 24 hours of radio each week in the first quarter of 2000, according to figures provided by the Radio Joint Audience Research Unit. Broadcasting's political, cultural and educational roles are, then, enormously significant. And ethical issues assume paramount importance. Concerns have recently focused on a wide range of issues. According to the critics, the preference for polemic over argument and superficiality instead of depth has created a superficial 'soundbite culture'. Over-confrontational, gladiatorial, entertainment-oriented interviewing techniques (by Jeremy Paxman and John Humphrys, for instance) are said to have led to 'hyperadversarialism' with the radio and TV interviewer becoming more important than the interviewed. Focusing on television's coverage of disasters, Tamar Liebes (1998: 75) argues that the new conditions make responsible journalism 'all but impossible . . . The decision to go to live coverage means scrapping all of the accepted norms. There is no time for investigative reporting which entails a lengthy process of interviewing sources, checking reliability, searching data, editing and so on.' Concerns also emerged over the ending of ITN's *News at Ten* in September 1998 and BBC moves in 2000 to shift its main evening news slot to 10 p.m., symbolising, it is claimed, the growth of 'soft', feature-led coverage and the marginalisation of 'hard' news coverage.

Commercial pressures are blamed for the spate of faked programmes (the most notorious being *The Connection* in which journalists concocted a story about heroin smuggling into Britain). Talk shows have been shown to have hired actors from talent agencies to pose as guests while controversies have exploded over TV 'reconstructions'. Trash TV has taken over from 'public service' programming particularly since television deregulation following the 1990 Broadcasting Act. Critics allege that television channels are now competing over the supply of soft porn, with philosopher Roger Scruton and the National Viewers and Listeners Association (founded by Mary Whitehouse as the 'Clean-up TV' campaign in 1963) claiming this amounts to a deliberate attack on 'family values'.

The glut of voyeuristic 'fly-on-the-wall'/'camera on the body' documentaries and docu-soaps (satirised in the Hollywood blockbusters, *The Truman Show* and *Being John Malkovich*) such as *Castaway 2000* and *Big Brother* (watchable 24 hours a day on the Web) are said to have raised serious issues relating to privacy and the lust for celebrity status. Dr Raj Persaud, a consultant psychiatrist at the Maudsley Hospital, London, commented on this new 'reality TV' genre: 'Is this just TV trying to keep pace with the Internet now that webcams can show you a couple losing their virginity or a woman giving birth?' Moreover, concerns were expressed over people's vulnerability before the seductive power of the media, with voyeur TV fuelling the creation of a superficial, vanity-pandering culture. As novelist David Lodge (2000) pointed out:

> The readiness of people to let programme makers into their homes, to answer the most intimate questions about their lives and to allow themselves to be filmed in the most undignified and unflattering situations never ceases to amaze and is some measure of the contemporary lust for celebrity. Very often the subjects complain after the transmission of the programmes in which they figure so disadvantageously that they were deceived by the producers.

Film-maker Roger Graef (2000) also argues that 'reality television' is increasingly failing to protect people's rights to privacy and dignity: 'These days, people put themselves in unbearable positions and simply do not realise they are doing it.'

Changes to the running of the BBC brought in by director-general John Birt were denounced as threatening the editorial integrity of the World Service, downgrading domestic radio services and unnecessarily boosting bureaucracy. As the BBC was transformed into an increasingly commercial enterprise, critics claimed it had been privatised 'by the back door' with over-emphasis on ratings and a major shift away from its public service ethos. According to media expert Professor Michael Tracey (2000), public service broadcasting was under threat not only in Britain but globally because of 'the rise of competitive new media and the ideological dominance of the market in almost every facet of life'. Plans announced in June 2000 to make BBC1 a popular, all-entertainment channel and divert more serious programmes on to alternative, niche channels were widely dismissed as 'culturally defeatist'. John Tusa, head of London's Barbican arts centre, commented (2000): 'The consequence of this numbers-led analysis by the BBC will be to bury 'culture' – clearly a dirty word in BBC strategy circles – in the distant regions of the unwatched BBC digital channels.'

From the political right have come allegations that the BBC is run by a bunch of left-wingers. Before the 1997 general election, Brian Mawhinney, chairman of the Conservative Party, protested that the corporation's journalists were displaying 'eager anticipation' at the prospect of a Labour victory. From the political left have come criticisms that the BBC is state propagandist, its board of governors a 'safe' collection of the Great and Good; its routine news values reflecting conventional racist, sexist and militarist assumptions. But governments have also routinely attacked broadcasters as the 'enemy within'. For instance, the controversial ban on Irish 'terrorist' organisations (the IRA, INLA, Sinn Fein, UDA) launched in October 1988 and finally dropped in 1994, denying 'terrorists' the 'oxygen of publicity' in Margaret Thatcher's celebrated words, followed TV news coverage of the killing of two British soldiers at the funeral of the IRA unit killed by the SAS in Gibraltar in March 1988 (Devenport 2000: 58–62).

Concerns are also growing that the concentration of ownership in the independent television sector is leading to a dull uniformity of coverage. After the 1990 Broadcasting Act, the ITV network fell into the hands of just a few media empires such as Michael Green's Carlton Communications and Lord Hollick's United News and Media and Granada. Legislation assisted these trends towards monopoly and cross-media ownership. From November 1996 newspapers with no more than 20 per cent of national circulation have been able to increase their holding in ITV companies while broadcasters have been allowed to expand up to 15 per cent of the total television audience. By 2000, the big newspaper and television companies were lobbying for all ownership constraints to be removed. Many saw Granada's purchase of the Meridian, Anglia and HTV franchises from United News and Media for £175 billion in July 2000 as a major step on the road towards a single owner for ITV with its £1.8 billion in annual advertising revenues. Concerns grew that ITV's centre of gravity would also shift south, and with it, advertising revenue and jobs, while the NUJ feared regional news would be the final casualty. Elsewhere the trend was similarly towards the 'convergence' of media companies: in June 2000, Seagram, Vivendi (formerly a utility company) and the French pay-TV channel Canal-Plus merged to form the world's second largest media company (valued at $100 billion) after Time Warner–AOL.

The Broadcasting Acts of 1990 and 1996 established a host of commercial local radio stations, and licences were granted to three new national stations: Talk Radio, Virgin Radio and Classic FM. But, as Williams argues (op. cit.: 247):

> On the surface the de-regulation of British radio would seem to offer diversity of programming. However, diversity is in reality limited by a number of factors. Most of Britain's local stations are owned by a small number of larger companies. Companies such as Radio Clyde, which controls virtually every radio station in Scotland, dominate large areas of the British Isles and commercial considerations make such companies play safe in the content of their stations. Output is dominated by talk and music.

Bob Franklin similarly complains (op. cit.: 14): 'Commercial local radio has little local identity and reports only a scattering of local news. Whether in Blackpool, Bristol or Basingstoke, ILR offers an unrelentingly tedious and uniform output.'

PRINT: STREETS OF SHAME?

In Britain, Fleet Street is now commonly known as the Street of Shame. Yet 80 per cent of adults read at least one national newspaper while 75 per cent read a Sunday (McNair 1996: 15). Mainstream newspapers comprise 101 dailies, 473 weeklies, 20 Sundays, 685 freesheets (Sparks 1999: 42) with some 69 per cent of all morning dailies edited in London. Their political, cultural and social roles are crucial – all the more so because they (and not TV) are the primary agenda setters. Moral concerns over recent years have focused on the spread of 'junk journalism' (Baistow 1985) epitomised with the emergence of the 'tits and bums'-obsessed *Daily Sport*. Launched on 17 August 1988, it was published originally only on three days a week but later became a six-day paper. Like *Sunday Sport* (launched in September 1986) it is owned by David Sullivan, his fortune based on the production of pornographic magazines, films and sex aids (Killick 1994). Both publications publish plainly invented stories – such as sightings of Elvis Presley and children conceived by aliens. Magazines such as *Loaded, FHM* and *Stuff* are blamed for spawning a male chauvinist, laddish culture while glossy women's monthlies have become increasingly dominated by one subject: sex (O'Sullivan 1999). In 1997, the right-wing Social Affairs Unit criticised them for portraying women as 'selfish, superficial and obsessed by sex'. GQ editor James Brown came under fire in February 1999 after his magazine named the Nazis among 'the smartest men of the 20th century'. Even teenage girls' magazines came under fire in 1996 from Peter Luff MP who proposed a private member's bill aiming to limit what he viewed as the over-use of sexual material in the publications.

Press obsessions with sleaze have led to growing calls by politicians – supported by the public in opinion polls – for privacy legislation to 'restrain' the prying press. Many argue that the hyper-competition amongst the national press, with the over-emphasis on scoop journalism, is the most serious factor behind the decline in standards. According to media commentator Roy Greenslade: 'Our scoop culture is a bizarre travesty of genuine journalism. It gives the impression of providing readers with wholly new and important news, yet most of it is the newspaper equivalent of theatrical illusion.' Concerns have also been expressed over the decline of investigative reporting (Foot 1999).

The cynical politics of the Fleet Street consensus – formerly largely pro-Tory now (bar three dailies and four Sundays) pro-Labour – has drawn criticisms just as its propaganda consensus in support of US/UK military adventurism – such as over Iraq in 1991 and Serbia in 1999 – is said to have marginalised calls for diplomatic restraint and constructive dialogue. The growing influence of the PR industry and spin-doctors on media content is reducing newspapers to being nothing more than publicity sheets for government and big business, so critics allege, while the growth of 'advertorials' (advertising copy written by journalists and flagged as such) is said to provide evidence of the power advertisers now wield over newspaper and magazine content. And concerns over racist and sexist content of newspapers have been accompanied by mounting protests over the institutional racism and sexism within the print industry.

The narrowing of the political debate in newspapers has been accompanied by a growing monopoly ownership of Fleet Street with the top four companies owning 90 per cent of total in circulation terms. Anti-monopoly legislation has actually been in existence for more than 30 years but has had little impact. As James Curran points out (2000: 45): 'Between 1965 and 1993, 151 transfers of newspaper ownership gained approval and only four (all relatively minor) were stopped.' Every major acquisition, such as Murdoch's purchase of The Times and Sunday Times, and the Guardian's purchase of the *Observer* were waived through by the government. Yet such trends towards monopolisation are global trends affecting not just media industries. As Peter Morgan stresses (2000), the top 200 companies now control a quarter of the world's economy. Also the growing control of the publishing industry by giant, multi-national companies (e.g. Rupert Murdoch's News International Corporation, Bertelsmann AG and the Dutch companies VNU and Elsevier) has led to calls for laws to prevent cross media ownership and such concentrations of power. Significantly the UK's magazine industry – with more than 3,000 mainstream periodical titles – is dominated by just two companies: IPC and EMAP. IPC (with 71 titles) was sold to Cinven, an investment company, in January 1998 for £860m. EMAP (with 90 consumer magazines) was valued in 2000 at £1.8 billion. Also in the magazine sector, recent years have seen an explosion of free customer titles where the stress is on publicity, not journalism. In 1998, only seven of the top 100 magazines in terms of circulation were from the customer publishing sector; in 2000, one third of the top 100 reached their readers free of charge.

Journalists have focused particularly on the slump in management standards, highlighting the scandal of low salaries in the provincial press. Despite the vast economic power of the mainstream press, a lively alternative print industry (ethnic minority/left-wing/peace movement/feminist/single-issue campaigning) survives against the odds – yet it tends to be ignored by both Fleet Street and academe. Critics allege this sector is too inward looking, concerned with esoteric, marginal issues and this is ultimately reflected in low circulations. Significantly, the left-wing *News on Sunday*, launched on 26 April 1987, lasted only six weeks (Chippendale and Horrie 1988) with blame directed at poor management, marketing and inadequate investment – the £6 million raised proving totally inadequate.

INTERNET: NEW MEDIA, NEW DILEMMAS

By 2000, just 25 per cent of British homes had Internet access (so still a small minority despite all the advertising-driven media hype), though this figure is expected to double in the following two years. When work access was included, the figure rose to around 40 per cent (Travis 1999). At the same time, a survey by the Consumers' Association magazine *Which?* found that one in four people refuses to acquire Internet access, considering it too expensive and irrelevant to their needs. Mainstream moral concerns over the Internet have tended to focus on the easy access it allows to extremist political views and pornography (particularly for children). Many Internet Service Providers (ISPs) say the network's main use is providing access to porn: amongst the top 15 words searched on Yahoo!UK were sex, *Playboy*, porn, porno, pussy. Concerns over children's vulnerability to paedophiles on the Internet have also mounted in the media. Critics argue that Internet usage for many is leading to information overload with users spending, on average, three hours a day e-mailing. On a national scale, such addiction is leading to a decline in social involvement and a rise in aggressive, selfish capitalism.

The Internet, it is claimed, will also accentuate moves towards the commodification and superficiality of the media's soundbite culture while the spread of anonymous and aggressive 'flaming' calls is said to be debasing the public sphere. There are also concerns that the Internet is reinforcing global structures of economic control rather than opening up new democratic possibilities. Some 85 per cent of the revenue from Internet businesses goes to American firms which hold 95 per cent of the stock market value of Internet properties. US sites are increasingly globalising their activities: Yahoo! for instance, has operations in 20 countries including Brazil, China, Denmark, Japan, Korea, Mexico, Norway, Singapore and Taiwan.

According to Anthony Thornton, editor of nme.com, one of Britain's most popular websites: 'Now the journalist needs to be a writer, sub-editor, designer, photographer, camera person, editor, technician and radio presenter to carry out online journalism effectively.' Concerns are mounting that such multi-skilling demands are, on a national scale, leading to a decline in standards. Since now anyone with Internet access can, in theory, set up their own media operation there are fears that this will lead to a 'deprofessionalisation' of the industry (Richstad 1999: 41).

2
Regulating the mainstream media: dawdling in the last chance saloon?

WHY BOTHER WITH ETHICAL CODES?

Ethical codes provoke a range of reponses from journalists (see Norden-streng 1997). Some regard them as vehicles of professionalisation, as a means of professional education, as instruments of consciousness-raising and as deliberate attempts by journalists to regulate the media and ward off legislation restricting their activities. Significantly, the first codes emerged in the first decade of the last century in Poland and the United States as part of the more general moves towards professionalisation. In Europe such codes were adopted gradually – after World War One (in Sweden, France and the UK), immediately after World War Two (Italy, Belgium) and around the late 1960s and 1970s (Spain, Portugal).

A contrasting response stresses the role of codes as mere rhetorical devices to preserve special privileges such as access to the powerful and camouflage hypocrisy. Some even argue that codes inherently restrict press freedom by encouraging certain patterns of behaviour and condemning others, while some suggest the media are more effectively regulated by the market, anyway. Critics claim that few journalists are aware of the content of codes, particularly when they are constantly being changed: the original Press Complaints Commission's code of 1991, for instance, has been amended 16 times. Guy Black, PCC director, however, claims the code's flexibility is its strength. 'Codes are meant to change from time to time. They need to be flexible documents especially in an industry like this.' Some journalists claim codes are there simply to be broken.

WHAT ARE THE PRINCIPAL UNDERLYING VALUES YOU CAN IDENTIFY IN THE CODES?

Some values are evident in codes throughout the world (Grevisse 1999; Laitila 1993):

- fairness;

- the separation of fact and opinion;

- the need for accuracy linked with the responsibility to correct errors; the deliberate distortion and suppression of information are condemned;

- maintaining confidentiality of sources;

- upholding journalists' responsibility to guard citizens' right to freedom of expression;

- recognising a duty to defend the dignity and independence of the profession;

- protecting people's right to privacy;

- respecting and seeking after truth;

- struggling against censorship;

- avoiding discrimination on grounds of race, sexual orientation, gender, language, religion or political opinions;

- avoiding conflicts of interests (particularly with respect to political and financial journalists/editors holding shares in companies they report on).

WHAT ARE THE MAJOR DIFFERENCES BETWEEN THE NUJ AND THE OTHER INDUSTRY CODES?

The National Union of Journalists' Code, first adopted in 1936, now incorporates 13 general principles (accessible at www.nuj.org.uk). Other codes tend to contain detailed specifications of what is deemed either ethical or unethical. But as Harris (1992: 67) points out:

> One of the consequences of bringing out detailed sets of regulations is that it fosters a loophole seeking attitude of mind. The result could be that journalists will come to treat as permissible anything that does not fit the precise specifications of unethical behaviour. Furthermore, short codes consisting of broad principles can often be applied to new types

of situation which could not have been envisaged by those drawing them up.

And Chris Frost (2000: 98) argues: 'A short code has the advantage of being easier for journalists to remember and use. They are able to measure directly their performance against the principles contained in the code and quickly realise when they are straying from the straight and narrow.'

The NUJ stopped using its code to discipline members after it was found to demoralise journalists in the 1980s. Now the code is seen more as a 'positive thing, a beacon for journalists to aim for rather than a means to punish', according to Tim Gopsill, the union's press officer. In contrast, the Institute of Journalists (www.cioj.dircon.co.uk) does discipline its members who breach its code. The PCC can force editors to publish adjudications. But it has no powers to fine a publication for breaching the code. In February 1998, the Lord Chancellor, Lord Irvine, demanded that the PCC should exact fines for breaches of the code, but this was simply ignored. Recently, national newspapers such as the *Guardian*, *Observer*, the *Independent* and *Daily Express* have supported calls for the introduction of fines but this has been strongly opposed by regional newspapers.

WHAT SUCCESS DID THE PRESS COUNCIL HAVE IN REGULATING STANDARDS?

Since World War Two, press standards have attracted constant concern from governments and politicians. A General Council of the Press was proposed by the first Royal Commission (1947–9) to safeguard press freedoms and encourage the development of a sense of public responsibility among journalists. Launched on 21 July 1953, its first ruling was that a *Daily Mirror* poll on whether Princess Margaret should marry Group Captain Townsend was 'contrary to the best traditions of British journalism' (how royal reporting has changed!).

A second Royal Commission, set up in 1961, followed continuing concerns over monopolies. It stressed the importance of including a lay element on the General Council but when the Press Council came into being in July 1963 it did so with 20 industry representatives and just five lay members. A third Royal Commission (1974–7) was particularly critical of the performance of the Press Council, making 12 recommendations to transform its operating procedures. These were largely rejected and the council remained a weak body, lacking the confidence of both managers and the NUJ and accused of being over-long in its adjudications on complaints.

Then in 1989, following a spate of controversies over press intrusions into private grief, the Thatcher government authorised a committee to investigate the possible introduction of a privacy law. Chaired by David Calcutt, master of Magdalene College, Cambridge, the committee in the end backed making physical intrusion an offence but opposed a privacy law. It also proposed the creation of a Statutory Press Complaints Tribunal, to be chaired by a judicial figure appointed by the Lord Chancellor, with powers to draw up a code of practice and investigate alleged breaches as well as stop publication of offending material, take evidence on oath and impose fines.

Quickly, to ward off such legislation and marginalise the NUJ (which had been represented on the Press Council but which was not invited on to the new body) the industry formed the Press Complaints Commission in the place of the Press Council to administer a code of practice. Based largely on the former Press Council's code and on the existing Newspaper Publishers' Association code, it covers such issues as accuracy, opportunity to reply, privacy, harassment, children in sex cases, misrepresentation, the coverage of victims of sexual assault, financial journalism, confidential sources and payment for articles (and is accessible at www.pcc.org.uk). Since 1990 many newspapers have incorporated the code into contracts of employment and express a commitment to it in their pages, though knowledge of its clauses remains low amongst journalists.

HOW CAN THE PERFORMANCE OF THE PCC BE RATED?

You may argue that the PCC has responded well to the rapidly evolving media environment of recent years. For instance, in December 1997, following the death of Princess Diana, the PCC responded to mounting concerns over invasions of privacy, harassment by reporters and paparazzi and cheque-book journalism by introducing major changes to its code. Lord Wakeham, its chairman, was moved to claim that the new code was 'the toughest in Europe'. New provisions included a tightening of areas considered 'private' and rules on the sensitive handling of news stories involving grief or shock. Payments to children for stories were also banned and the clauses on accuracy were expanded to include photographs. Rules on the investigation of stories were tightened with reporters banned from being involved in the 'persistent pursuit' of sources. In many cases, the former use of the words 'should' and 'may' were changed to 'must'. Stuart Higgins, the then editor of the *Sun*, commented on the new code: 'I and all *Sun* journalists are committed to implement it.'

In its 1997 annual report the PCC said it had 'extended its jurisdiction to certain publications on the Internet'. In November 1999, it condemned the magazine *FHM* over an article on student suicides; cheque book journalism, and the coverage of the royal family have both drawn rulings. In 2000, it issued special guidance to editors to protect Prince William's privacy after he left Eton. Provincial and national editors are some of the PCC's most vocal supporters. According to *Western Mail* editor Neil Fowler: 'Most journalists have it written into their contracts and editors discuss it every day.' Even David Yelland, editor of the *Sun*, said: 'Anybody who thinks the PCC doesn't have teeth is wrong because I can tell you it's the most horrible thing.' He was particularly impressed by its success in reducing the use of intrusive pictures by the paparazzi. 'I can turn down pictures in the full knowledge that none of my competitors can use them either. The way the two princes are pretty much left alone by the British press is an amazing achievement.' Supporters of the PCC also stress that it conducts business swiftly, resolving most complaints within three months. And the cost of any complaint is just the price of a first class stamp. Given the millions of words written and photographs published every year, very few people choose to complain, reflecting, it is claimed, the success of self regulation.

But you may choose to join the many critics who are equally vehement in their condemnation of the PCC as a toothless watchdog. According to Geoffrey Robertson (1993: 111): 'The PCC is a confidence trick which has failed to inspire confidence and 40 years' experience of "press regulation" demonstrates only that the very concept is an oxymoron.' Julian Petley (1999: 155) has these harsh words: 'To read its code's high-flown rhetoric about "accuracy", "opportunity to reply", "privacy", "harassment", "intrusion into grief or shock", "discrimination" and so on, and then to immerse oneself in the daily, debased reality of much of the British press, which quite clearly cares not a jot for such self-deluding nonsense, is all that is needed to understand why the PCC cannot be seriously regarded as a regulatory body.' Media sociologist James Curran is equally damning (2000: 41):

> All that the Press Council did, other than to adjudicate public complaints, was to develop from the 1960s onwards a low-key corporate role that included occasional pronouncements on ethical and freedom issues. Even this was largely abandoned when the Press Council was reincarnated as the PCC in 1991. It became simply a customer complaints' service, a far cry from the professionalising vocation to which it had been called with such wide-eyed hope by the first Royal Commission on the Press.

Tim Gopsill, of the NUJ, argues that the code is nothing more than a PR stunt. The best standards in journalism are at the *Guardian*, *Financial Times* and BBC, all places where there is full union recognition and bargaining, he says. The MP Clive Soley has constantly criticised the PCC over its failure to take a proactive role and accept complaints from third parties. But Lord McGregor of Durris, its first chairman, and Lord Wakeham, his successor, have argued that third-party complaints would open the way to a flood of letters from special interest groups.

WHAT OTHER FORMS OF REGULATION ARE IN PLACE IN BRITAIN?

Most media attention has focused on the PCC and the press' often wayward behaviour. But all the other sectors have regulatory bodies administering codes. Given the wide range of regulatory bodies for broadcasting and the growing media profile of telecoms (regulated by the Office of Telecommunications), a growing consensus emerged amongst mainstream commentators in 2000 that a single regulator for the two sectors would emerge. A name had even been coined for the new body: Ofcom.

The Broadcasting Standards Commission (BSC)

The BSC has two codes – on privacy and fairness – to administer (covering such issues as the use of hidden microphones and cameras, doorstepping, the handling of people suffering a personal tragedy and reporting on children) though its main priority is to monitor that programmes shown before 9 p.m. are suitable for children. Introduced in June 1998, interestingly they were the first journalists' codes (accessible at www.bsc.org.uk) in Britain demanded by statute – Section 107 of the Broadcasting Act 1996, to be precise. The Act also created the BSC by merging the Broadcasting Standards Council – formed by the Broadcasting Act of 1990 and dealing with alleged offences against taste and decency in the areas of sex, violence, bad language and treatment of disasters – with the Broadcasting Complaints Commission. This had been set up following the Labour government's Annan committee in 1981 and dealt with complaints over lack of factual accuracy, unfairness in presentation and intrusions into privacy. The act also relaxed the rules on cross-media ownership, much to the delight of the big media groups.

The BSC is chaired by Lady Elspeth Howe and has 13 members. It regulates all radio and television – both BBC and commercial – as well as text, cable, satellite and digital services. It can call a hearing at which the complainant, a representative of the broadcaster and other witnesses are able to give their version of events while its verdicts are published in a monthly bulletin. The broadcaster can also be ordered to publish the verdict on-air at the same time as the original programme.

The Independent Television Commission (ITC)

The role of the ITC, which replaced the Independent Broadcasting Authority in 1990, is to license and regulate all commercial television in the UK, including teletext, terrestrial, cable, digital and satellite services. Chaired by Patricia Hodgson, former head of the BBC's policy unit, it has its own code (accessible at www.itc.org.uk) and, unlike the PCC and BSC, can fine offending companies up to three per cent of their annual revenue for serious breaches of their licences. Moreover it has powers to issue reprimands for minor breaches or genuine mistakes over its code terms; to give formal warnings, ask for on-screen corrections or apologies, disallow repeats, impose fines for more serious matters; and to shorten a company's licence or withdraw it altogether. This it did controversially on 22 March 1999 when it closed down the Kurdish satellite station, Med-TV, for 21 days for allegedly supporting terrorist acts against Turkey. The station denied it was a direct supporter of the Marxist-oriented Kurdish Workers Party (PKK).

Its annual performance review is taken seriously by the industry. In May 1998, for instance, it commended ITN for its 'high-quality news coverage of foreign and domestic stories'. But it complained that foreign news was concentrated in *News at Ten*. 'The *Early Evening News* gave greater prominence to crime, show business and royal stories. In the ITC's view this bulletin requires a much more balanced agenda.' On regional news programmes, the ITC criticised Central News for an 'unwelcome move' away from hard news towards more lifestyle coverage, while Yorkshire Television's *Summer Special* editions were 'unoriginal and contrived' though popular with audiences. In May 2000, the ITC criticised the decision to cut *News at Ten* and gave the network a short deadline to improve its news coverage. In its annual report, published in the same month, the watchdog criticised ITV for over-use of security camera footage and lightweight, human interest stories in current affairs programmes, singling out *Tonight with Trevor McDonald*. But it praised ITN for its coverage of the Balkans and Eastern Europe, Jonathan Dimbleby's US interview series and John Pilger's documentary from East Timor. Then on 22 June 2000, it took the unprecedented decision of ordering the ITV companies to bring forward their evening news slot before 11 p.m.

The BBC *Producers' Guidelines*

The BBC also regulates its own performance through issuing detailed guidelines to producers (accessible at www.bbc.co.uk/info/editorial/ prodgl/contents.htm). Regularly revised, these cover a broad range of issues: including accuracy and fairness, taste and decency, privacy, the reporting of crime, political coverage and commercial relationships. They also incorporate a specific code on impartiality and accuracy and take account of the legal and statutory requirements on broadcasters, such as laws on defamation, national security and copyright and rules on advertising and sponsorship. The BBC governors (appointed by the Queen on the recommendation of ministers with the overall responsibility of monitoring the Corporation's performance) describe the guidelines as setting out 'the editorial and ethical principles that must underpin all BBC programmes'. New guidelines issued in February 2000 stressed the key BBC values as:

- impartiality,

- fairness,

- giving a full and fair view of people and cultures,

- editorial integrity and independence,

- respect for privacy,

- respect for standards of taste and decency,

- avoiding the imitation of anti-social and criminal behaviour,

- safeguarding the welfare of children,

- fairness to interviewees,

- respect for diverse audiences in the UK,

- independence from commercial interests.

Every year the BBC governors publish a report on the Corporation's performance. In recent years the report has been particularly critical, saying BBC1 was failing to win public support and lacking in quality. In turn, the governors have faced mounting criticisms that they are not sufficiently independent of BBC management and, by late 2000, they were expected to be placed under an independent regulator overseeing the entire broadcasting industry.

The Radio Authority (RA)

Set up in 1990 to replace the IBA's commercial radio responsibility, the RA is the watchdog for all national and local, cable, digital, satellite, hospital, community and student radio services (see www.radioauthority.org.uk). Though its main task is to organise frequencies so they do not overlap, it has several codes of practice covering news broadcasts, election campaigns, the portrayal of sex and violence, issues relating to taste and decency, religious programming, charity appeals, representations of royalty, privacy and accuracy in news and advice programmes. From June 2000, when a 'Memorandum of Understanding' was signed between the RA and BSC, privacy and fairness complaints have been handled by the commission, while the RA has continued to deal with licence-related standards matters.

There is also a code on advertising standards and programme sponsorship, as required by the 1990 Act. But it rejected calls in 2000 to draw up guidelines on how much local news should be aired by commercial radio stations. The RA has similar powers to the ITC, including sanctions such as on-air apologies and corrections, fines and the shortening or withdrawal of licences. For instance, it fined Huddersfield FM £5,000 for poor service including failure to broadcast a topical phone-in, not running educational features, inadequate sports coverage and no arts or entertainment features. Yet the Internet appears to have broken by stealth the RA's control over licensing. Spinner.com, for instance, offers more than 120 simultaneous channels offering every musical genre from Baroque to Latin pop. Moreover, Geoffrey Robertson (1993: 273) argues against the cosy consensus of the broadcast media: 'Speech is not free on British television and radio: it is cribbed and confined not merely by the laws which apply to all media but by a notion of what is "seemly" for a general audience to hear and view.'

Teenage Magazine Advisory Panel (TMAP)

The TMAP was set up by the Periodical Publishers Association (www.ppa.co.uk) after MPs expressed concern over the allegedly explicit sexual content of teenage magazines in 1996. TMAP guidelines to editors comprise (McGowan 2000: 27):

1. encouraging readers to take a responsible attitude to sex and contraception;

2. promoting safer sex in relevant articles;

3. stressing that under-age sex or sexual abuse is illegal;

4. giving the names of relevant professional organisations and using their guidance in advice pages;

5. encouraging readers to seek support from parents and other responsible adults;

6. explaining the emotional consequences of sexual activity.

In May 2000, the panel rejected complaints against an issue of *Bliss* which included articles such as 'Lewd quizzes' and 'Help, he wants oral sex'. Significantly, a survey in *Bliss* found that 75 per cent of readers considered teen magazines the best source of sex education, while only 28 per cent felt comfortable talking about sex with their parents.

The Internet Watch Foundation (IWF)

In January 2000, Internet Service Providers set up the IWF as an industry-funded, self-regulatory body aiming to remove child pornography from UK-administered web servers. But soon afterwards, the government asked the foundation to expand its remit. Internet Freedom founder Chris Ellison criticised the body for promoting a form of 'silent censorship'.

And are there still more?

Well, yes. This is not the end of media regulation! There are a host of other bodies and industrial practices which impact on journalists' behaviour. The Brussels-based International Federation of Journalists has its own succinct Declaration of Principles on the Conduct of Journalists. Its first clause stresses: 'Respect for truth and for the right of the public to truth is the first duty of the journalist.' The NUJ issues guidelines on such issues as covering race, disability and dealing with freelances. Strict guidelines are in force covering the broadcasting of parliament (Jones 1996: 17). Newspapers and magazines usually have their own style books which principally outline policies on such fundamental issues as the use of italics, capital or lower case letters for titles, spellings of words (jail or gaol?) but they can also cover ethical issues ranging from the avoidance of sexist and racist language and stereotyping, the coverage of children and disabled people, to the importance of maintaining the confidentiality of sources.

The readers' representative

Newspapers claim to represent their readers but are often slow to respond to their complaints. At least that was the view of Alan Rusbridger, editor of the *Guardian*. He commented: 'Newspapers generally are hopeless in customer relations. You would get a much better service at the gas board and Dixon's than you would from newspapers.' So he decided to appoint Ian Mayes as an American-style readers' representative who, every week, comments on the issues raised and supervises a daily 'Corrections and Clarifications' column. In addition, an external ombudsman looks after the serious complaints involving the integrity of the newspaper's staff – such as followed the deputy foreign editor, Victoria Brittain's brush with MI5 and the use of her bank account to channel funds for a libel action against the *Independent*. Mayes' column on 19 July 2000 was typical, carrying six corrections. In one, it was stated that the newspaper had failed to acknowledge that the author of an article was married to one of the people quoted. 'While we do not suggest this connection in any way influenced the content of the piece, failure to declare the connection is against the *Guardian*'s policy.'

Media campaigning bodies

In addition, there are a range of campaigning bodies seeking to improve media standards. They include PressWise; the Campaign for Press and Broadcasting Freedom (publisher of *Free Press*); Article 19 (*IXX Bulletin*); the World Association for Christian Communication (*Media Education*); Women in Publishing (see Reading 1999: 170–83) and think-tanks such as the International Broadcasting Trust, set up in 1989 by groups including Oxfam, Action Aid, WWF, Save the Children, Voluntary Service Overseas, Christian Aid and RSPB to promote more ethical foreign coverage.

WHAT CAN BRITAIN LEARN FROM THE EXPERIENCE OF MEDIA COUNCILS IN OTHER COUNTRIES?

Many critics argue that, in Britain, management and editorial functions have become too closely intertwined. In some other countries steps have been taken to prevent such developments. In Holland, for instance, newspaper companies have introduced statutes into their collective labour agreements separating the interests of the editor and management. Thus, if journalists object to any particular assignment they can raise the issue with an editorial council which also has a say in any merger or sale plans and on advertising matters. In Germany, some newspapers have agreed understandings with staffers giving them a voice in editorial decisions and in the editor-in-chief's selection. Similarly, the code to which Norwegian Editors' Association and National Association of Norwegian Newspapers are signatories (drafted in 1953 and revised in 1973), entitles editors to 'free and independent leadership of the editorial department and editorial work and full freedom to shape the opinions of the paper even if they in single matters are not shared by the publisher or board . . . The editor must never allow himself/herself to be influenced to advocate opinions that are not in accord with the editor's own conviction' (cited by Bromley 2000: 113). Editorial staff are also given considerable powers to challenge interventions by proprietors. Publishers who have tampered with editorial decisions have found themselves without an editorial staff; in one case a paper went bankrupt when its staff quit following the publisher's order to remove an article about his family business. The strength of journalistic support for the code and for editorial autonomy has tended to reduce the potentially negative impacts of ownership concentration.

HOW CAN YOU ACT FURTHER TO IMPROVE MEDIA STANDARDS?

There are a range of steps you can take to exploit what Claude-Jean Bertrand (1999) calls 'media accountability systems':

- letters to the editors;

- boycotts: for instance, a major boycott was conducted in Liverpool over the *Sun*'s coverage of the Hillsborough football stadium disaster in April 1989 in which many fans were crushed to death. Under a report headed 'The truth' the tabloid alleged drunken Liverpool fans had harassed the police and abused the bodies of the victims. Sales of the *Sun* on Merseyside dropped by almost 40 per cent and editor Kelvin MacKenzie was forced to go on BBC Radio 4's *The World This Weekend* to apologise. 'I made a rather serious error,' he said (Pilger 1998: 448);

- complain to relevant bodies;

- join campaigning groups such as the Campaign for Press and Broadcasting Freedom (http://www.cpbf.demon.co.uk/). Stephen Stannard, in a *Guardian* letter of 16 March 2000, described how gay protests against coverage of issues in the paper and meetings with representatives had led to improvements in coverage;

- attend one of a series of public meeetings, organised by the BBC around the country (and occasionally by national and local newspapers) at which people are invited to comment on output;

- and, as a journalist, through constant self-evaluation and learning; study closely writers and broadcasters you admire. You may also choose to contribute to debates in the NUJ's magazine, the *Journalist*, in trade magazines such as *Press Gazette* and *Broadcast* – or to broadsheet media sections. But investigative reporter John Pilger (1998: 480) is sceptical of their value.

> Media sections of broadsheet newspapers occasionally allow dissenting voices but that is not their purpose. Like the media itself, they are essentially marketing vehicles whose primary interest is not serious journalistic scrutiny of the industry but formulaic 'media village' tittle-tattle, something on circulation figures, something from the what I have had for breakfast school of journalism and perhaps a 'controversial' interview with a wily political 'spin doctor'. The reason why journalists are so malleable is rarely discussed.

3

At the root of relationships: sourcing dilemmas

HOW CAN JOURNALISTS RESPOND TO THE MANY ETHICAL ISSUES THROWN UP BY INTERVIEWING?

As a source of information, despite its prominence in journalistic routines, the interview is problematic. The source may be lying, hiding crucial facts, uninformed, confused, intimidated and so not expressing true feelings – or speaking in a foreign language and so unable to speak their thoughts clearly. The reporter's bias, personality and body language, even their age and colour, can affect the kinds of responses solicited. The journalist needs to be aware of these problems. Extra pressures on reporters to produce 'exclusives' and brighten up copy is increasing the tendency of journalists to invent quotes.

On- and off-the-record

Following conventional routines, journalists conduct three main types of interview: on-the-record, off-the-record and those for unattributed/background comments. Members of the public are often unaware of the distinctions and thus the journalist will sometimes have to clarify their position to the source. Most interviews are conducted on-the-record and on trust. The source trusts the journalist to report what is said fairly and accurately. Occasionally they will be reported verbatim; usually sections are used in either direct or indirect quotations. An off-the-record interview is completely different. Information is supplied but, because of its sensitive nature, the source asks for it not be reported. Obviously, if the undertaking is broken, then trust (and the source) is lost. Occasionally, in a routine on-the-record interview or during a public meeting a source may say: 'By the way, that's off-the-record', but the reporter is not obliged to agree. Ideally they need to be told of the reporting conventions and persuaded to withdraw their request. An off-the-record agreement also leaves the journalist free to secure the same information from an alternative, on-the-record source or to return to the original source and try to persuade them to go on-the-record. Sometimes problems can arise when sources assume that asides or comments made outside the formal interview context are off-the-record and patience may well be needed in explaining the conventions.

Off-the-record interviews can benefit both journalist and source. For the source, the occasion provides the opportunity to impress their perspective on the reporter while the journalist can be briefed on complicated details about which they may not have any specialist knowledge. David Hencke, of the *Guardian*, points out (2000) that journalists often find it better to work with a network of moles. 'Then when they see the story, they can say truthfully that they have not leaked everything. It is amazing how much better that makes them feel, and how much more information they are then prepared to leak.'

But there are dangers: powerful institutions, groups and individuals have the power to organise such briefings and so influence the media's agenda. Weaker groups and individuals have no such opportunities (Tiffen 1989: 112). Campaigning journalist John Pilger (1996), following the tradition of the great American muckraker, I.F. Stone, advises: 'Beware all background briefings, especially from politicians. Indeed, try to avoid, where possible, all contact with politicians. That way you find out more about them.' Moreover, leaks accompanied by the use of anonymous quotes from compliant journalists can lead to institutionalised lying.

Tiffen (op. cit.: 122) warns:

> The competitive rewards accompanying the publication of leaks makes journalists more open to manipulation. They may be seduced by the appearance of access and intimacy or the lure of an 'exclusive' and so not exploit others' perspectives. The wish to gain exclusives and maintain favoured access can induce selectivity, limited search and the possibility of manipulation.

He continues: 'Because the source remains covert, there is the possibility of them adopting different faces in public and private unbeknown to the public.' Moreover, secrecy can provide the cover for invention, and blur the boundaries between knowledge and surmise. Governments regularly issue leaks to test responses to controversial issues and then denounce the plans if an outcry emerges. Figures released by the Labour Government in 2000 showed 60 leak investigations in the first two years of office ('Straw tops inquiry list as leaks mount', the *Guardian*, 14 February 2000). As secrecy mounted in the New Labour administration, so did the number of leaks. By July 2000, damaging leaks to the Murdoch press (allegedly by the 'professional' rubbish bin searcher Benjamin Pell) of internal battles in Tony Blair's government were becoming front page news.

Background/unattributed briefings: leaking in the public interest

Between off-the-record and on-the-record interviews lie those 'for background only' or unattributed and most confusion surrounds these. Reports can carry quotes from these interviews but attribution is vague to hide identities on particularly sensitive subjects. Journalism is, paradoxically, a secretive profession. Thus colleagues quoted on media personalities or issues are often described as 'a former associate editor on *The Times*', 'an insider at *Panorama*', or 'sources close to the editor of the *Mirror*'. 'Sources close to Prince Charles', a 'ministerial source' and 'diplomatic sources' are other constantly appearing phrases. An *Observer* attack on Chancellor Gordon Brown (described as having 'psychological flaws') was sourced to 'someone who has an exceedingly good claim to know the mind of the Prime Minister'.

Ideally, if journalists are to carry unattributed quotes, then the source should be already known as reliable and they should be identified as clearly as possible without revealing their identities. Thus 'a city councillor' is preferred to 'an informed source'. The reason why the source wishes to remain anonymous should be explained and the information should be corroborated by at least one other source. *The Times* style book rules: 'Unattributed quotes are normally banned. Where they proliferate, for instance in the more pedestrian political reporting, they should be treated with caution.' Unattributed pejorative quotes about someone need particular attention and should provide a sufficiently valuable insight to warrant the shield of anonymity. On 15 July 2000, *Guardian* editor Alan Rusbridger announced a new 'stricter code' on using anonymous pejorative quotes: 'And we will encourage reporters to be as specific as possible about the source of any anonymous quotation.'

HOW SHOULD JOURNALISTS HANDLE CONFIDENTIAL SOURCES? FURTHER DILEMMAS

A survey of journalists' attitudes by researchers at the London College of Printing in 1997 found a large majority agreeing that payments for confidential information can be justified, while more than 80 per cent were prepared to use confidential documents. Moreover, according to John Wilson

(1996: 86), former editorial policy controller of the BBC, '[O]ne of the few accepted absolutes in journalism is that confidential sources must be protected.' Clearly, if promises over confidentiality are broken then the crucial trust between the source – and implicitly all other ones – and the journalist is lost. Such a stance is reaffirmed in media codes (such as Clause 7 of the NUJ's), though Britain is one of the few European countries not to enshrine the principle in law. Some journalists prefer this state of affairs, arguing that the threat of imprisonment is merely an occupational hazard. Better this than facing a law which could potentially seek to define who was and was not a journalist – regardless of what journalists and their organisations felt.

Under Section 10 of the Contempt of Court Act 1981, courts have the right to demand that journalists reveal sources if 'disclosure is necessary in the interests of justice or national security or for the prevention of disorder or crime'. Also, in line with the Police and Criminal Evidence Act of 1984, police investigating a 'serious offence' can obtain an order requiring the journalist to submit evidence considered useful to the court. This can include unpublished photographs, computer files and notes. In a few celebrated cases journalists have risked fines and imprisonment to preserve confidential sources (and in the process, helping reaffirm the myth of the 'free press', some would argue). Occasionally they have succumbed to threats and revealed all.

- In 1963, Brendan Mulholland, of the *Daily Mail*, and Reginald Foster, of the *Daily Sketch*, were both jailed over their coverage of the Vassall spy tribunal.

- Eight years later Bernard Falk went to prison after he refused to tell the court whether one of two Provisional IRA men he interviewed for the BBC was a man subsequently charged with membership.

- In 1984 the *Guardian*, under pressure from the courts, handed over a document that helped reveal that civil servant Sarah Tisdall had leaked information about the delivery of cruise missiles to RAF Greenham Common. National security seemed hardly threatened but Tisdall was jailed.

- In 1988, Jeremy Warner, of the *Independent*, was ordered to disclose the source of a story on insider dealing in the City, refused and was ordered to pay a £20,000 fine and £100,000 costs by the High Court.

- In 1990, Bill Goodwin, a trainee on the weekly trade magazine, the *Engineer*, refused to hand over notes of a telephone conversation revealing confidential details about a computer company's financial affairs. He was fined £5,000. But, supported by the NUJ, Goodwin took his case to the European Commission of Human Rights which ruled, in September 1993, in support of Goodwin and called on the government to negotiate a 'friendly settlement'. Three years later, the European Court of Human Rights ruled that Goodwin had been right to protect his source. But still the government refused to budge on the Contempt of Court Act.

- Following the poll tax riots of 31 March 1990, the police applied for possession of 'all transmitted, published and/or unpublished cine film, video tape, still photographs and negatives of the demonstration and subsequent disturbances' under PACE. Some national newspapers complied. But the NUJ moved fast, sending prints and negatives out of the country and so saving the other organisations from prosecution.

- In 1991, Channel 4 was fined £75,000 under the Prevention of Terrorism Act after refusing to reveal its source for a programme by the independent company, Box Productions, alleging collusion between Loyalist death squads and members of the security forces in Northern Ireland. A researcher on the programme, Ben Hamilton, was later charged with perjury by the Royal Ulster Constabulary, and though the charge was dropped in November 1992, the police retained all items seized from Mr Hamilton including his PC, disks, cuttings and notes of telephone calls and meetings with interested journalists. The programme later became the subject of an acrimonious libel action by the *Sunday Times* which, in May 1993, denounced the programme as a hoax (Lashmar 2000).

- In 1996 Dani Garavelli, then chief reporter for the *Journal*, Newcastle, won a 20-month battle in the High Court. She had refused to name a source after being subpoenaed to give evidence to a police disciplinary hearing.

- In March 1998, a judge's decision to throw out an application by Norfolk Police for the *Eastern Daily Press* and reporter Adrian Galvin to name a source was lauded as a 'landmark judgment' by editor Peter Franzen. Judge Michael Hyman ruled: 'There is undoubtedly a very formidable interest in a journalist being able to protect his sources.'

- In September 1999, Ed Moloney, northern editor of the Dublin-based *Sunday Tribune,* faced jail after refusing to hand over notes dating back 10 years of interviews with a Loyalist accused of murdering a Catholic solicitor. Moloney's ordeal ended the following month when the Belfast High Court overturned an order by Antrim Crown Court.

- Then in April 2000, the *Express* overturned a High Court ruling that it had to reveal the source from which financial reporter Rachel Baird obtained confidential documents about a High Court action involving Sir Elton John.

Significantly, the Public Interest Disclosure Act, of July 1998, displayed New Labour's intention to protect whistle-blowers. It covers a wide range of issues from the mistreatment of patients and financial malpractice to miscarriages of justice and dangers to health and safety, but the army, police, intelligence services, volunteers and self-employed are exempted from its clauses. Leaks by brave whistle-blowers can be used to expose corruption – as Paul Van Buitenen found at the European Commission. They can also be used to discredit opponents. David Leigh (1998) and Stephen Dorril and Robin Ramsay (1991) have shown the extent to which secret service leaks to sympathetic journalists in national newspapers were used systematically to smear Harold Wilson and his close associates during his premiership before he unexpectedly resigned in 1976.

SHOULD JOURNALISTS SUPPORT THE PARLIAMENTARY LOBBY SYSTEM?

One of the most famous, and controversial, manifestations of the background briefing is the parliamentary lobby, providing privileged access to ministers, the PM and other politicians to a few journalists. Every day on which the House sits, Downing Street gives two briefings to around 240 accredited lobby correspondents (just 30 of them women). Joe Haines, press secretary to Labour PM Harold Wilson, commented: 'They have privileged access which they are very jealous of and yet most are of low ability and totally precious.' The lobby was launched in 1884, five years before the first Official Secrets Act. As Michael Cockerell, Peter Hennessy and David Walker comment in their seminal study of the lobby (1984: 34): 'The paradox was that as Britain was moving towards becoming a democracy by extending the vote to men of all classes (women still had 40 years to wait) mechanisms were being created to frustrate popular participation in government and to control, channel and even manufacture the political news.'

Until recently, the briefings were unattributable – and provoked enormous passions, both pro and anti. Bernard Ingham, Margaret Thatcher's press secretary, was alleged to use the system for blatant disinformation campaigns, even against Conservative colleagues, and in protest, the newly-launched *Independent*, as well as the *Guardian*, *Scotsman* and *Economist* withdrew from the lobby for a few years (Harris 1990). Since then, lobby rules have been continuously relaxed. Ingham's successor, Christopher Meyer, in 1995, allowed the briefings to be attributed directly to 'Downing Street'. Then Alastair Campbell, Tony Blair's press secretary, on March 13, 2000, ruled that he could be named as the source of his briefings (rather than the 'Prime Minister's official spokesman'). Soon afterwards, Fleet Street printed verbatim versions of a lobby briefing. In the previous month the twice daily briefings for journalists were put on the Downing Street website. Why this remarkable openness? Some journalists welcomed the move, others argued it was an attempt by the government to bypass media 'spin' and communicate directly with the electorate. Those with Internet access could now find out what was said in the lobby just an hour after the meeting ended.

New Labour is accused by some of seeking to downplay the role of the Commons and enhance the power of the Executive. Just as Alastair Campbell was seeking to bypass the lobby (Oborne 1999: 197–200) so Tony Blair rarely attended the Commons: his voting record was the lowest by far of any PM since the early eighteenth century, attending just five per cent of all votes. Even Margaret Thatcher (notoriously contemptuous of parliament despite her rhetoric) voted six times more. Some commentators suggested it was only a matter of time before the Prime Minister's press secretary adopted the US system of nightly TV screenings of his comments. The lobby would then be transformed into showbiz, leaving the most important business to be conducted behind the scenes in informal, bilateral contacts between journalist and politician. As former lobby correspondent Andrew Pierce (2000) commented: 'ministers, their special advisers and senior Labour Party workers are still being wined and dined by political journalists in fashionable restaurants within the shadow of Big Ben.' Then, in July 2000, a major row erupted after novelist Ken Follett, husband of a Labour MP, accused the Blair Government of exploiting unattributed briefings to smear a series of ministers – including Mo Mowlam, David Clark, Tessa Jowell and Ann Taylor. Should journalists consider boycotting the lobby again?

TO WHAT EXTENT DO MAINSTREAM JOURNALISTS, THROUGH THEIR SOURCING ROUTINES, REFLECT THE FULL DIVERSITY OF THE SOCIETY THEY REPORT ON?

Conventional sourcing routines divide sources into two categories: primary and secondary (Aitchison 1988). At a local level, primary sources include councils, MPs and Euro MPs, courts, police, fire brigade, ambulance service, hospitals, local industries and their representative bodies, the local football, cricket and rugby clubs. Schools and colleges, churches, army, naval and air force bases, local branches of national pressure groups and charities are secondary sources. In rural areas, other contacts in this category will include village post office workers, publicans and hotel keepers, agricultural merchants, livestock auctioneers, countryside rangers or wardens. In coastal areas they might include coastguards, harbourmasters and lifeboat stations. Sources' details are held in contacts books, the journalist's most prized possession.

A system of calls institutionalises these sourcing routines. The police, ambulance station and fire brigade are rung at regular intervals for breaking news. Local reporters will habitually drop in for chats to help personalise the contact. Primary and secondary sources are often described as 'on-diary' since details of their activities are listed in diaries held by the news desk. 'Off-diary' sources are all those which fall outside these routines. Many journalists argue that the media are like a mirror reflecting reality, presenting a credible first draft of history – and that their sourcing routines reflect the social and political realities (Frost 2000: 37). Accordingly, John Whale (1977: 85) argued that 'the media do more towards corroborating opinion than creating it'. He cited the *Morning Star* (a communist newspaper originally published as the *Daily Worker*) with its very low circulation as proof that the views it promoted were simply not popular. Jay Newman (1992: 213) argues that the national media have generally succeeded in 'balancing the interests' of minorities and majorities, 'which is no easy task'.

Yet others claim that mainstream journalists use a remarkably limited range of sources. Johan Galtung and Mari Ruge (1973) in their seminal analysis of news values, highlighted the bias in the Western media towards reporting elite, First World nations and elite people. The elements of the hierarchy were different within and across different media. Television soap stars and showbiz personalities feature far more in the tabloid media than in the broadsheets. Yet there exists a distinct consensus over sourcing routines in the mainstream media. Some sources are always prominent, others will be marginalised, eliminated or covered generally in a negative way. Philip Schlesinger (1978) found that as much as 80 per cent of BBC news came from routine sources while Bob Franklin and David Murphy (1991), in a study of 865 stories in the local press, found local and regional government, voluntary organisations, the courts, police and business accounted for 67.7 per cent of the total. Inevitably journalists can become friends with their elite sources and that can subtly 'soften' coverage and cement loyalties.

Some critics express concern over the failure of the mass media to represent working-class views. Newspapers such as the *Daily Herald*, *Daily Sketch* and *Sunday Graphic*, aimed specifically at the working class, failed through lack of sales. As James Curran and Jean Seaton comment (1991: 108): 'They all had predominantly working class readership and, in terms of mass marketing, relatively "small" circulations. They thus fell between two stools: they had neither the quantity nor the social "quality" of readership needed to attract sufficient advertising for them to survive.' The Glasgow University Media Group also identified within the broadcasting institutions an underlying ideology critical of working-class institutions. Television coverage of strikes was 'clearly skewed against the interests of the working class and organised labour' and 'in favour of the managers of industry' (1980: 400).

The spread of phone journalism also narrows the range of journalists' sources. Many journalists (such as Sarah Knight of the *Derby Trader*) say that as much as 90 per cent of their work is now conducted on the phone, their job reduced to a form of glorified clerking, the links with their audience dramatically cut. 'Phoney journalism' is popular with proprietors and managers because it's cheaper – and provides quick access to information and quotes. Investigative reporter Sylvia Jones comments (1998: 50):

> I was helping out doing a sleaze story for the *Mirror*. There was a contact of mine who had some information and I needed to go out and see him. When I suggested that I actually go out and see him the other journalists looked at me absolutely astounded and said: 'It's bottoms on seats these days luv. You don't go out on a story, you do it all from the office by phone.' Deadlines are earlier and staff numbers have been cut.

Concerns have also mounted in recent years about the power of the PR industry to influence the news agenda. Nick Cohen (1999: 126–7) suggests there are 25,000 PRs in Britain and 50,000 journalists, and quotes a prominent City public relations consultant who estimates that 80 per cent of business news and 40 per cent of general news comes straight from the mouths of PRs. Former editor of the *Daily Mirror*, Mike Molloy, has even claimed that PR has taken over from journalism so that the original purpose of newspapers as the primary source of truth has been eliminated. 'We are in a world which is controlled, organised and manufactured by public relations,' he said.

Some critics argue that the media's obsession with elite sources and dependency on advertising mean that the experiences of the poor are marginalised in news coverage. Two decades of Conservative rule left Britain with the worst poverty record in the developed world, according to figures produced by the Organisation for Economic Co-operation and Development and released on 11 January 2000. Poverty affected 20 per cent of the population on average between 1991 and 1996. During the six years of the study, 38 per cent of the population spent at least one year below the poverty line. To what extent do the media reflect those realities?

Certainly, the media display an obsession with 'rich lists' pandering to the competitive, consumerist fantasies of their readers: on 12 March 2000, the *Sunday Mirror*, *Mail on Sunday* and the *Observer* all ran such lists. During the following week, the *Sunday Times* published its twelfth such list. Emily Bell, *Observer* business editor, commented: 'People like to read about people who have more money than they have. People are absolutely appalled that somebody is not only 27, nice-looking and talented but is also worth £50m. There's something intrinsically upsetting but also fascinating about it.' Yet a UN report of 1999 revealed the gap between rich and poor in Britain is the widest in Europe with the richest 20 per cent of the population earning 10 times as much as the poorest 20 per cent. 1.3 million pensioners are totally reliant on their state pension of less than £70 a week (the *Big Issue*, 6–12 March 2000). Do journalists need to re-examine their sourcing routines?

SHOULD JOURNALISTS ALLOW THEIR SOURCE ACCESS TO THE REPORT BEFORE PUBLICATION OR BROADCASTING?

Most journalists place a blanket ban on allowing sources access to the report or script before it appears. Such promises can land the journalist in all kinds of problems. Sources sometimes allow the copy or script to go through untouched but invariably they will want minor if not major changes inserted. And the journalist can feel their professionalism and autonomy are being questioned. Chris Frost (op. cit.: 76) argues strongly: 'Showing the copy to an interviewee is a tacit admission that the piece is Public Relations and not journalism.'

But a different approach may see the value in the journalist demystifying their role and adopting a collaborative attitude toward the source. The final piece then becomes the product of a joint exercise between journalist and source, each one learning from the other. Clearly, a political perspective may inspire action. Such collaboration would not be appropriate for conventional sources who are well equipped to deal with the media. But a member of a progressive group normally marginalised or demonised by the media may appreciate the involvement. And occasionally journalists will submit selected quotes and factual sections of pieces to sources for checking when particularly complex issues are being handled. Some argue that the conventional view, denying access to copy, is based on the myth of the journalist as the independent professional while, in reality, the media serve as sophisticated publicity for the status quo. In this context, there is a need for overtly partisan media (such as provided by campaigning, leftist, environmental groups) in which journalists identify more closely with their audience – and thus are likely to subvert the conventions of traditional news gathering.

American Janet Malcolm (1991: 1), in *The Journalist and the Murderer*, controversially argued that every relationship with a source was exploitative and 'morally indefensible'. 'Every journalist who is not too stupid or too full of himself [sic] to notice what is going on knows that what he does is morally indefensible. He is a kind of confidence man, preying on people's vanity, ignorance or loneliness gaining their trust and betraying them without remorse.' Need it always be so? Award-winning documentary maker Roger Graef challenges Malcolm, advocating a collaborative relationship with sources. His films for the BBC, such as *Breaking Point*, on the marriage guidance body, Relate, usually deal with extremely sensitive, controversial areas. He comments (1998):

> The notion of any kind of collaboration evokes a kind of journalistic capitulation that would send shivers down the spine of many film-makers. But in our experience, the sense of collaboration allows the participants to keep their dignity not only during filming – when they could ask for the camera to be switched off, or us to leave – but crucially during and after transmission.

Yet the dilemmas persist. Say you are a radio journalist and the source says the interview is so good it should go out unedited: how do you respond?

SHOULD JOURNALISTS TREAT ALL SOURCES THE SAME?

Children: no small challenge

Adults thrown into the limelight are often unprepared for media attention, so don't children need even more protection? In Britain, certain laws are in place to protect children in courts: thus those under 18 who are alleged offenders or witnesses at youth courts cannot be identified under the Children and Young Persons Act 1933 and the Criminal Justice Act 1991. Similarly, the Children Act 1989 imposed restrictions on identifying children, as did the Criminal Evidence and Youth Justice Act 1999 whose Section 44 made it an offence for the media to reveal the identity of a person under

18 suspected of an offence. Media law expert Tom Welsh described the provision (which came into force in December 2000) as 'draconian'. In 1993, the PCC advised journalists covering children who have been victims of a crime, accident or other event: 'Editors should consider carefully whether or not their pictures offer clues, albeit unwittingly, that will allow some readers to put a name to the individual concerned. Such clues may be found in unusual hairstyles or in distinctive clothing.'

Following a complaint by Tory MP Roger Gale over a *Mirror* story outlining his son's suspension for firing a 'gun' on a bus, the PCC issued 'tough guidelines to protect the vulnerable position of children at school' in 1997. They suggested that, where possible, stories about public figures raising issues about or involving children should be published without detail, including name, which might lead to the identification of the child. And 'where the story about the parents of the child is justified in the public interest, the vulnerable position of a child must be taken into consideration – and the child only identified in exceptional circumstances'. One of the changes to the PCC's code, introduced in January 2000, focused on the reporting of young children. A new Clause 10 directed editors to pay particular regard to children who are victims or witnesses to crime. The children of the royals and Prime Minister Tony Blair have also been the subject of rulings by the PCC. Significantly, after Euan Blair was found by police lying drunk and semi-conscious in Leicester Square at 11 p.m. one evening in July 2000, the press carefully followed the PCC guidelines, according to *Times* columnist Brian MacArthur. But such coverage would have been illegal under provisions of the Youth Justice and Criminal Evidence Act, due to be implemented a few months later. Also, following media frenzies over coverage of Blair baby Leo, the PCC planned to issue special guidelines to the press.

Al Tompkins, of the Poynter Institute, suggests that journalists should leave a business card with the child so the parents have a way of making contact if they object to the interview being used. Radio reporter and lecturer Jim Beaman (2000: 38–9) suggests it can be easier and more profitable to interview children in groups. 'Ask open questions and show an interest in what they tell you.' And CNN has a specific policy on questioning children. Reporters should make sure they are safe and away from the news scene while 'a highly inquisitive or investigative style' of questioning should be avoided. Significantly, the Broadcasting Standards Commission's report in June 2000 stressed that the inclusion of distressed children in both documentary and entertainment programmes had become a major issue over the previous year and it upheld a complaint against *Panorama* about an 'emotionally charged and intrusive' interview with a child.

Clinical psychologist Oliver James also criticises the media's typical coverage of children's murders, usually by a paedophile stranger. Yet of the 80 children killed on average every year, just seven are by someone unknown to them. The vast majority are killed by their parents, usually with low incomes. James comments (2000): 'The only reason why parents are worrying so much is because the tabloids, followed sheepishly by the broadcast media, have realised that playing on parents' fears sells newspapers.' These views appeared in the *Guardian* which, on the same day, ran a large, close-up picture of the family of a murdered child hugging each other in their grief. Was that a tasteless intrusion on their private grief? Moreover, outrage greeted the *News of the World*'s decision to 'name and shame' 49 paedophiles on 23 July 2000, the first instalment of a proposed list of 110,000. Many argued the campaign was a blatant publicity stunt while a letter to *Private Eye* took a wry view on the controversy: 'Am I alone in thinking that there should be a register of *News of the World* readers? Surely we should be told if such people live in our midst.' A dossier compiled by the Association of Chief Officers of Probation listed 40 cases in which released sex offenders went underground or innocent people were attacked as a result of mistaken identity following newspaper 'pervert watch' campaigns. Earlier, after predatory paedophile Sidney Cooke was released and the Government introduced a sex offenders register, the *Sunday Express* ran a similar campaign providing photographs, names and addresses of the 'evil men'. Does it serve the public interest to demonise these men as 'monsters'? *News of the World* editor Rebekah Wade was adamant: 'Our intention is not to provoke violence. The disturbing truth is that the authorities are failing to properly monitor the activities of paedophiles in the community.'

The ambush interview

Certain sources accused of crimes or other wrong-doing are reluctant to meet reporters and require special treatment. Occasionally journalists, as a last resort, will decide to 'ambush' the source, suddenly confronting them with questions which they will find difficult then to avoid. This strategy is mainly used by television journalists when the drama of the spectacle provides extra news value. Journalists should also work in pairs at least on such assignments; sources can turn violent.

Doorstepping

This is a favourite device of reporters, waiting outside the homes or workplaces of people in the news, all set to interview them. When journalists wait in packs this can amount to intimidation and harassment, punishable by law. Very often the comments gained from the reluctant source are unsubstantial but the hype surrounding breaking big stories usually encourages reporters to doorstep. PressWise, a media ethics watchdog, advises members of the public: 'If you would prefer not to get involved, simply tell them, politely but firmly. Don't be surprised if they persist – that is their job. However, if they refuse to leave your premises or stop pestering you on the telephone, you are entitled to call the police.'

SHOULD JOURNALISTS SHARE THEIR CONTACTS AND QUOTES WITH COLLEAGUES?

Journalism involves a fascinating mix of individual drive and co-operative action. For instance journalists, often for safety reasons, work in pairs (or even threesomes) on risky investigative assignments. Reporters and production staff can work together on the details and presentation of a graphic. There is intense competition between staff on different media outlets. But there are some occasions when journalists routinely share information. This can be formalised with the creation of pools: a few journalists are given access to a special source or event and their reports are distributed to other media. Sometimes at long-running conferences, reporters will 'pick up' details from colleagues of any items missed. Similarly, at press conferences journalists may work as a pack to ask a speaker a series of questions on a complex, controversial issue. Afterwards, they may confer if some of the quotes were unclear.

But what if a colleague on a rival media institution asks you for contacts in one of your specialist areas? Some journalists would impose a blanket ban on such requests. Some responses may be politically motivated: they may be prepared to share with a colleague on one outlet but not another because of its unacceptable political bias. Some journalists decide to share a few of their sources but not their main ones, acquired only after considerable effort. After all, a colleague you fail to help today will not be there to help you in the future.

SHOULD IT BE POSSIBLE FOR JOURNALISTS TO PAY SOURCES?

There is a rich tradition in Britain of cheque-book journalism. In November 1996, the then editor of the *News of the World* said, on average, subjects were paid in about 10 per cent of stories. Writers of works serialised in the Sundays can receive substantial payments just as prominent people in the news (often backed up by publicist Max Clifford) can receive large 'buy-outs' for their stories. In August 1996, a furore greeted a deal between the *News of the World* and prospective mother Mandy Allwood (at one time expected to give birth to eight children) but this payment was dependent on the number of babies born. Sources are routinely paid to appear on the radio or television. But does this not lead to the situation where information becomes the monopoly of the wealthy? Is there not a danger sources will exaggerate and lie to justify the payment?

Most of the critical attention in the mainstream media has fallen on the issue of payments to witnesses in criminal court cases, and to criminals or their associates, significantly outlawed in the PCC's first Code of Practice in 1991. Controversies had blown up over payments to witnesses in the Moors murders case (1966), in the trial of Jeremy Thorpe, former leader of the Liberal Party (1979) and in the Yorkshire Ripper trial (1981). But the controversy reached fever pitch after newspapers made deals with 19 witnesses in the trial of mass murderer Rosemary West in 1995, including daughter Anne Marie Davies, who was paid £3,000 by the *Daily Star* but promised up to £70,000 (Hanna and Epworth 1998). A Green Paper published by the Lord Chancellor's department in October 1996 claimed the PCC's code had failed to prevent 'widespread and flagrant breaches' and recommended legislation to deal with the problem.

The PCC adamantly opposed legislation, saying payments to witnesses and criminals occurred in any case only rarely. All the same, in the light of evidence from the Chief Constable of Gloucestershire, the commission revised its code in November 1996 to incorporate new clauses which placed a burden of justification on the editor to prove payment is in the public interest and must be disclosed to the parties involved in the trial. However, the all-party National Heritage Committee, chaired by Gerald Kaufman in January 1997, urged the Government to bring in legislation to ban media payments for the stories of witnesses and called for the Contempt of Court Act 1981 to be strengthened so that the media could not escape punishment where pre-trial publicity caused a trial to collapse. Then, in February 2000, the Lord Chancellor, Lord Irvine, announced the Government was to review payments by the press to witnesses in criminal trials. Interestingly, a survey by Hanna and Epworth (op. cit.: 14) of journalists working in England and Wales showed 70 per cent saying that media payments to witnesses put justice at risk, though only 58.1 per cent agreed there should be a statutory ban on such payments.

Over recent years, the PCC has clarified its position on payments in a series of much-publicised rulings. After nurses Deborah Parry and Lucille

McLauchlan were released in May 1998 from a Saudi jail after sentencing for the murder of a colleague, their stories were 'bought' by the *Express* and the *Mirror*, respectively. But a PCC ruling in July did not condemn the payments. Controversies also emerged after *The Times* ran a serialisation of *Cries Unheard* (London: Macmillan 1998), Gitta Sereny's biography of 1960s child murderer, Mary Bell, and the *Daily Mail* paid £40,000 to the parents of nanny Louise Woodward, convicted of the manslaughter of baby Matthew Eapen in Boston. In both these cases the PCC ruled there was a clear public interest defence.

But the *Daily Telegraph* was censured in July 1999 for paying Victoria Aitken around £1,000 for writing about her father's plight. Her article was published a day after Jonathan Aitken was sentenced to 18 months in prison for lying about payment of his bill by a Saudi arms financier at the Ritz, Paris, when minister for arms procurement in the Major government – and as revealed by the *Guardian*. This payment could not be defended in the public interest. In May 2000, the PCC ruled that the *Sunday Times* did not infringe its code in agreeing to pay for the rights to serialise Aitken's memoirs. The *ST* maintained its payment would go directly to the trustee in bankruptcy for Aitken's creditors. In December 1999, the *News of the World*'s £25,000 'conviction bonus' to the key witness, Allison Brown, against Gary Glitter (jailed for four months for child pornography offences) was condemned by the PCC and described as 'a clearly reprehensible state of affairs' by the judge. But *NoW* editor Phil Hall said his conscience was clear. 'We acted in good faith and took her on when there was no suggestion the police would interview her. People say we should have dropped out of the contract then but I thought the best thing to do would be to leave it to the authorities to make a decision.'

SHOULD JOURNALISTS ACCEPT FREEBIES FROM SOURCES?

Rare is the British journalist who has not enjoyed a free foreign trip, free hotel booking, a free book or seat at the theatre. Many continental media ban such freebies, only a few (such as the *Independent Traveller* section and *Condé Nast Traveller*) do in Britain. Reviewers of new cars are sometimes given them on indefinite 'loans'. Virgin Airlines has even provided journalists with mobile phones and unlimited calls. Is a 'freebie' (or, when it involves travel, a junket) a euphemism for bribe? Clearly, the institution paying for it is gaining some publicity, whether good or bad. And many journalists object to news being bought in this way. There is an alternative view which stresses that journalists don't always lose their critical faculties when cash is thrown in their faces. As John Wilson says on the influence of the freebie culture (op. cit.: 168):

> Much of the time it is harmless. Some of the time it fails the public because editorial scrutiny is relaxed. The proper journalistic stance is that, whatever facilities are provided, they will be declared, no conditions will be accepted, no editorial favour granted and the nature of the coverage decided independently.

Significantly, the British Guild of Travel Writers promotes a code of conduct which incorporates a ban on paid and promotional work for travel companies. Members can accept freebies – but only on the understanding that this will not influence their judgement.

Most journalists unite in their condemnation of financial journalists and editors who use insider knowledge for their own profit. Both the NUJ (Clause 12) and the PCC (Clause 14) codes condemn such practices. Piers Morgan, editor of the *Mirror*, and two of his colleagues on the *City Slickers* column were censured by the commission in May 2000 after they were found to have shares in companies they were reporting on. Some journalists argue they were simply unlucky. The practice is, in fact, more widespread than generally acknowledged. And some journalists are calling for a 'new transparency' in which journalists declare their financial interests. As investigative reporter Phillip Knightley commented:

> Many journalists were indignant at the *Mirror* shares affair. But are their own deals, consultancies and commercial contracts above reproach? Should we not ask ourselves whether a craft that demands such high standards of transparency from others (MPs for example) should be prepared to conform to high standards itself? A 'Register of Journalists' Interests' in each editorial department, freely available to the public and placed on a company's website, would be a start. Who will lead the way?

WHEN IS IT LEGITIMATE TO CONDUCT A CONFRONTATIONAL INTERVIEW?

Interviews for print are rarely confrontational. The journalist's main concern is to listen attentively and sensitively to the source. In broadcasting, where entertainment/spectacle priorities surface, different criteria apply. Interviewers such as John Humphrys and Jeremy Paxman have acquired the reputations of being the journalistic equivalents of 'Rottweilers'. Humphrys was even criticised by the BBC programme complaints unit in August 2000 over a 'confrontational' interview with Lord Robertson,

NATO Secretary General. Yet, in commenting on his technique, Humphrys stresses the democratic/Fourth Estate function of the media: the interview with a politician, he says, constitutes 'an important bridge between the electorate and their political leaders. We have to try to distil the national argument, to represent voters' concerns'.

Dr Grego Philo, of Glasgow University, however, argues that political interviews on television and radio remain deferential with 'very few people taking chances'. Certainly politicians are increasingly being trained to counter adversarial interviewing techniques (pioneered by Sir Robin Day and later Brian Walden) and thus it could be argued the 'confrontation' is in danger of becoming ritualised. Trevor McDonald, of ITN, was actually criticised by the Independent Television Commission for an over-sycophantic interview with John Major, on 18 July 1996, in which he praised his 'great courage' over Northern Ireland. Humphrys, for all his 'Rottweiler' reputation, was voted 'political journalist of the year' by politicians in 2000. Margaret Thatcher was, significantly, troubled only once – and this was by a member of the public during a discussion over the sinking of the *Belgrano* during the Falklands conflict of 1982. In 1987, David Dimbleby's *Nine O'Clock News* interview with Thatcher revealed her contempt for 'whingers' 'drooling and drivelling that they care', but this was cut from the bulletin and only shown 'at a late point in the campaign when it could make no significant difference to the outcome' (McNair 2000: 101). Significantly Tony Blair was most rattled, not by any television interviewer, but by Carol, a nurse from Liverpool, who criticised him over interest rates and rising mortgages during the Nicky Campbell show on 15 July 1998. Leigh and Vulliamy (1997: 234) argue that inherently superficial television interviews are unable to delve into the complexities of modern politics. Others welcome the rise of confrontational interviews as representing the decline in deference amongst the electorate to authority figures.

DOES THE INTERNET THROW UP NEW ETHICAL ISSUES IN THIS AREA?

With the rapid explosion of the Internet in recent years, it is not surprising that media workers have found it difficult to identify its precise implications on their routines and ethics. The BBC's decision in May 2000 to allow content from its licence-payer-backed (and extremely popular) online operation to be distributed to the Yahoo! website raised concern that the corporation was sacrificing its journalistic independence by singling out one commercial service. And certainly with so many people able to publish on the Web, journalistic 'professionalism' has come under increasing threat. How can journalists respond? Some argue that well-established brand names, already respected for their journalistic standards, will win out in the end over the brash new players in cyberspace. Others say such an approach is too complacent, with the new media environment demanding a radical rethink of media routines and of the relationship between journalists and their audience and sources. Certainly the interactivity of the Internet means journalists can have much closer contact with their audience and sources. Yet only a minority of the population enjoys Internet access (though the numbers are growing rapidly) and thus there may be a danger in generalising over its impact, and privileging the experience of the relatively affluent few over the many.

According to commentators such as Jon Katz (1997), the Internet is transforming the journalist–audience relationship: from being an unquestioned expert the journalist now becomes simply a facilitator of debate. Increasingly media are providing e-mail addresses of staffers encouraging feedback and input from consumers. Nora Paul (the *Guardian*, 28 February 2000, reprinted from www.poynter.org) argues that the 'us to them' model of television producers and viewers is dying. News consumers now expect to have control on many aspects of the newscast: when they watch it, from what angle, the depth of the coverage, the type of news they want to see. 'Time shifting, multi-casting, camera vantage point selection – all will provide the viewer with more power over the product. News consumers will have new means of communicating with you about news and will expect a response.' The Internet certainly provides reporters with the chance to extend their range of sources, giving them easy access to so many formerly marginalised groups and to internationalising their sourcing strategies. But there are dangers journalists will come to rely too much on the Internet: much of journalism's human dimension will then be lost with reporters retreating into a virtual, lifeless world. And concerns are mounting that the temptations towards plagiarism will grow. Ian Mayes (2000), readers' editor at the *Guardian*, pointed to the deadline pressures on reporters. 'Over-reliance on cuttings and now, even more to the point, the ease of electronically cutting and pasting from the Internet, may be not simply attractive options, but the only options open to hard-pressed journalists in certain circumstances.'

SHOULD JOURNALISTS ALWAYS IDENTIFY THEMSELVES AS SUCH WHEN JOINING A DISCUSSION GROUP?

When investigating sensitive and dangerous issues, journalists may be justified in seeking anonymity when gathering background information. But Randy Reddick and Elliott King argue (1997: 219):

Journalists should always identify themselves as such if they plan to use information from discussion lists. In most cases, journalists have the ethical obligation to allow people to choose to go on-the-record or not. To lurk in a discussion list, then quote people who did not know that what they wrote would be used in a different context is as deceptive as posing or going undercover to report a story.

The Americans have developed the concept of 'precision journalism' in relation to the Web, reflecting an over-confidence in the reliability of information. Indeed, journalists have to be specially careful in assessing the value of material drawn from the Internet. Robert Kiley (1999) advises Internet users to always check that the information is current. 'A well organised web page will state when it was first written and last updated.' See if there is a named author. If so, then search an appropriate database for their previous publications. 'If there is no identified author the information should be treated with caution.' Who is funding the site? The owner should be clearly displayed along with details of any sponsorship or advertising.

The legal position on Internet content remains confused. In theory, online media discussion groups could face problems if they carried material considered defamatory, grossly indecent or offensive, with the website providers subject to a civil action for defamation or charged under the Telecommunications Act 1984. In November 1999, the Lord Chancellor's department had a website closed down because material posted on it criticised five judges. Anxieties mounted in March 2000, after Demon Internet paid Lawrence Godfrey, a university lecturer and physicist, £15,000 plus legal fees of around £250,000 in an out-of-court settlement after he was the subject of an allegedly libellous bulletin board posting. Within days British Internet Service Providers (ISPs) closed two websites – a gay one called *Outcast* and another devoted (fittingly) to opposing censorship.

Fears mounted that the libertarian view of the Internet as a medium immune to censorship would be exposed as a myth. Giles Wilson, a BBC journalist, compiled a spoof web page ridiculing a colleague and found that most ISPs would pull it if any complaint were made. As John Naughton commented in the *Observer*: 'ISPs are run by businesses whose main interest is making money, not defending free speech.' To confuse the issue further, in May, a US Supreme Court ruling gave ISPs full protection against libellous or obscene messages sent out over the Web, putting them on the same legal footing as telephone companies.

Journalists' investigative work and promises of confidentiality also appeared under threat by the Government's regulation of investigatory powers legislation. As Ian Reeves warned (2000), the contents and details of e-mails and telephone calls would potentially become accessible to a 'horrifying' variety of government agencies, police officers and even low-grade council officials. Dan Hogan (1998: 28), on the other hand, expresses fears that 'the neo-anarchistic world of cyberspace can effectively by-pass the print media and all manner of legislation – from strict privacy laws to the Contempt of Court Act'. He cites the example of the *Daily Mirror* scoop about the Home Secretary's son dealing in cannabis. The paper only 'half-heartedly' broke the story. 'But the naming and shaming was more effectively carried out by the Internet.'

4
The ethics of sleaze coverage: privacy, bugging, surveillance and subterfuge

HOW MUCH WERE JOURNALISTS TO BLAME FOR MAKING THE 1990s THE NAUGHTY DECADE OF DIRT AND SLEAZE?

The 1990s seemed submerged in an endless series of scandals involving randy royals, MPs (always male and mostly Tory) and showbiz personalities. Issues surrounding invasions of privacy came to dominate media and political debate over the decade. But it is debatable how much the public was concerned. Relatively few complaints to regulatory bodies focused on privacy. People, after all, are ambivalent: often condemning invasions of privacy but lapping up the published results.

The 'dirty decade' may, in fact, be seen to have started on 23 July 1989, when the *Sunday People* carried a photograph of Prince William's 'sly pee' in a park under the headline 'The Royal Wee!'. Robert Maxwell, the proprietor and fervent royal supporter, promptly sacked the editor. But the tone for media coverage was set for the following decade. Hardly a month passed without some celebrity, Minister or MP being 'exposed': many lost their reputations, some their jobs (and Princess Diana her life). In the three years following John Major's election victory in 1992, there were 14 resignations on grounds of scandal; half the cases involved sexual activities; about half financial irregularities. The *Independent on Sunday* (23 July 1995) claimed that between 1990 and 1995 there were 34 Conservative, one Liberal Democrat and four Labour scandals; of these around a quarter involved sex.

One theory accounting for this rash of sleaze stories stresses the impact of the end of the Cold War. Changes in the operation of the national security state mean the media become the theatre where inter-elite squabbles are fought out. Significantly, hardly any country has been unaffected by corruption scandals since 1989. Since the Cold War had a global reach it is not surprising that the consequences of its demise should be global. In the United States, for instance, President Clinton's affair with internee Monica Lewinsky dominated the headlines globally after Matt Drudge's maverick Internet site broke the story in February 1998. But President Kennedy's rampant sexuality and many affairs had not been covered in the media because national security in the Cold War would have been considered endangered by such revelations (Keeble 1998).

With the decline of ideology, critics claim there has been a breakdown in the old-fashioned divisions between the private and the public, and people's understanding of politics has to centre around personal narratives. At the same time it is argued 'human interest' stories can address deeper issues such as sexual harassment and the abuse of power. The Major Government's stress on 'Back to Basics' certainly put the spotlight on Conservative moral hypocrisy. While some criticised the media's descent into 'bonk journalism' and trivia, journalists argued that if a politician publicly promoted family values but in private was cavorting with prostitutes, then they had a duty to expose such hypocrisy in the public interest. According to Hywel Williams (2000):

> The cult of the personal and intimate dragged into the light of day is a powerful one here. The impulse is democratic, egalitarian and anti-heroic: leaders are shown to have feet of clay. It's a comforting conclusion that they are really just like ourselves. Politically, the result is that we've grown sceptical about leadership. Suspicion of politics has always been a powerful British trait. But television in particular and journalism in general have de-sacralised the tribalism of party politics. Daylight, let in on old mysteries, has revealed new banality.

Brian McNair (2000: 54) argues that sleaze journalism 'should be viewed as a welcome by-product of an era when journalistic deference toward political elites has been eroded and the normative watchdog function of the Fourth Estate is increasingly applied, in conditions of heightened competitiveness, to the secretive, insider networks which if left alone burrow away at and undermine the democratic process'. He also links sleaze journalism with the theories of Burke (1988) which focus on the feudal carnivalesque forms of popular culture when 'the world was turned upside down' (op. cit.: 58–9).

The explosion of sleaze journalism was also a product of the hyper-competition on Fleet Street. In the face of falling sales and the need for rising profits, the focus on sensationalism became inevitable. Yet, while stories tended to be exposed in the red-top, brasher tabloids, the rest of the media, operating similar news values, rapidly picked them up. It was the BBC's flagship investigative programme series, *Panorama*, which hosted Princess Diana's famous 1995 interview in which she described in detail her marriage breakdown and relations with the royal family. It was the highly-regarded *Channel 4 News* which paid Monica Lewinsky a reported £400,000 to be the first British broadcast institution to interview her. Dan Hogan complains (1998: 28): 'The major concern is that politicians are being let off the hook by an obsession with private lives. Other more crucial matters get less airtime and column centimetres.' Some media commentators suggested that the focus on sleaze in the run up to the 1997 election (with scandals surrounding Tory MPs such as Allan Stewart, Tim Smith, Piers Merchant and Neil Hamilton) meant that the BBC lost its normal neutral stance. According to Professor Hugh Stephenson, of City University, London: 'Normally during an election, the broadcasters are stuck with the agenda the major parties produce.' Sleaze had changed all that. 'The running story is anti-Tory which wouldn't normally be the case during an election.'

IS A PRIVACY LAW NECESSARY TO RESTRAIN THE MEDIA?

According to Matthew Kieran (2000: 163): 'Privacy concerns certain areas of our lives over which we exercise autonomous control and which it is not the business or right of others to concern themselves with unless we so choose.' Consequently, privacy is regarded as a fundamental human right – the essential bulwark against the state or social groups acquiring power over us to our disadvantage. Yet how can this privacy be best protected? And since there will be on occasions justifiable invasions of privacy, how can criteria for these be identified? The French elite certainly believes in the importance of legislating to protect privacy. Its law helped keep President Mitterrand's womanising and illegitimate daughter away from media scrutiny. The constitutions of Italy and Belgium also protect citizen's rights to privacy. In the United States, Australia and Canada there are statutory defences to privacy. But in Britain, the political elite has remained consistently opposed to such legislation, concerned over the difficulties in precisely defining 'privacy' and the 'public interest', though the debate has raged for many years.

- The first Royal Commission on the Press (1947–9) decided against privacy legislation, leaving it to a newly-created General Council of the Press to condemn bad practice.

- The Younger Committee on Privacy which reported in 1972 also came down against legislating.

- Following a spate of controversies over invasions of privacy, backbench Tory MP John Browne introduced a Privacy Bill to the House of Commons in 1989 but it was voted down.

- On 13 February 1990, the *Sunday Sport* took unauthorised photographs of comedian Gordon Kaye when recovering from a serious head wound in hospital. Ten days later the newspaper successfully appealed against an injunction obtained by the actor's agent preventing publication. The judge ruled there was no right to privacy in English law, implying that parliament should consider the introduction of a law to prevent such intrusions.

- The Calcutt Committee of Inquiry into Privacy and Related Matters, set up by the Thatcher Government, reported in 1990 and came down in favour of making physical intrusion an offence, but did not propose a privacy law. The Government held back and the newly-formed PCC (which replaced the Press Council as recommended by Calcutt) largely concerned itself with issues of privacy in its Code of Practice. Separate clauses looked at privacy, inquiries at hospitals, harassment, intrusions into grief or shock, interviewing or photographing children and covering victims of crime. Invasions of privacy could be justified only when in the 'public interest'. This it defined as:

  i)   detecting or exposing crime or serious misdemeanour,

  ii) detecting or exposing seriously anti-social behaviour,

  iii) protecting public health and safety,

  iv) preventing the public from being misled by some statement or action of that individual.

- On 7 June 1992 the *Sunday Times* began its serialisation of Andrew Morton's book on Princess Diana, revealing her unhappiness, suicide attempts and eating disorders. Though it later became known that the Princess had covertly assisted Morton, a huge row over the alleged unjustifiable invasion of privacy erupted. In July 1992, PCC chairman Lord MacGregor went so far as to describe reports of the royal marriage as 'an odious exhibition of journalists dabbling their fingers in the stuff of other people's souls'. In its defence the newspaper argued that the story raised important constitutional issues.

- David Mellor, the Heritage Minister (and Chelsea supporter), appointed Calcutt to head a new inquiry, warning the press they were drinking in the 'last chance saloon' in the face of the mounting threat of privacy legislation. But then, after Mellor's affair with an actress was revealed in the *People*, in July 1992, he was forced to resign in September. Privacy controversies continued after Prince Andrew's wife 'Fergie', the Duchess of York, was pictured in the *Daily Mirror* and *Observer* (clearly desperate for sales) frolicking topless with her 'financial adviser', and the *Sun* published the 'Squidgy' tapes of conversations supposedly between Princess Di and James Gilbey.

- Calcutt's second report, published in January 1993, recommended the replacement of the PCC with a statutory press tribunal. In addition, it proposed new offences carrying maximum fines of £5,000 for invasions of privacy and the use of surveillance and bugging devices in certain cases. In defence, journalists could claim the material was obtained for preventing, detecting or exposing crime or anti-social behaviour, or to prevent people being misled by some statement or action of the individual concerned.

- The Major Government responded positively and, later in the year, proposed the introduction of a privacy law. Yet it was determined not to apply the restrictions to the security services.

- In March 1993 the Commons national heritage committee on privacy and media intrusion included in its 43 recommendations the suggestion that the Government appoint a Press Ombudsman and a Protection of Privacy Bill, while in July the Lord Chancellor, Lord Mackay, published a consultation paper, *The Infringement of Privacy*, which proposed a new civil tort to protect privacy. In November the committee added an addendum to its March report calling for a new privacy tort.

- A new controversy erupted in November 1993 after the *Sunday Mirror* and *Daily Mirror* published 'peeping tom' photographs of Princess Di in L.A. Fitness Club, Isleworth, West London. Colin Myler, editor of the *Sunday Mirror*, defended publication on grounds of the security issues it raised.

- The PCC introduced new clauses to the code on bugging and the use of telephoto lenses and a lay majority (though only of the Great and the Good) was created amongst its members. In addition, Professor Robert Pinker, of the London School of Economics, was appointed special privacy commissioner in January 1994.

- In March 1994, the Association of British Editors, the Guild of British Editors and the International Press Institute issued 'an alternative white paper', *Media Freedom and Regulation*, which concluded that it was unnecessary to introduce a privacy law since it would 'risk seriously undermining legitimate public investigation by the media'.

- In October 1994, the *Guardian* began its own long campaign to expose MPs taking cash handouts from lobbyists in return for asking parliamentary questions. After editor Peter Preston admitted his reporters had sent a 'cod fax' to the Ritz Hotel, Paris, and used a mock-up of the House of Commons notepaper to protect a source, all in search of financial information about Cabinet Minister Jonathan Aitken, the privacy debate hit fever pitch. Preston duly resigned from the PCC, though Premier John Major soon afterwards set up a committee, chaired by Lord Nolan, to investigate the ethical behaviour of MPs and lobbyists. Aitken was duly jailed for 18 months in July 1999 (though in the end he served only 30 weeks) after being discovered lying over the payment of a bill at the Ritz during a libel case against the *Guardian* (Leigh and Vulliamy 1997). Intriguingly, security expert Gordon Thomas (2000: 4) suggests that the case collapsed after investigators acting for the newspaper were tipped off over the crucial Ritz stay by Mossad, the Israeli secret service 'through a third party source'.

- The appointment in November 1994 of Lord Wakeham, former Tory Cabinet Minister, as PCC chairman was welcomed by many mainstream journalists as likely to smooth the relations between press and parliament, particularly over privacy issues.

- In 1995, the PCC criticised the *News of the World* for publishing pictures, gained through the use of a long-lens camera, of yet another aristocrat, a frail-looking Countess Spencer, sister-in-law of the Princess of Wales, in the garden of a private health clinic. After her husband, Earl Spencer, complained, Professor Pinker contacted Rupert Murdoch, owner of the *News of the World*, who publicly reprimanded its editor, Piers Morgan. Murdoch described Morgan as 'a young man' who 'went over the top' in his coverage. Morgan duly apologised – and went on to even greater fame as editor of the *Mirror* (Browne 1996).

- In April 1995 the Commons privileges committee condemned the *Sunday Times* for 'falling substantially below the standards to be expected of legitimate journalism' over stories exposing Graham Riddick and David Tredinnick. The Tory MPs had accepted £1,000 from an undercover journalist to ask questions in parliament. The newspaper was originally backed by the PCC but in March 1996, it reversed its decision, ruling that the newspaper did not gather enough information since an issue of serious public interest was involved.

- In July 1995, a new White Paper, presented by Heritage Minister Virginia Bottomley, called for the PCC to pay compensation to victims of privacy intrusion; for a clearer definition of privacy in its code; and for a telephone line to be set up between the PCC and editors to head off breaches of code. Tory backbenchers greeted the announcement with jeers; the Labour Party expressed disappointment.

- Much of the privacy controversy had focused around the media's coverage of Princess Diana. Her own attitude to the media was ambivalent: at times appearing to welcome and even encourage coverage; at other times frankly detesting it. In November 1995, nine days after her *Panorama* interview, she telephoned *News of the World* royal reporter Clive Goodman and gave him an exclusive interview. But then just months later in 1996 for instance, she won an injunction preventing a member of the paparazzi from approaching within 300 metres of her. After her death on 31 August 1997 in a Paris road crash, blame initially fell on the paparazzi who were allegedly pursuing the royal Mercedes at the time. New guidelines on the use of paparazzi photographs were introduced by the PCC and, in revising the code, Lord Wakeham redefined 'a private place' as covering the interior of a church, a restaurant and other places 'where individuals might rightly be free from media attention'.

- In February 1998, the Lord Chancellor, Lord Irvine, caused enormous confusion after proposing a privacy law allowing for prior restraint by the PCC and the payment of compensation to victims of privacy invasions. He was promptly rebuked by Premier Tony Blair who remained committed to opposing privacy legislation.

- In June 1998, the Broadcasting Standards Commission introduced its code with a specific focus on the protection of privacy.

- Then in April 2000, the PCC condemned the *News of the World* in what Roy Greenslade, media commentator of the *Guardian*, called a 'landmark' judgement on privacy. A typical kiss 'n' tell story (headlined 'Street star's eight-month marathon of lust') by the former fiancé of *Coronation Street* actress, Jacqueline Pirie, was said to have breached clause three of the code: 'Everyone is entitled to his or her private and family life, home, health and correspondence.' As Greenslade concluded: 'In other words, the one-sided account by Pirie's ex-fiancé, even though its truth has not been disputed, was considered to have invaded her privacy.'

While in opposition, the Labour Party had backed calls for privacy legislation as a way of curbing press excesses. When in office, its tune changed. Soon after its May 1997 landslide victory, New Labour made it clear it was not planning to introduce privacy laws unless newspapers behaved in an 'intolerable fashion'. Journalists disguising themselves as doctors was given as an example of such behaviour. Fears grew amongst prominent journalists that the European Convention on Human Rights, which the Government was due to incorporate into British law, could introduce privacy legislation 'by the back door'. But on 11 February 1998, Tony Blair pledged in the Commons that the Government had no such intention. Article 8 of the convention, incorporated into British law in October 1999, states: 'Everybody has the right to respect for his private and family life, his home and his correspondence.' Balancing this, Article 10 guarantees freedom of expression.

Significantly, on 16 January 1998, the European Commission of Human Rights ruled that Earl Spencer and his former wife had insufficient grounds for starting a case under the European Convention of Human Rights over the Government's failure to protect them against press intrusions. And in June 2000, after Lord Levy, a multi-millionaire fund-raiser for the Labour Party, was found by the *Sunday Times* to have paid just £5,000 tax for the previous year, his application for an injunction to prevent publication was rejected. Mr Justice Joulson ruled that there was an over-riding public interest in the information being published. Others objected to this invasion of privacy. The *Guardian* editorial of 26 June took the judge's ruling – 'He who actively involves himself in public life, as Lord Levy has, cannot altogether complain if he is caught by the heat' – as a major definition of the media's public interest defence.

IS THERE A CASE FOR RELAXING THE LIBEL LAWS IN EXCHANGE FOR THE INTRODUCTION OF A PRIVACY LAW?

Some journalists, such as Alan Rusbridger, editor of the *Guardian*, argue that a properly worded privacy law, which might reduce some of the media's excesses, could be exchanged for a new libel legislation that encouraged free expression on matters of public importance. The case stands on the US Supreme Court ruling in 1964 by Justice William J. Brennan. In the case of *New York Times* v. *Sullivan*, Brennan revolutionised American libel law by ruling: 'Debate on public issues should be uninhibited, robust and wide open and . . . it may well include vehement, caustic and sometimes unpleasantly sharp attacks on government and public officials.' He said that the fear of libel litigation dampened the vigour and limited the variety of public debate. Public officials would have to prove actual malice: in other words, the reporter would have to be shown to be reckless as to whether what they were writing was true or not.

In India, too, journalists have an established defence after defamatory claims have been made about the conduct of public officials, and in Australia a special 'qualified privilege' has emerged for political discussion in a series of rulings culminating in a 1997 victory by ABC against David Lange, former New Zealand Premier (Crooks 1998). Concerns were raised in 2000 after ITN's successful libel action against the left-wing *LM*, over its coverage of the Bosnian prisoner-of-war camps, killed off the magazine. Under US libel laws, *LM* may well have survived. In a major 1997 survey conducted by researchers at the School of Media at the London College of Printing, more than a third of the journalists backed the introduction of a privacy law, while 41.3 per cent believed that in some circumstances such a law might be justified.

DO YOU CONSIDER UNDERCOVER 'STING' INVESTIGATIONS UNNECESSARILY INVADE PEOPLE'S PRIVACY?

The codes (of the ITC, BSC and PCC) are unanimous in stressing that subterfuge is only legitimate in the public interest and when the material cannot be obtained by other means. A ruling by the BSC against the *Watchdog* programme suggests evidence of malpractice is needed before secret filming is attempted, while under the ITC code the consent of the broadcasting company's senior programme executive is required before commencing secret filming. There are many associated problems. For instance, when a journalist takes on a job in order to expose malpractice, they are, strictly speaking, obtaining money on false pretences. In one case, a *World in Action* reporter escaped prosecution after taking a job in an abattoir, though the programme returned the money earned.

In 2000, Lesley Saunders, freelance for the *Reading Chronicle*, took a job at the town's legal aid office, where she was made to:

- invent a false name for a client;

- enter a false date of birth;

- over-ride computer warnings that cash limits were being exceeded;

- omit clients' National Insurance numbers;

- authorise a claim where the client's name differed from his signature.

The furore which followed her undercover investigation led to questions in parliament and a promise by a Government minister to look into the way solicitors' fee claims were being processed. Clearly the reporter's strategy was justified. In 1998, *Observer* reporter Gregory Palast claimed to represent an American company in his meetings with lobbyists at Westminster and was able to expose several boasting of the access to government information and ministers they could offer if the company became their client. In April 2000, Burhan Wazir, of the *Observer*, went undercover to show how a £350 bribe helped smuggle him into Britain in a truck with two Pakistanis and an Iranian.

In broadcasting, two of the most prominent undercover reporters are Roger Cook, of *Checkpoint* and the *Cook Report*, and Donal MacIntyre, of *World in Action* and *MacIntyre Undercover*. Bravely adopting the roles of football hooligan, care worker, bodyguard and fashion photographer, MacIntyre gathered secret evidence of violence, corruption and exploitation which led to the suspension of four senior executives of an international model agency and the closure of the care home investigated. In addition, four other homes run by the same owners were also shut, leaving 42 mentally handicapped people homeless and 84 workers redundant. MacIntyre stresses both that undercover work is 'a tool of absolute last resort' and the importance of the reporter deciding their principles before taking on an assignment. His own principles are (Spark op. cit.: 171):

1. Never make friends with anyone who isn't a criminal. Your friend might otherwise suffer retribution after you have gone.

2. Never break the law. You may buy drugs in certain limited circumstances but you must send them for analysis to check whether they are true narcotics. Give orders that they must be destroyed or given to the police.

3. Do not compromise your sources.

4. Simply be a witness of what you see. It's not your job to convict anyone.

5. Remember that anything written or recorded is a matter of record and may become evidence in a court case. Never be flippant in an inquiry.

But questions were raised over MacIntyre's techniques after the police said they planned to sue the BBC for the £50,000 cost of an investigation into the 'misleading and distressing' claims made in November 1999 documentary on the Brompton Care Home for mentally handicapped patients in Gillingham. The BBC rejected the police claims – and criticisms from the *Sunday Telegraph* – as 'ludicrous'. Producer Alex Holmes said investigative journalists should not have to worry about whether they had enough evidence to secure a conviction before transmitting a programme. But others drew on Howard Kurtz's criticisms of the US media to argue that the *Undercover* series was making investigative journalism 'part of the vast entertainment culture which seeks to amuse and titillate and shy away from the risks of old-style muckraking as media corporations have grown wary of abusing influence and offending the public' (Kurtz 1993: 5).

You may even consider journalists are in danger of acting as 'agents provocateurs' inciting victims to commit crimes. In March 1998, Freddie Shepherd and Douglas Hall, directors of Newcastle United Football Club, were taped by an intrepid *News of the World* investigative reporter, Mazher Mahmood, mocking fans, Geordie women and England captain Alan Shearer. Mahmood had posed as a rich foreign businessman, taking them to a luxurious hotel suite and on a crawl around Marbella's nightspots. As Spark comments (1999: 11), a touch of showmanship and cheek helped here. It was one of a series of 'exposés' by the red-top that raised concerns over journalistic entrapment of celebrities. Critics of the 'sting' strategy claimed that people's privacy was being invaded, being enticed into committing acts they would have avoided but for the presence or encouragement of the undercover reporter. Other celebrity victims of the *NoW*'s 'cocaine sting' strategy in the same year included Richard Bacon (fired from presenting *Blue Peter*), DJ Johnnie Walker (suspended from Radio 2) and England rugby captain Lawrence Dallaglio (fined £15,000 for bringing the game into disrepute).

Significantly, as concerns mounted, a judge in September 1999 passed a lenient sentence on the Earl of Hardwicke after he accepted that he had been entrapped into taking cocaine, and thus committing the offence, by the *News of the World*. The paper defended its position, claiming it was exposing 'one of the greatest social evils in Britain'. Earlier, John Alford, of TV's *London Burning*, was jailed after another *NoW* 'cocaine sting'. Also, following a *Sunday Times* investigation in July 2000 which revealed that Lord Levy, Tony Blair's special envoy to the Middle East, had paid just £5,000 in taxes for 1998–9 there were allegations that reporters had committed a crime to gather the information. Some journalists oppose the use of deception on principle. Benjamin C. Bradlee, executive editor of the *Washington Post*, criticised an operation by the *Chicago Sun-Times* in which undercover reporters had operated a bar for four months to expose bribery and fraud among building inspectors: 'In a day in which we are spending thousands of man-hours uncovering deception, we simply cannot deceive' (Meyer 1987: 79).

WOULD YOU APPLY DIFFERENT CRITERIA FOR COVERING THE PRIVATE LIVES OF POLITICIANS AND CELEBRITIES AND 'ORDINARY PEOPLE'?

Most journalists would reply immediately 'Yes'. Most politicians and celebrities expect constant public exposure as an inevitable part of their lifestyles. Most crave publicity, many are remarkably open (and even confessional) about the most intimate aspects of their private lives when interviewed. Thus, you may argue, they can hardly complain when they fall victim to 'bad publicity'. Journalists often argue that exposés are justified to highlight hypocrisy. A celebrity may thrive on a squeaky clean image but, in private, may be found to be abusing children, say. But, say a former male friend of a woman Labour MP approached the media with a 'kiss and tell' story of lust and betrayal, all of it happening ten years ago. Would this be legitimate? Could it be justified in the public interest? If the brother of a famous soccer personality was found to be an addicted gambler, would that be OK to carry? In November 1996, Lord Wakeham outlined seven key public interest tests which he wanted editors to consider before publication:

1. Is there a genuine public interest involved in invading someone's privacy as defined by Clause 18 of the Code of Practice – detecting or exposing crime, protecting public health, preventing the public from being misled – or is this simply a story which interests the public?

2. If there is a genuine public interest, have you considered whether there are ways to disclose it which minimise invasion into the private life of the individual concerned?

3. If you are using photographs as part of the story, which will have to be (or have already been) obtained by clandestine means and therefore compound the invasion of privacy, does the public interest require their automatic publication or are they simply illustrative?

4. Is there a genuine public interest which cannot be exposed in any other way than intrusion; have you considered whether there is any other way to minimise the impact on the innocent and vulnerable relatives of the individual, in particular the children?

5. If you are intending to run a story about someone connected or related to a person in the public eye in order to illustrate a story about a public figure, are you satisfied the connection isn't too remote and there is a genuine public interest in mentioning the connection?

6. Where you are preparing to publish a story seeking to contrast what a public figure has said or done in the past with his current statements or behaviour, have you satisfied yourself it is fair to make such a comparison and that the original statement or behaviour was recent enough to justify publication in the public interest?

7. If you are intending to run a story about the private life of an individual where there used to be a public interest, have you applied each of these questions afresh in case a defence no longer exists?

On these criteria, both the above story ideas fail. Red tops, however, are likely to publish in the hope of boosting sales – and then take the PCC flak. The privacy issue becomes further confused when 'public office' comes to include everyone from vicars, council officers, teachers, lawyers, soldiers and police officers. Stories of randy vicars and teachers eloping with schoolchildren are part of the constant diet of red top Sundays. Can these be justified? Behind the titillation of all these exposés, it could be argued, is a reactionary moral agenda, condemning any behaviour that threatens conventional 'family values'.

WHAT CRITERIA SHOULD YOU APPLY TO THE INTERVIEWING OF RELATIVES/FRIENDS AFTER SOMEONE'S DEATH?

Such interviews (called 'deathknocks' in the jargon) can be particularly harassing for journalists. Mourners can be obviously acutely depressed with little interest in sharing their feelings with a stranger. Sometimes journalists simply decline to follow the news desk's lead and phone in with an excuse, though journalists have been known to be sacked over such refusals. In December 1999, Ian Bailey, a reporter on the *Stoke Sentinel*, who refused his editor's order to seek an interview with a football manager after his son's suicide, lost his claim for unfair dismissal. Sometimes people welcome the attention of the reporter and use the interview as an opportunity to celebrate the life of the deceased person. Clearly discretion is required. The PCC significantly ruled against one newspaper after its reporter broke news of death to relatives and carried out inquiries without 'sufficient discretion'.

One of the most celebrated examples of journalists respecting the privacy of individuals caught up in tragic circumstances came after Thomas Hamilton killed 16 children and a teacher in a primary school massacre at Dunblane in 1996. Immediately after the event, television broadcast shots of a mother breaking down as she heard her child had died and the *Sun* and *Daily Mail* used close-up pictures of the same woman in distress. But thereafter, the media showed restraint. As John Taylor comments (1998: 105):

> The response was also marked by a new, rare respect for privacy: the media voluntarily stopped invading the privacy of vulnerable people whose loved ones had died in the massacre. The anniversary of the massacre was marked by the continuing conspicuous absence of invasive 'doorstep' journalism from Dunblane, which in this case was regarded as unfitting or outlandish.

No images of dead bodies were seen in the media but the signs of youth, innocence and unity were reproduced by using an official school photograph of the class. But was this appropriate? Some parents were distressed by seeing the photograph of their smiling children, particularly alongside pictures of their killer.

5
Dumbing down or dumbing up? The tabloidisation controversy

ARE THE MEDIA INCREASINGLY OBSESSED WITH SEX AND SENSATIONALISM IN THE HUNT FOR PROFITS, AUDIENCES AND CIRCULATIONS?

Scandal has always been the staple ingredient of the mass media and few periods have escaped moral panics over alleged declining media standards. Journalists through the ages have tended to be asssociated with the 'street of shame'. As Samuel Johnson (1709–84) put it: 'If an ambassador is said to be a man of virtue sent abroad to tell lies for the advantage of his country, a newswriter is a man without virtue who writes lies for his own profit.' And Professor Hugh Stephenson stresses (1998: 19): 'Sex, lies and the invasion of privacy of individuals have certainly been an important part of the staple diet of popular British newspapers since British newspapers have existed.'

But the most recent panic over the alleged dumbing down of the media (Mosley 2000) is generally seen as starting with Rupert Murdoch's purchase of the *News of the World* in 1968, serialising shortly afterwards the memoirs of Christine Keeler, so reviving memories of the Profumo affair. In the following year Murdoch purchased the tabloid *Sun* from the owners of the *Daily Mirror*, the International Publishing Corporation, and shortly afterwards the infamous topless 'Page 3 girl' was introduced, allegedly institutionalising a new sexual 'permissiveness'. By 1978 the brash, 'soaraway' *Sun* had overtaken the *Mirror* and in June of that year sales passed the 4 million figure, while the 'downmarket' *Daily Star* was launched by Express Newspaper Group in 1978, targeted at northern male/chauvinist readers. According to the critics, this 'plague' of trivia and tabloidisation shifted from the newspapers to the media in general.

Nick Cohen (1999: 129–30) blames the dumbing down of the media on the rise in power of shareholders who have brought about the greatest change in Anglo-Saxon capitalism since the 1970s: 'Shareholders, encouraged by deregulatory governments, have broken out of the social democratic prison by becoming footloose. If a corporation does not produce short-term profits, they sell and the company faces takeover or closure.' And, he continues: 'Bad journalism is a consequence of an unregulated market in which would-be monopolists are free to treat the channels of democratic debate as their private property.'

But many question this approach. For instance, the Archbishop of Canterbury, in February 2000, said newspapers should delve into the private lives of politicians to expose extramarital affairs, sexual high jinx and homosexuality. Such exposés were a legitimate matter of public interest, he argued:

> I believe it is a self delusion for politicians and those at the centre of public life to think they can divest themselves of the responsibility to make and respect moral judgment. The question has to be asked often enough whether in the Church's view, sexual sins have any relevance to standards in public life. I do not believe they can be disregarded. The question reasonably arises in the public mind why should we have confidence in someone in public life who cannot be trusted not to cheat in their private life?

Alan Rusbridger, editor of the *Guardian*, and Will Hutton, former editor of the *Observer*, have both argued that recent years have witnessed a 'dumbing up' of the media. Hutton claimed the media were carrying more attractive writing, clearer 'hooks' and better narrative stories than in the past. An editorial in the *Independent* of 6 March 1999 highlighted this view, claiming that the increased emphasis on popular culture within the broadsheets was making cultural life more open and democratic.

You may also argue, along with Helen Montgomery, news editor of the *Cambridge Evening News*, that making reports more interesting and accessible should not be dubbed 'dumbing down', which becomes an elitist, snobbish notion. Peregrine Worsthorne, former editor of the *Sunday Telegraph*, comments (1999: 122): 'Newspapers are far more sophisticated, far cleverer, far better written than they ever were before; incomparably more entertaining and readable.' In the same spirit, BBC executives such as Tony Hall, chief executive, news, consistently argue that, even in a period of hyper competition from the commercial sector, the Corporation has managed to maintain its public service commitment to high-quality broadcasting. Support for this view came from Steve Barnett, of the University of

Westminster, who with other colleagues analysed changing trends in tele-vision news from 1975 to 1999. Their research, published in July 2000, dis-puted the 'dumbing down' thesis, claiming that journalists were 'working harder to make difficult stories more understandable to people watching them'. At the same time, Barnett predicted a decline in news over the next ten years with the 'marginalisation of serious and foreign reporting', and a fall in the amount of political coverage.

Jon Grubb, deputy editor of the *Nottingham Evening Post*, also argues 'emphatically' that local newspapers have not 'dumbed down':

In the last two years particularly, many of the leading regional newspapers have recognised the need for the paper to examine issues with expertise, responsibility and depth. After all it is the ability to put things in context and examine issues in depth that sets newspapers apart from their other media rivals – TV, radio and the Internet. As newspapers develop their own individual websites I think we will see this trend grow. Newsrooms may soon be expected to produce short, sharp news items for their Internet site and detailed articles for the newspaper. Far from dumbing down I think we could be entering a real renaissance period for newspapers with a greater range of issues, more in-depth writing and a deeper commitment to investigations and campaigns.

IS THERE TOO MUCH BAD NEWS IN THE MEDIA?

Switch on the box and you are most likely to hear terribly depressing news: a murder, famine in Africa, a teacher jailed for sexual abuse, and so on. How different from the news routines in the old Soviet Union where the stress was always on positive social phenomena. As Brian McNair (1994: 34) comments:

The Soviet news media had no need to concern themselves with winning audience share or making profits, so they did not consistently have to outdo each other with exclusives and shock-horror headlines. Western news media, by contrast, are required to win audiences with entertainment as well as information. Entertainment is often about drama and drama is, more often than not, about conflict and negativity.

In 1993, the debate about good/bad news was highlighted by the broadcaster Martyn Lewis who used his prominent public position to call passionately for a complete rethink about news values. 'We are sitting on the outer circle of a whirlpool of negativity and in danger of being sucked into the vortex,' he said. Journalism award ceremonies leaned too heavily towards images of disasters. 'It has become locked in the journalistic lexicon that these are the kind of winning stories many talented reporters should aspire to. It is surely just as great a journalistic challenge to pursue positive stories – which don't present such dramatic pictures but are every bit as important to society as a whole – and turn them into TV news reports that people want to watch.' In February 1999, he maintained his crusade at a conference sponsored by the *Financial Times*, claiming that a BBC review of news policy stated that audiences were alienated by journalism which appeared fixated by problems. They wanted more of a sense of how issues could be resolved.

Reportedly warned by senior BBC executives against launching his campaign, Lewis received a generally hostile response from his national colleagues such as Jeremy Paxman, Peter Sissons, John Cole, John Humphrys and John Simpson. Perhaps he offended them because, at root, his views highlighted the bias and selectivity behind their supposedly 'objective' news values. But at the same time Lewis received much support from local journalists. As Robin Fletcher, editor of the *Northampton Chronicle and Echo*, commented: 'For local newspapers it is not a question of "should we, shouldn't we?" when it comes to good news. Those who ignore good news cannot survive. End of story.' Significantly, in 2000, three newspapers in the Courier group, the *Standish Courier*, *Shevington Courier* and *Wigan Courier*, put down their success to pursuing only positive news stories about the communities they covered. Publisher Mark Ashley commented: 'People tell us they can get depressing news if they want it from the national newspapers.' His stance went 'against all my years of training and work as a journalist but there is no doubt in my mind now that there is a market in the regions for a non-stop diet of good news'. A website at http://www.good-newsnetwork.org is devoted entirely to good news. The *Guardian* described it as 'worthy and boring'.

During the 1990s the good news/bad news debate became enmeshed in controversies over the media's growing obsession with lifestyle and 'soft', infotainment features (such as on fashion, gardening, DIY, travel, wine, restaurants, shopping) at the expense of 'hard', serious news. As Michael Bromley comments (1994: 99):

> In the 1980s most journalists would have been extremely uncomfortable to find themselves relocated in show business. By the early 1990s many were already there, writing daily updates on the plots of television soap operas and paying enormous sums of money for anodyne interviews with celebrities. Some were becoming marketers of 'useful information' on the opening hours of chemist's shops and how to survive in a snow storm.

You may consider the local media's commitment to good news is driven by economic necessity: to survive they have to be actively involved in their local communities, praising their achievements (particularly in industry, the suppliers of the all-important advertising revenue), running campaigns, sponsoring events. Others claim Lewis' views over-simplified the complex issues surrounding news values (hence their popularity). Concepts of 'good' and 'bad' are always going to be subjective: the Glasgow University Media Group, for instance, during the 1970s and 1980s highlighted the ways in which the mainstream media consistently portrayed trade unionists in a 'bad' light. 'Bad' events such as disasters are part of the staple diet of news, yet much of the coverage subverts this 'negativity' by focusing on 'positive' angles – such as the 'heroic' activities of rescuers and the emergency services or on 'miracle escapes'.

WHAT DO THE CONTROVERSIES OVER FAKE TELEVISION PROGRAMMES TELL YOU ABOUT TRENDS IN JOURNALISTIC STANDARDS?

During the late 1990s and into 2000, broadcasters became involved in a series of controversies over faking information which seriously damaged their reputations.

- In December 1998, the television watchdog, the ITC, fined Granada Television £2 million for breaches of its code in the 1996 documentary, *The Connection*. Made by Carlton for ITV's *Network First*, it focused on a supposedly new route for running heroin into Britain from Cali in Colombia. It was seen by 3.7 million viewers, won eight international awards and was broadcast on 14 stations around the world. But an exposé by the *Guardian* in May 1998 revealed that 'drug runners' were, in fact, actors playing the part and the 'heroin' shown was sweets. The company also had to pay £5,000 damages to a man it wrongly accused of supplying heroin.

- After a Channel 4 series debunking the green movement was screened in 1997, the Independent Television Commission required the channel to make an on-air apology in April 1998 to four environmentalists whose views had been misrepresented through selective editing.

- The 1997 BBC1 series *Driving School* made a celebrity of serial test failure Maureen Rees. But the BBC later admitted that certain scenes were staged, including the waking of husband Dave Rees at 4 a.m. to test her on the Highway Code.

- A *Cutting Edge* film, *Rogue Males*, about cowboy builders and petty criminals, was exposed in the *Mirror* in February 1998 as containing faked scenes including a violent row between two decorators and a customer and an incident in which a pair were shown stealing a pallet. Channel 4 apologised for 'several scenes that were effectively constructed for the camera'.

- On 9 June 1998, the *Guardian* revealed that another Carlton award-winning documentary, which claimed it had secured an exclusive interview with Fidel Castro, Cuban President, was a fake. Shots of Castro talking to camera were actually unlabelled archive footage provided by the Cuban Government.

- In June 1998, the Broadcasting Standards Commission criticised daytime confessional shows such as *Vanessa, Kilroy, Esther, Ricki Lake, Oprah Winfrey* and *Jerry Springer* for cultivating 'victim entertainment'. 'Exploitation of the misfortune of others is not an endearing human trait. A society which has long since abandoned the stocks as a form of public entertainment should think twice about the modern version designed to titillate rather than inform.' Then in February 1999, the *Mirror* revealed that, in a number of cases, guests on the *Vanessa Show* who laid bare their personal histories were actors and impersonators.

- Also in the same month, Matthew Parris, on Radio 5 Live's *Late Night Live*, revealed that stumped celebrities on Channel 4's quiz show *Countdown* were whispered suggestions through an earpiece.

- On 23 March 1999, the *Guardian* revealed that a Channel 4 documentary, *Guns on the Street*, that investigated how Manchester gangsters obtained illegal guns (and which led to the imprisonment of a man for seven years) was faked in key sections. One of the reporters who posed as a concerned citizen in the documentary withheld the fact that he had convictions for burglary and armed robbery.

- In April 1999, the BSC upheld a complaint of 'unfairness and unwarranted infringement of privacy' from a man portrayed as a criminal in the Channel 4 film *Stolen Goods* broadcast in May 1998. The commission concluded that broadcasters who did not seek to inform or use the police before screenings should take 'great care' before accusations of illegal behaviour are broadcast.

Most critics blame financial cutbacks for the drowning of investigative journalism under the floods of sensationalism. Significantly Alan Yentob,

director of programmes at the BBC, admitted that the use of fake particip-
ants on the *Vanessa Show* was ultimately due to a lack of resources (*Press
Gazette* 25 February 2000). Others argue that reconstructions are an
inevitable part of television. Roger Graef, a founding director of Channel
4, argues (2000) that the fuss over staging in documentaries 'misses the
point' that most factual programmes have been staged since the heyday of
great film-makers such as John Grierson and Humphrey Jennings. And
Matthew Kieran (2000: 172–3) comments:

> Often people wish to remain anonymous and won't trust being filmed in
> shadow or having their voice synthesised, so someone is brought in to act
> out the part and utter the anonymous source's words for them. A
> sequence of events may be quite hard to describe, the relevant detail may
> be cumbersome or tricky and it may be much easier to convey the right
> kind of impression of what happened by dramatisation – not to mention
> making the documentary more telegenic. Or it may be that the actual
> filmed or tape recorded evidence is scratchy, fits badly together and is
> hard to discern.

He compares such practices to the reporter rewriting or making up quotes
because they seem to express more clearly the interviewee's actual
thoughts. 'As long as this is checked with the interviewee, to rule out mis-
understandings on the part of the journalist, there seems to be nothing
wrong.' But he stresses that reconstructions should be allowed only under
strict conditions, namely:

1. The journalistic team can substantiate the dramatisation independently in a manner which shows they have sufficient grounds to claim
   that they either know this was or probably was the case.

2. Those independent grounds are made perfectly clear in the programme
   and the validity of the reconstruction is shown to rest on these grounds.

3. The reconstruction is labelled on screen as such to the audience and it
   is made clear whether the dramatisation is being presented in terms of
   what is known to be the case, believed to be probable or merely a
   representation of what might plausibly or possibly have happened.

HAS INVESTIGATIVE JOURNALISM GONE OUT OF FASHION WITH COMEDIANS SUCH AS MARK THOMAS TAKING OVER ITS ROLE?

No, according to Hugo de Burgh, senior lecturer in journalism at Nottingham Trent University, former broadcaster and editor of a major study of

investigative journalism (2000). In fact, following the development of investigative journalism during the 1960s and 1970, by the 1990s, he suggests, it was 'booming'. Amongst the documentary series he cites were the BBC's *Inside Story, Public Eye, 40 Minutes, Taking Liberties, Rough Justice, Private Investigations, Timewatch* and *Here and Now*; ITV's *Big Story, Network First, First Tuesday, The Cook Report* and Channel 4's *Cutting Edge, Street Legal, Countryside Undercover, Undercover Britain, Secret History* and *Witness*. For 1995 alone, on UK terrestrial television there were 300 discrete programmes that could be classified as investigative, excluding programmes with investigative elements. On BBC radio there were *File on Four* and *Face the Facts* while other programmes with a tradition of investigative work included *You and Yours*, the *Food Programme, Farming Today*, the *Today Programme* and the *World This Weekend*.

In print, Paul Foot's books *Who Framed Colin Wallace?* (1989) and *Murder at the Farm: Who Killed Carl Bridgwater?* (1993) have examined serious cases of injustice. John Pilger's print and screen journalism (much of it collected in a special site: www.carlton.com/pilger) has consistently examined injustices at both home and abroad: in East Timor, Australia, South Africa and Iraq. The *Guardian's* investigations have exposed broadcast fakes and parliamentary corruption. Its exposure of Tory MP Neil Hamilton and the shady activities of covert lobbyists such as Ian Greer are said to have played an important role in the collapse of support for the Conservative Party in the 1997 general election. In early 1999 its exposure of ministerial corruption led to the resignations of Geoffrey Robinson and Peter Mandelson.

The special investigative role of Internet sites (free from the constraints of mainstream print and broadcast media) is being heralded by many. In the States, Matt Drudge's site was the first to reveal Monica Lewinsky's affair with President Clinton. And it was the tiny Internet e-zine, *TheSmoking-Gun*, founded by *Village Voice* investigative crime reporter William Bastone and freelance Daniel Green, and set up on a budget of $500, which revealed the hidden past of the groom on Rupert Murdoch's Fox Television's *Who Wants to Marry a Millionaire?* in February 2000. The revelation led to the sudden halting of the 'shockumentary' (Wittstock 2000).

Moreover the global aspects of the Internet are seen as stimulating a new kind of investigative work. The Washington-based International Consortium of Investigative Journalists [http://www.icij.org/] has been formed, linking journalists from Moscow, Tel Aviv, Panama, Britain, Japan and the US to examine major global issues. Its first investigation provided the lead story in the *Guardian* of 31 January 2000 and exposed British American Tobacco condoning tax evasion and exploiting the smuggling of billions of cigarettes in a global effort to boost sales. The Internet also provides easy access for British journalists to excellent US investigative magazines such as *ZMag* [www.ibbs.org/zmag], *Counterpunch* [www.counterpunch.org] and *Covert Action Quarterly* [http://mediafilter.org./caq]. Moreover, 1999 saw the formation in Britain of the Association of Investigative Journalists, modelled on the American Society of Investigative Reporters and Editors and with close links with the MA course in investigative journalism at Nottingham Trent University.

Others argue that the media's growing commercialisation has marginalised expensive investigative journalism such as undertaken by the *Sunday Times* Insight team under Harold Evans in the 1970s (Knightley 1998). Its investigations on behalf of the thalidomide victims and into the DC-10 air crash of 1974 were amongst its most celebrated campaigns. In contrast, newspapers are now left 'exposing' human interest scandals or, paradoxically, the failings of broadcast investigations. According to David Northmore (1994: 319), the 'arms to Iraq' controversy exposed the weakness of investigative journalism in Britain:

> In fact, details of British arms exports to Iraq only surfaced at the trial of three executives of Matrix Churchill because of skilful legal manoeuvring by the defence lawyers. The role of journalists and their respective media institutions in that case, as in the case of numerous fraud trials of the time, was to observe merely the proceedings from the sidelines and provide a detailed 'analysis by post mortem'.

Specific investigations have also drawn fierce criticisms from journalists. For instance, in March 1990, the *Daily Mirror* joined forces with Central Broadcasting's *Cook Report* to expose the National Union of Mineworkers as being in receipt of foreign funds during its strikes. Money donated by Soviet miners and Colonel Gaddafi, of Libya (dubbed a 'mad dog' by President Reagan) had also been siphoned off by leading NUM officials such as the widely demonised Arthur Scargill. But *Guardian* journalist Seamus Milne argued (1995), in a meticulously researched book, that the award-winning journalists had been duped by the secret services who had been seeking to smear the miners' leaders. Donal MacIntyre's investigations, into the international fashion industry and football hooligans, have drawn many plaudits – and many criticisms, as well. Some suggested that the style in which he carried out his investigations was given more prominence than the story he was delving into. Tessa Mayes, investigative reporter on *Panorama*, the *Cook Report* and Carlton TV's the *Investigators*, says journalists 'work within the restrictions imposed by self-regulatory codes and laws which increasingly make it difficult to air stories'. She cites the Protection from Harassment Act and the 1994 amendment to the Video Recordings Act (which makes anyone showing an uncertified video in a public place liable to imprisonment) as new threats.

Some journalists argue that a new breed of satirist is taking a new, vital role in journalism. John Pilger, for instance, says of satirist Mark Thomas:

> He's essentially a satirist but he's helping to fill a vacuum in investigative journalism. Journalism has become obsessed with lifestyle, gardening, trivia, celebrities and distractions. Mark has taken head-on the issues that touch our lives but in ways we may not immediately understand, then put them to us in a form we can engage with. So much journalism today doesn't do its basic job of keeping the record straight, peering under rocks, looking behind screens and telling people when they're being conned.
>
> (*Press Gazette* 25 February 2000)

Thomas' stunts for his Channel 4 series have shown multiple sclerosis sufferers smoking cannabis in Home Secretary Jack Straw's constituency and a politician dressed as a giant bear being interviewed. Critics suggest he is reducing politics to entertainment. But this is precisely what Thomas hopes for and what he believes journalism requires. Drawing inspiration from Situationism, an anarchist/art student movement of the late 1960s which used comic spectacles to highlight political issues, Thomas argues that journalists, in general, are too close to their sources. Being a comedian frees him from such constraints. In one sketch he interviewed a representative of the Indonesian army posing as someone from a firm offering training to deal with tough questions from human rights activists. In the course of the questioning the man admitted torture was a necessary evil. But such routines have not gone uncriticised. An item in Chris Morris' *Brass Eye* series hoaxed MPs into condemning a new and dangerous drug called 'cake' which was said to be illegally flooding into the country from the Czech Republic. But in April 1997, the ITC ruled that that programme had breached its code by not making the MPs aware of its format or purpose. And Tessa Mayes comments:

> In recent years experiments with humour, emotion, new types of presenters, covert filming techniques and subject matter have modernised programmes successfully. But before they can follow in the footsteps of the greats, journalists need to concern themselves with the Big Picture, not just the auto-focus on the mini-cam.

6
Race/anti-racism matters

Many journalists are concerned to remove discrimination on grounds of gender, sexual orientation, race, disability, age, mental health and so on. At the same time there is a dominant culture which tends to regard sceptically lobby groups interfering with journalistic professionalism and seeking to bend coverage to match their own biases. Such groups are often condemned as PC (political correctness) fanatics. Inevitably, in such emotionally charged contexts, argument, protest and defensiveness result – as well as lots of ideas for creative responses.

WHAT ARE THE MAJOR ETHICAL/POLITICAL ISSUES SURROUNDING THE MEDIA'S COVERAGE OF ETHNIC MINORITIES?

Many critics focus on the alleged institutional racism within the media industry when trying to explain the coverage of ethnic minorities. This racism is rooted in the country's imperial past, with feelings of racial superiority and crude nationalism now deeply embedded in the dominant culture. Columnist Polly Toynbee, in an article headed 'The West really is the best' (the *Observer*, 5 March 2000), argued: 'Deeply flawed maybe, but the best so far, Western liberal democracy is the only system yet devised that maximises freedom for the many.' But how accurate is this?

Some media workers have been identified as overtly racist. For instance, the *Sun*'s acting editor was recorded as saying: 'I'm not having pictures of darkies on the front page' (Hollingsworth 1990: 132). And some of the headlines which appeared in the tabloids during the Euro 96 football tournament and again over stories about asylum seekers during the late 1990s and early 2000 were racist. Significantly, the United Nations, on 19 November 1998, criticised the way in which Britain treated refugees. Yet, on 30 November 1998, the *Daily Mail* led its front page with the headline: 'Brutal crimes of asylum seekers'. In December of the same year the

Sun, under the headline 'Inn-sane' condemned the decision of a Gravesend hotel to allow 21 Romanian women and children to spend a night in the hotel after being discovered among a group of 103 people packed into a goods container (Donovan 1999). Amnesty International even considered taking legal action over whether the *Mail's* coverage could be considered to be inciting racial hatred. Local papers in Kent were accused of whipping up anti-immigrant sentiment in their coverage of asylum seekers (Platt 1998). 'Illegal immigrants, asylum seekers, bootleggers . . . and scum of the earth drug smugglers have targeted our beloved coastline,' raged the *Dover Express*. Concerns were also expressed after the *Sun*, *Daily Telegraph* and *Daily Mail* expressed 'ecstatic support' for William Hague, Conservative leader, after his 18 April 2000 speech recommending the detention of all new asylum seekers in secure units and the formation of a special removals agency to get rid of rejected asylum seekers.

The media are also criticised for being 'colour blind'. Few official statistics are available about ethnic minority employment in newspapers. John Tulloch, head of journalism at the University of Westminster, has conducted research into the figures and commented: 'One tabloid paper said: "We don't notice the colour of our journalists – we are all journalists together". I was intrigued subsequently to get from the same organisation a marketing pack which revealed they knew precisely how many black readers they had. So their marketing department takes notice of colour but their editorial doesn't' (McCue 2000: 20).

The roots of racism are cultural, economic, political – and extremely complex. As Stuart Allan comments (1999: 182): 'The ways in which racist presuppositions are implicated in the routinised priorities of news production from the news values in operation to "gut instincts" about source credibility are often difficult to identify let alone reverse.' The dominant culture is white and tends to marginalise (or eliminate altogether) the experience of other ethnic groups. For instance, there are 12 million Roma gypsies all over the world, eight million in Europe: 'They are the continent's largest ethnic minority group. Yet they are a forgotten people,' according to Martin Smith (*Socialist Worker* 3 June 2000). 'The long-hallowed cult of journalistic objectivity has too often been a veneer for what is essentially a predominantly white male point of view in our news culture,' says John Phillip Santos of his experience in the United States, but his words could equally apply to Britain. Only 1.8 per cent of NUJ membership is black. Asian, black and Arab journalists comprised just two per cent in the first industry-wide study by Anthony Delano and John Henningham (1995), a figure which was 'disproportionately low' compared to the national minority population of 5.26 per cent. Very few journalists working in provincial papers are black. And according to critics, there is no industry-wide effort to improve on this. In response, editors often claim there is a shortage of suitable applicants from ethnic minorities and not a shortage of institutional will.

The BBC, under director general John Birt, aimed to employ around eight per cent of staff from black and minority ethnic groups. But by early 2000 only two per cent of managers were from ethnic minorities. On 7 April 2000 Greg Dyke, newly-appointed director general, pledged to increase the number to ten per cent by 2003. In the same month, the NUJ accused the BBC of institutional racism. Ethnic minority staff stood in for colleagues at higher grades but were rarely promoted. And according to the union, there was a bottleneck of ethnic minority staff at low levels in the World Service newsroom at Bush House in London (Wells 2000). Somaye Zadeh, of BECTU (2000), also criticised the BBC for limiting work permits given to World Service journalists from abroad to a maximum of three years. This denied them the ability to stay in the country for four years as required to gain permanent residency. 'Many World Service journalists come from countries which are governed by totalitarian regimes and are in the midst of civil war. Furthermore, many are journalists who have been specifically targeted by their government.' And according to Yasmin Alibhai-Brown (2000), white, middle class Britons still hogged all the stories at the BBC. Professor Thom Blair, editor of the *Chronicle* Internet magazine (http://www.chronicleworld.org), says: 'Clearly there is evidence of diversity fatigue in the upper echelons of the BBC. Managers are failing to keep up the momentum of their commitments to race equality practices.'

Minority employment in newsrooms of commercial broadcast companies is 'derisory', according to Jim Pines, author of the UK's contribution to a major trans-European study of media employment, *More Colour in the Media*. A survey by BECTU (Broadcasting, Entertainment, Cinematograph and Theatre Union) showed that, with the exception of LWT, most companies were falling short of reasonable targets for minority employment and, in some, the levels were going down (Trevor Phillips, the *Guardian* 20 September 1999). In 2000, GMTV's Deborah Bain was the only black female national television reporter. She commented: 'Five or six years ago I was the only black person regularly on screen. Now I see more women and blacks and Asians on and off the screen. Blacks are being used as pundits and guest reporters. I believe a more diverse newsroom will create a more diverse agenda.'

Data from UCAS and HESA suggest that minority students are under-represented on journalism courses and are less likely than white candidates to gain admission. There are mounting criticisms that, following the introduction of student fees, both undergraduate and postgraduate studies are becoming the privilege of the middle class, with black students increasingly excluded. Many jobs in the industry are not advertised but filled through 'old boy networks' from which blacks also tend to be excluded. As black *Guardian* journalist Gary Younge comments: 'Editors tend to hire in their own image and thus reinforce the status quo. Blacks aren't in the network, it's as simple as that.' Adding to the complexity of the issues, it is often claimed that greater racial diversity in the news organisation does not automatically translate into more diverse forms of news coverage.

Paul Macey, regional affairs editor of the *Voice*, comments: 'I recently spoke to some black youths and asked them how they thought they were represented in the media. They said as muggers, rapists and on their way to prison. But when I asked them what their lives were really like they said they were afraid of being attacked, anxious about the future and scared of being stopped and searched by the police.' According to the Runnymede Trust, the media's failure to represent the daily experience of fear, insecurity and intimidation cramps the lives of virtually all blacks and ethnic minorities in Britain (*Runnymede Bulletin* March 1996).

Black stereotypes often associate them with crime. For instance, the *Bristol Evening Post* of 17 April 1996 under the headline 'FACES OF EVIL' showed 16 police 'mug shots' of convicted crack cocaine dealers: all were black. As Simon Cottle commented (1999: 192): 'For the *Post*'s 227,000 or so regular readers, the front page was unlikely to do other than confirm the prevalent views routinely fed by local news portrayal associating both the locality of St Paul's and its African–Caribbean population with crime and criminality.' In November 1998, a Channel 4 *Dispatches* documentary examined gang rapes in England and Wales. The programme identified 14 cases involving 79 youths, 80 per cent of them black. Did this not sensationalise the issue? Certainly the National Assembly Against Racism mounted a demonstration outside Channel 4's headquarters and called for it to be dropped from the schedules. Further criticism that television is failing to reflect the multi-cultural nature of the society, came in a report, *Include Me In*, published by Broadcasting Standards Commission in December 1999. Too often, programmes are guilty of presenting characters from ethnic minorities as two dimensional and without a role in society as a whole.

SHOULD RACIST POLITICAL PARTIES BE ALLOWED TO GIVE ELECTION BROADCASTS AND HAVE A VOICE IN THE MEDIA?

You may feel it vital that in a democracy all voices should be given a platform. Sinn Fein, the political wing of the IRA, has a voice so why not the National Front or the British National Party? You may disagree with their policies but feel the public has a right to hear them and judge for themselves. If they are cranks then they will be exposed as such by their policies. An alternative view stresses that the NF's racism is, in effect, outlawed by race relations legislation. Freedom within democracy, it is argued, does have its limits and so voices that stir up race hate must be banned. A middle-view is promoted by the National Union of Journalists. In its *Guidelines on Race Reporting*, it suggests that when quoting representatives of racist organisations, journalists should carefully check all reports for accuracy and seek rebutting comments. The anti-social nature of such views should be exposed. Journalists should seek to publish or broadcast material which exposes the myths and lies of racist organisations while letters columns and phone-in programmes should not be allowed to be used to spread race hatred.

DO YOU CONSIDER THE MARGINALISATION OF AFRICAN AND ASIAN NEWS TO BE PART OF THE GENERAL 'DUMBING DOWN' OF FOREIGN NEWS IN THE MEDIA?

In 1993, broadcaster Martyn Lewis said: 'I recently bumped into one well-known TV correspondent . . . who told me he had repeatedly proposed going to Africa specially to cover success stories . . . But he ran up against the stereotyped newsroom view of Africa as a continent racked by war, famine, corruption and AIDs.' Critics argue that such attitudes still prevail in newsrooms. Broadcaster Jonathan Dimbleby, for instance, has highlighted the 'dumbing down' of coverage of global issues. 'Reporters find themselves, not liberated by the ever-advancing technology but imprisoned by it: attached umbilically to this post-terrestrial means of instant transmission. The pressure to be first, to beat the rivals with even more sensational pictures, puts a premium on voyeurism,' he said. Labour minister Clare Short similarly accused the media and aid agencies of presenting an image of Africa which induced despair and 'compassion fatigue' and of ignoring the positive.

Guardian writer John Vidal (28 February 2000) commented:

> We almost certainly know less about what is happening in the world today than we did 10 years ago. TV hardly gives us a clue what is happening in most parts of the world, the social and economic forces

shaping people's lives, how other cultures think or are responding on political or personal levels to some of the greatest scientific, ecological, cultural and social changes in world history. Even as business and politics has been globalised and as more people than ever are travelling abroad, so British TV – the prime source of information about the 5bn people living in the developing world – has become more insular, shallower, more opinionated, narrower, consumer-led, less intelligent and more self-obsessed. Our world map is massively diminishing as our ignorance is increasing.

Channel 4 News presenter Jon Snow has criticised the 'scandalously low profile that foreign affairs have in broadcasting'. Virtually all the media over recent decades have made substantial cutbacks on their foreign reporting. 'Firemen' (and they are usually male) tend to fly out to foreign locations when major stories break and become instant experts – but how large is their knowledge of the country, its history, customs and language?

A study entitled *Losing Perspective* by Jennie Stone of the International Broadcasting Trust (2 Ferdinand Place, London NW1 8EE) shows that the vast majority of factual programmes about poorer countries at peak times are celebrity-led and about travel or wildlife. At the same time, foreign news coverage relies to an increasing extent on reporting disaster and conflict. Why is this? Stone suggests it is the result of diminishing budgets, the advent of new technology allowing images to be transmitted cheaply and quickly but which results in less in-depth coverage and a changing production culture, with staff more likely to move across pro-gramme genres with less overall commitment. Increasingly, resources are being diverted to online services and away from mainstream foreign coverage. Figures show that over the last decade factual programming on developing countries has declined on television by 50 per cent; ITV by 74 per cent, BBC by more than a third, Channel 4 by 56 per cent. Channel 5 has commissioned almost nothing from non-Western coun-tries since it was set up. *Observer* investigative journalist Greg Palast (2000) highlighted the way in which the media failed to cover the fight against water privatisation in Bolivia when a general strike forced the government to retreat.

It showed globalisation could be stopped in its tracks. Yet it was barely reported in the press. This is not because of direct pressure from institutions like the World Bank (although the leader of the bank did rush to condemn what he called 'rioters'). Rather it is because of the strange and horrid consensus which has emerged that there is no alternative to the New World Order that the people of Bolivia – and Third World peoples everywhere – simply don't understand.

And a report from the Glasgow Media Group in July 2000 for the Department of International Development found that most television coverage of the developing world concentrated on conflict, war or terrorism, often with little explanation and only rare follow-ups. Out of 137 developing countries, there was no coverage of 67 of them. Of the 72 countries covered, 16 were mentioned only in the context of reporting visits by westerners, wildlife events, sport – or the fact that a round-the-world balloon had flown over them.

Concern is also expressed over the influence of relief agencies in setting agenda for foreign coverage. Bridget Harrison (1997) comments:

> In crisis situations, the British element to a story is further perpetuated by aid agencies and charities who work in the Third World. Relief agencies actively court western media to publicise their activities and generate donations from the public. As a result, not only do we equate the Third World with disasters but imagine that these are rarely resolved without our help.

Some critics also point to the anglocentrism and inherently racist assumptions underlying the media's portrayal of death. John Taylor describes the 'hierarchy of death' (1998: 90–1):

> In general, dead bodies in Britain are treated with more respect or restraint than corpses of foreigners. The simple explanation for this may be that editors choose pictures on the basis of good taste and decency or at least they realise it may be counterproductive to upset readers with horrifying pictures of identifiable British people. They also seem to assume that the audience's stomach for pictures of dead foreigners is stronger and guess that such images are unlikely to provoke complaints from relatives. A rider to the general rule would be that the dead are accorded more respect if they are white, or if they are from western liberal democracies.

Critics also suggest that the coverage of African wars is crucially influenced by the level of the West's political and military involvement. For instance, as US/UK military ambitions focused on Somalia in 1992/3, coverage of that country increased; as the soldiers withdrew (humiliated) so did the press, and reporting disappeared altogether. Novelist Thomas Keneally (2000) has pointed out how the border war between Eritrea and Ethiopia (running two years by 2000) was being ignored: 'In reality, there is no difference in international law between the invasion of Eritrea and the invasion of Kuwait by Saddam Hussein.' But as the main Western powers turn away, so do the media.

Yet many mainstream journalists maintain they are still committed to campaigning on Third World issues and raising awareness about distant conflicts. In 2000, for instance, the *Mirror* campaigned to highlight the plight of child victims of war. Mike Moore, whose powerful photographs (of child soldiers in Sierra Leone, for instance) were used prominently in the campaign, commented: 'If my pictures raise awareness then my job is done.' Robert Fisk, of the *Independent*, has won many awards for his outstanding and brave reporting, often against the dominant consensus, from trouble-spots around the globe. And John Pilger's films on East Timor and Iraq have been used by campaigning bodies to inspire action. Ken Metzler (1997: 139) stresses the potential of the Internet to globalise the news: 'The sources represent a worldwide selection so that even the most local of media can achieve a worldly feel by quoting people from far-away places.'

TO WHAT EXTENT HAVE ARABS/FUNDAMENTALISTS/ TERRORISTS REPLACED COMMUNISTS AS THE NEW 'ENEMIES' OF WESTERN CIVILISATION IN DOMINANT MEDIA REPRESENTATIONS?

Representations of the 'enemy' pose many political/ethical dilemmas for journalists. Following the collapse of the Berlin Wall in 1989 many elite commentators in the West, such as Samuel P. Huntingdon (1997), saw the major threat shift from communists to Islamic fundamentalists and terrorists. The rise to power of the Ayatollahs in Iran, of the Taliban in Afghanistan, of President Gaddafi in Libya, of the radical Hizbollah guerrillas in southern Lebanon and of the Saudi Arabian terrorist 'warlord' Osama bin Laden (blamed for masterminding the bombings of US embassies in Africa) were all seen as part of the growing global threat to Western interests. Moreover, in a series of Hollywood blockbusters in the years leading up to the Gulf crisis of 1990–1 (and later shown on British television), Middle Eastern characters served as symbols for greed, primitive behaviour and violence (Kellner 1995: 75–88). As Stephen Prince (1993: 240) argues:

> Films like *Top Gun* and *Rambo* dramatised the heroic ideals of empire and the aggressive heroes of these narratives functioned as personifications of a national will and warrior spirit encoded by the foreign policy rhetoric of the Reagan period.

Concerns over the threat to Western interests posed by 'rogue' dictators focused on Iraq's Saddam Hussein after the invasion of Kuwait in August 1990. All Fleet Street editors were united in backing the military attacks to eject Iraqi forces from Kuwait. The invasion posed an unacceptable threat to the New World Order as proclaimed by US President George Bush. But many critics, such as Edward Said (1981) and Rana Kabani (1994) have argued that the demonisation of the Iraqi leader as 'the evil, barbarous, mad, megalomaniac Butcher of Baghdad' and the 'new Hitler' fed on orientalist myths and anti-Islamic clichés so embedded in dominant Western perceptions. Stuart Hall (1995: 21) has argued that representations of the 'savage barbarian' lie at the root of racist ideology. Significantly, Roy Greenslade who edited the *Daily Mirror* at the time of the Gulf conflict, later commented: 'I can now see that our coverage in the *Mirror* was built on a lot of anti-Iraqi bias, an anti-Moslem bias and an anti-Arab bias' (Keeble 1997: 71). He said it never occurred to him at the time to question the dominant Fleet Street consensus.

ARE THERE ANY PARTICULAR LANGUAGE ISSUES TO CONSIDER WHEN COVERING RACE ISSUES?

Criticisms of journalists who focus on language issues come from both the political left and right. The first group claims that terminology matters are of minor importance in a largely visual culture and in comparison with the campaign for equal opportunities. From the right come allegations that such obsessions are the preserve of the laughable Politically Correct and 'loony left' who seek to impose their Stalinist rules on society. Others argue that journalistic writing/'journalese' (which is poorly regarded in academic circles) has many positive qualities: it's direct, accessible and able to present complex issues in straightforward, non-abstract ways. Cliché, over-simplification, distortion and stereotyping inevitably result. But the essential routines of journalism are honourable.

All the same, most style books follow the line of Reuters', which says (MacDowall 1992: 125): 'Mention a person's race, colour or ethnic or religious affiliation only if relevant to the story.' But John Wilson (1996: 253) argues that the media tend to ignore this principle when covering urban deprivation and race:

> A deprived estate that is nearly all white will be referred to simply as a deprived estate. A deprived area that has a majority of black people is likely to be referred to as a deprived black area regardless of whether its

black majority is relevant. If it is a mixed area it will be referred to as
racially mixed whether the racial mix matters or not.

Moreover journalist Trevor Phillips, a candidate for mayor of London in
2000, complained of constantly being referred to as the 'black' candidate
while his opponents were never described as 'white'.

The NUJ *Guidelines on Race Reporting* suggest a range of useful strategies in
this area. It reminds journalists that words which were once in common
usage are now considered offensive. Thus instead of 'half-caste' and
'coloured' use 'mixed-race' and 'black', though it is always best to ask
people how they define themselves. 'Immigrant', it says, is often used as a
term of abuse and should only be used when a person is strictly an immigrant. Most black people in Britain were born here and most immigrants
are white. On the reporting of gypsies, it says journalists should only
mention the word 'gypsy' or 'traveller' if strictly relevant and accurate. Is
not care also needed when using the word 'riot'? Simon Cottle (1993: 164)
argues that it can serve to de-politicise an event, with the media failing to
identify the deeper structural causes of the conflict, namely social deprivation and acute levels of inner-city unemployment.

HOW CAN JOURNALISTS IMPROVE COVERAGE OF PEOPLE FROM ETHNIC MINORITIES?

The *Daily Mail*'s campaign over Stephen Lawrence is often cited as an
example of brave, anti-racist coverage. With the famous 'Murderers' headline of 14 February 1997, the newspaper dared to accuse five men of the
April 1993 murder of the 18-year-old black student in south London –
and challenged them to sue the paper. Significantly they chose not to.
But the campaign for justice, led by the parents of Stephen Lawrence and
backed by the *Mail* (though many years after the black ethnic press had
focused on the murder), ultimately led to the Macpherson report which
identified serious institutional racism within the police force and throughout society.

The *Mail* is not normally identified with anti-racism campaigning. Some
commentators suggested the u-turn occurred because Stephen's father had
once worked as a plasterer and decorator for Paul Dacre, the paper's editor.
Others suggested it was all part of the *Mail*'s strategy to extend its appeal to
middle-class ethnic minority audiences. It certainly had little impact on its
campaign against asylum seekers.

Is positive discrimination an answer? No: it's illegal, as is the setting up of specific race- or gender-specific quotas. But positive action is the answer, according to Professor Thomas Blair, editor of the Web magazine, the *Chronicle*: 'Positive action for greater newsroom diversity deserves a trial in Britain.' He cites the success of the Chips Quinn initiative (www.chips-quinn.org) launched by the Freedom Forum in the United States which has provided intensive journalism training to 'students of colour' from African–American, Hispanic, Asian–American and Native American backgrounds. Following on from the US initiatives, in Britain, a special work placement scheme for ethnic minority students was launched in 2000 by the Creative Collective backed by the Freedom forum. Would the appointment of more ethnic minority specialists provide some solution?

There is certainly a need for mainstream journalists to extend the range of their contacts to incorporate more ethnic minority voices. The *Washington Post* has shown a commitment to improving coverage by setting up a diversity committee which reviews the ethnic and racial composition of staff; it has appointed a correspondent dedicated to race relations issues. And it arranges a series of informal lunches where staff and ombudsman meet to discuss the way the paper reported race issues. A call by the American Society of Newspaper Editors 20 years ago to have newsrooms reflect the country's ethnic diversity resulted in a 270 per cent rise in journalists of black and Hispanic origin. In Britain, the *Guardian* has scholarships reserved for minority journalists at City University, London. The *Leicester Mercury* has half a dozen correspondents from the town's Asian communities who file news and pictures regularly. The *Bradford Telegraph and Argus* has Asian columnist, Anila Baig, tackling such subjects as trips back to Pakistan and the cultural difficulties young Asians can encounter (Moore 1999). The *Nottingham Evening Post* has introduced special training on ethnic issues for all its editorial staff, and is helping to promote a publication targeted at the black community. All Channel 4 proposals now have to indicate what contribution they make to the channel's new remit which demands three and a half hours of identifiably multicultural programmes a week. And the BBC, along with other broadcasting institutions, has set up the Broadcasting Cultural Diversity Network to promote diversity and track the progress of ethnic minority staff. Some call for a more 'anti-racist' focus, arguing that 'diversity' projects are politically naïve and aim primarily at promoting the career interests of the ethnic middle class.

Journalists need to challenge the myths surrounding 'compassion fatigue' which serve largely to excuse the media from covering the Third World systematically. Fergal Keane, BBC news special correspondent, agrees that most of what is shown of Africa is negative. The media, he stresses, need to show 'the numerous small miracles of African life' placing the imagery of despair in its proper political and economic context. Is there not also a need for more ethnic minority students in journalism training schools? A BT survey published in May 2000 showed the number of such students enrolling on journalism courses had risen by 94 per cent in the past four years: 208 non-white students enrolled in 1999 compared with 107 in 1995. Journalism courses at the prestigious City University, London, and University of Westminster reported that one in five of their intake was from an ethnic background. Such figures are heartening but many journalism courses have far to go in recruiting ethnic students – and systematically integrating anti-racist perspectives (along with a critical study of the history of US/UK imperialism) throughout their curricula.

Should not all journalists be more aware of religions such as Catholicism, Islam, Hinduism and Judaism, their customs, principal festivals and titles of their leaders? Journalists also need to be made aware of alternative ethnic media, their different ethical standpoints and the opportunities they offer for alternative careers away from mainstream stereotyping. *Muslim News*, *Q News*, *Eastern Eye*, *Asian Times*, *The Voice*, *New Nation*, *Jewish Chronicle* should all be closely watched, along with black Internet sites such as *Blackserve*, *Blacknet*, *Blink*, *BlackBritain*, *DarkerthanBlue.Com* and *Voice-online* – and anti-racist journals such as *Searchlight* and *Race and Class*, *Socialist Worker*, *Fight Racism Fight Imperialism*, *Campaign Against Racism and Fascism*, *Peace News* and the *New Left Review*.

Broadcasters need to produce more programmes aimed specifically at ethnic audiences. Figures produced by BBC Broadcasting Research in March 1996 showed that, in general, BBC Radio was not performing well amongst ethnic groups while ethnic stations like Choice FM, Sabras Sound, Sunrise Radio and Spectrum International were the most popular. Bill Morris, head of Radio 2, admitted: 'Radio 2 is too much of a white station.' BBC Radio Leicester producer Vijay Sharma told a seminar her station provided a 'positive model', producing 86 hours of Asian programming per week – with a history of such targeted output since 1976. Most of the Asian listeners to the special programmes stayed with the rest of the output, proof that targeted programming could 'develop loyalty amongst minority listeners to the station' (*Runnymede Bulletin*, March 1996). Journalists have also united against racist media coverage. The NUJ agreed an important statement in defence of asylum seekers in the wake of press attacks on refugees in 1999; the PressWise group (25 Eastern Business Centre, Felix Road, Bristol

BS5 0HE; tel 0117 941 5889; fax: 0117 941 5868; e-mail: pw@presswise.org.uk) has trained refugee and community groups in handling the media, while the Law, Asylum and Media Group (c/o 2 Garden Court, Temple, London EC4Y 98L; tel: 020 7415 6265) has drawn together radical lawyers and journalists to campaign against press harassment and xenophobic coverage.

7
Getting the representation right: tackling issues over gender, mental health, disability, HIV/AIDS and gays/lesbians

HOW SERIOUS A THREAT DO YOU CONSIDER INSTITUTIONAL SEXISM TO BE TO MEDIA STANDARDS?

Critics tend to focus on the alleged institutional sexism within the media industries as a crucial factor behind the coverage of women. A survey by Liz Curtis (1994) found serious cases of sexual harassment of women within the BBC and other broadcasting organisations, while research by Margareta Melin-Higgins (1997) found women alienated by the dominant male newsroom culture. Former managing director at the *Independent* Amanda Platell (1999: 144) talks of institutional sexism as being 'endemic' in newspapers:

> . . . it's about pigeonholing women journalists, denying equality of pay and conditions and opportunities, demeaning them and making assumptions about them. It is about a widespread and inherent belief by some men that women can't quite cut it, that newspapers are a man's world, that women are good for only one thing – 'features' – and that ritual humiliation is a way of keeping girls in their place.
>
> (Sebba 1994)

The percentage of women on national dailies remains low at 22. *Mirror* editor Piers Morgan in October 1998 said his newspaper employed just 62 women to 204 men, though female staff had quadrupled over the last 15 years. But magazines often employ more women than men. At Condé Nast, of 480 employees only 50 were men and only four of those in senior management. Women also comprise 44 per cent of journalists in independent television, 38 per cent in independent radio and 37 per cent at the BBC (Franklin 1997: 61). The numbers of women trainees are rising all the time: by 2000, half the entrants to newspapers were female. And the 1990s also witnessed a few advances for women in the mainstream press. In May 1991, Eve Pollard became the first woman editor of the *Sunday Express* while Rosie Boycott, in April 1998, became the first woman editor of a broadsheet (the struggling *Independent on Sunday*) before moving on, first to edit the *Independent* and then – in April 1998 – the struggling *Express*.

At the *Sunday Mirror*, editorial control in November 1996 was in the hands of three women: managing director Bridget Rowe, deputy managing director Pat Moore and acting editor Amanda Platell. This was the first time in Fleet Street history that an all female executive triumvirate had held power on a national newspaper. In May 2000, Rebekah Wade, at 31, became editor of the *News of the World*, and in the same month Rebecca Hardy, at 34, became the first woman editor of the *Scotsman*. At the local level, the *Diss Express* was staffed entirely by women. On 8 March 2000, to mark International Women's Day, the *Western Mail* changed its name to the *Western Femail* and was edited by Pat English with Michelle Bower as head of content. But Linda Christmas (1997), journalism lecturer and co-founder of Women in Journalism, questions whether the media are becoming as women friendly as it may seem: 'It's about who controls the purse strings. Yes, women edit magazines but hardly any are magazine publishers which is where the real power is.'

Women in similar jobs are often paid less: in 1997 it was revealed that while John Humphrys and James Naughtie were paid £120,000 a year, Sue McGregor, also a presenter on Radio 4's *Today* programme, received £100,000. A MORI survey of 537 national newspaper and magazine journalists by telephone in the autumn of 1997 suggested that women earned significantly less than men (Allan 1999: 136). Award-winning interviewer Ginny Dougary, author of *Executive Tarts and Other Myths* (Virago 1994) objected after she was criticised for being an 'ambitious girl reporter' (she was 38) following her profile of Chancellor Norman Lamont in *The Times* magazine in September 1994. Dawn Alford (2000), the *Mirror* reporter who duped Jack Straw's son into selling her cannabis, claimed she was victimised afterwards: 'Columnists used up hundreds of inches inferring I was a cross between Mata Hari and a black widow spider and my family and friends were doorstepped by agency reporters hoping I had a murky past.'

A report from the Fawcett Society in April 1997 showed that in BBC, ITV and Channel 4 news bulletins, 80 per cent of election coverage was carried out by male journalists. Female politicians appeared on screen only eight times compared with 127 by men. Of 17 academics asked opinion, not one was female. Such figures merely reinforce research which suggests that journalists' conventional sourcing routines tend to prioritise male sources above females. Other research by the Fawcett Society, published in August 2000, showed that TV news reporters tended to seek women's views on 'soft' news items, leaving politics and business to the men. The historic role of feminism is often marginalised by the media. A report from the campaigning group, Women in Journalism, *Real Women – The Hidden Sex*, in November 1999, expressed concern over the constant sexist use of images of women to 'lift' pages.

- The NUJ has published a document on sexual harassment, including a section of 'How to prevent it' and a model clause for house agreements.

DO YOU FEEL THE EMPLOYMENT OF MORE WOMEN WILL IMPROVE NEWS VALUES?

Research by Linda Christmas (1997), senior lecturer in journalism at City University, London, suggests that the employment of more women in newspapers has had a dramatic impact on 'humanising' news values: 'Women have already made a difference, particularly on the magazine and feature side of newspapers . . . the features content of all national daily and Sunday newspapers has increased in the last 15 years. There has been a huge increase in human interest stories, tales of triumph over tragedy and advice on handling relationships.' Women have also helped change the content of news pages with material of interest to women spread throughout national newspapers. She argues that women write differently from men. They tend to put readers' needs above those of policy makers, are more 'people' than 'issue' oriented, see more importance on seeing news in context and prefer to examine the consequences of events. *Sunday Times* columnist A.A. Gill has also highlighted the 'feminisation' of television, but sees it as a worrying development. TV boardrooms may still be occupied by men but mostly women are making the important day-to-day decisions: 'They are middle-ranking commissioning editors and producers who see themselves as role model women in a traditionally male-oriented business. Television is deeply concerned with women's issues, desperate not to offend women, not to get it wrong' (Ellis 1998).

But many challenge these views. Women journalists often claim they do not have a news agenda distinct from their male colleagues and that it is patronising to suggest they are more interested in 'softer', featurish stories. Lindsey Hilsum, diplomatic correspondent of *Channel 4 News*, accused

Christmas of promoting 'old fashioned, clichéd notions of gender'. Jaci Stephen (1997) questioned women's role in 'humanising' journalism: 'My experience has been that executive female journalists are a terrifying bunch of unscrupulous, spiteful, cruel, manipulative and often grossly unprofessional cows.' Others claim that the economic, ideological factors behind the growth of 'human interest' stories are more important than the rise in the numbers of prominent women journalists. Women editors often reproduce the same values as men. Bridget Rowe, for instance, led her 52 staff at the *People* in 1996 at a time when the paper was packed with stories about royals, Pamela Anderson, Hugh Grant's prostitute Divine Brown (shown naked except for a strategically placed star marked 'censored') and more sex. In any case, numbers in themselves don't count: more important is the need to have women (and ethnic minority) journalists employed with a political understanding of the ways in which their subordination is reproduced – and with a will to change it.

Others expressed concern over mounting anti-male rhetoric – dubbed 'womanism' by journalist Ros Coward – in the media. Coward writes (1999):

> Womanism came out of feminism's attack on male pomposities but now has a much wider constituency. Womanism is feminism's vulgate, found everywhere, from the humorous disparagement of men by stand-up comedians and novelists through to more savage criticisms of men in the context of fears of social disintegration. It unites unlikely allies. The ubiquitous New Age philosophies promote the idea of woman as caring, in touch with natural, healing forces, while men are men, responsible for destructive technology and science.

SHOULD PAGE 3-TYPE IMAGES BE BANNED?

In 1970, the *Sun*, acquired a few months earlier by Australian Rupert Murdoch, carried its first Page 3 picture – of Stephanie Rahn. Over the following year, the paper doubled its circulation – and thus began Fleet Street's descent in sexploitation and trashy titillation. Or at least, so its critics argue. Others claim Page 3's undoubted success (becoming a national institution by the 1990s) proves its popularity with both men and women readers. Isn't the model exploiting her sexuality for financial gain? What's wrong with that? A lot, claim some feminist critics who see the Page 3-type image (which quickly spread to other tabloids) as legitimising the crude sexist stereotyping of women.

These criticisms came to a head in 1986 when Labour MP Clare Short, backed by the anti-porn crusader Lord Longford, tried, unsuccessfully, to introduce legislation to outlaw such images. Under the editorship of the abrasive Kelvin MacKenzie, the *Sun* hit back at Short, with Samantha Fox, the most famous Page 3 'lovely', denouncing her as a 'killjoy'. The *News of the World*, then edited by Patsy Chapman, set out to find a picture of the MP in her nightdress (Holland 1998: 27). And when a council in Sowerby Bridge, West Yorkshire, banned the paper from its library, the *Sun* dubbed them the 'Barmy Burghers of Sowerby Bridge' and pictured three local 'lovelies' posing in mini-skirts. All the same, the controversy raises a number of issues: can an issue as complex as the representation of women be tackled through legislation, to what extent do Page 3-type images contribute to a culture in which women are routinely exploited and suffer intolerable levels of physical harassment and violence, and, if legislation is not the answer, how can such sexist attitudes and images be challenged?

IS THE MEDIA COVERAGE OF SPORT PARTICULARLY SEXIST?

Male sport dominates the media. Women cricketers, footballers and golfers hardly get a look-in. BBC's Radio 5 Live and talkSport are virtually exclusive male bastions. When women do feature their presence is usually heavily sexualised. The coverage of sportswomen from the early 1980s to the present day, such as the late Florence Griffith-Joyner, Katarina Witt, Gabriela Sabatini, Mary Pearce and Anna Kournikova has tended to focus on their sexuality. Yet the issue becomes further complicated when some of these women show themselves happy to capitalise on the commercial advantages of such profiles. David Rowe comments (1999: 128): 'Such debates are especially intense when sportswomen explicitly play the role of soft pornographic subject on the covers of sports magazines, in calendars, posters and publicity shots.' Witt, for instance, posed for *Playboy*, while top UK athlete Denise Lewis stripped for *Total Sport*. In 1999, women's sport received less than five per cent of sports sponsorship and only a fraction of the 30,755 hours of televised sport in the UK. According to Adrian Gatton (2000), women have to uncover to get coverage: 'Often it is the only way to get crucial sponsorship and keep balding TV commentators drooling.' In response to these pressures, the Women's Sport Foundation has issued guidelines on how 'women athletes can create a positive image without losing their dignity'.

In the lead-up to Wimbledon 2000, and before her quick exit, the British mainstream press carried 52 pictures of 19-year-old Kournikova (ranked 14 in the world and dubbed 'Cor!-nikova by the tabloids) compared to 46 of all the other top female players combined. Mary Ann Sieghart comments:

> I've often heard the question on considering a story: 'Is she photogenic?'
> I've never heard the same said of a man. A picture of a beautiful woman
> is undoubtedly a plus – men and women like that. But many women find
> an overtly sexy picture offensive and gratuitous. They ask is this aimed at
> me or at lecherous men? Sometimes newspapers – both broadsheets and
> tabloids – go the wrong side of that line.

Kournikova was also caught in a typical, manufactured row with Elizabeth
Hurley, the representation of women competing for the attention of males
being a prominent sexist stereotype. The Russian tennis star had apparently
described Ms Hurley to Russian *Vogue* as 'so ugly' but, in response to journalists' probing, Ms Hurley had merely described Kournikova as 'looking
smashing'. There was no stopping the media frenzy. The *Sun*, *Mirror* and
Scottish Daily Record ran polls asking readers who was the prettier; columnists such as Dominic Mohan, Lynda Lee-Potter and Melanie McDonagh
all waded in with their words of wisdom on the matter. Significantly,
women are found to promote such stereotyping as well as men. Yet Eve
Pollard, chair of Parkhill Publishing, argues the problems of sexist images of
women will persist while men hold a monopoly on the seats at picture
desks. Picture editors stress they are reflecting dominant assumptions and
the editorial agendas of their publications, their decisions shaped by the
dual pressures of access and tight deadlines (Carter 1999).

WHAT OTHER STRATEGIES CAN JOURNALISTS ADOPT FOR IMPROVING COVERAGE OF WOMEN?

A number of issues arise:

- Are separate women's sections and programmes the answer – or do they
  tend to perpetuate sexist stereotyping with the focus on sex, health,
  beauty, domestic issues, personal advice columns and lifestyles? Should
  men be allowed to contribute to special women's sections?

- Should women have a firmer grasp of the writings and journalism of the
  leading feminist theorists such as Germaine Greer, Ros Coward, Sheila
  Rowbotham, Andrea Dworkin, Dale Spender and Kate Millett?

- Should not journalists be 'gender sensitive' in their sourcing routines?
  It's often all to easy to find willing male commentators.

- How important is the use of non-sexist language in countering stereotypes? For instance, was not the widespread use of 'Blair's Babes' to
  describe new women MPs in the Labour-dominated House of
  Commons post-1997 sexist? Challenging this bias is no easy task.

Some style books avoid all mention of sexist language issues except in relation to the use of 'Ms', 'Miss' and 'Mrs'. Most now accept the use of 'Ms' where appropriate and avoid using 'he' when 'he or she' or 'they' (as a singular bisexual pronoun) is more accurate. Phrases such as 'the common man' and the 'man in the street' are also widely avoided.

Discussions over style book changes can provide opportunities to raise language issues. But style book revisions can often be dominated by an editorial elite so it might be appropriate to work with colleagues in the NUJ to confront sexist stereotyping in language. To assist such campaigns, the union has drawn up an *Equality Style Guide* suggesting words to be avoided and alternatives. For example, there is:

businessman	business manager, executive, boss, business chief, head of firm
cameraman	photographer, camera operator
newsman	journalist or reporter
fireman/men	firefighter/fire services staff/fire crews
dustman	refuse collector
workmen	workers/workforce
mankind	humanity/people
gentleman's agreement	verbal agreement
foreman	supervisor
ice cream man	ice cream seller
policeman/men	police officer or just police
salesman/girl	assistant/shop worker/shop staff/ representative/sales staff
spaceman	astronaut
stewardess/air hostess	airline staff/flight attendant
nightwatchman	caretaker/security guard

Even where editors fail to acknowledge these issues, there is often a certain degree of stylistic freedom available to the reporter to use such language.

WHAT ISSUES SHOULD JOURNALISTS BE AWARE OF WHEN COVERING MENTAL HEALTH MATTERS?

First some facts as presented by the Mental Health Foundation (020-7631 3868; e-mail: mhf@mentalhealth.org.uk; Web: http://www.mentalhealth.org.uk): mental health problems, according to the MHF, occur when feelings such as depression, anxiety and stress become more extreme or long lasting that they affect a person's ability to carry on their everyday life. Mental illness, on the other hand, is a term used by doctors and other health professionals to describe clinically recognisable psychological symptoms and patterns of behaviour. Mental illness is not a single condition and mentally-ill people are not a homogeneous group. Like mental health problems, mental illness can be regarded as a continuum, ranging from minor distress to severe, long-term disorders.

- One in four of the UK's adult population will experience some kind of mental health problem in any year.

- Over any year, 12 million adults attending GP surgeries have symptoms of mental illness.

- Some two million children are estimated to have some form of mental health problem and evidence suggests the figure is rising.

- Mental health remains one of the least popular causes for charity despite being one of the most universal issues.

Do the media not have a responsibility to make people aware of the scale of the mental health problem? Yet headlines containing words like 'psycho', 'madman', 'loonies', 'nutters' and 'maniac' are very common and only fuel negative myths and stereotypes about mental illness. Moreover, people with mental health problems are not normally deemed newsworthy, unless attached to a spectacularly negative event. Given the number of people suffering mental illness of some kind, if you are not personally affected then someone close to you is likely to be.

The Health Education Authority and the mental health charity, Mind, are also concerned over the media emphasis on crime and violence when covering mentally-ill people. The Press Complaints Commission also criticised the *Daily Star* for describing (in November 1995) a patient at Broadoak hospital who cycled up to Princess Diana and asked for a kiss as a 'raving nutter' and a loony. A survey the two organisations published in 1997 showed half of total press coverage in 1996 dealt with crime, harm to others and self harm, while more than 40 per cent of tabloid articles used pejorative terms such as 'nutter' and 'loony'. Articles providing advice and guidance on mental health subjects accounted for less than eight per cent of the coverage. Reports of Home Office homicide figures tend to focus on the mentally ill – even though their numbers have not increased while those committed by others have more than doubled. Yet the suicide rate amongst the mentally ill runs at two a day: in other words, they are more likely to harm themselves than other people.

A survey of mental health sufferers published by Mind in February 2000 showed that half believed their condition was made worse by the way they were covered in the media. A quarter of the respondents to the survey, *Counting the Cost*, said they had experienced hostility from local communities as a result of the coverage. Sue Baker, of Mind, said:

> Nobody can deny that when something goes tragically wrong with the care of a person with a diagnosed mental health problem that this is of valid public concern. What equally cannot be denied is that often news reporting of these rare and tragic events has stated or suggested that all mentally ill people are a danger to others and are 'time bombs waiting to explode'.

Local journalists were considered better than national counterparts, though radio was felt to be the fairest medium.

David Brindle, of the *Guardian*, suggested that the focus on violence and crime was not all the fault of the journalists: 'Part of the problem is the system of having an independent inquiry every time there is a homicide involving a mentally ill person. The news agenda is set that way and that is an issue both the press and the government need to think about' (Johnson 1997). Other journalists are keen to defend their coverage as being in tune with public sentiments and editorial lines.

Reporters are advised by the MHF not to use diagnostic labels such as 'schizophrenic' or 'manic depressive' but less stigmatising phrases such as 'someone who has a diagnosis of schizophrenia' or 'someone who has bouts of depression'. At the same time, reporters should not understate or trivialise the pain and damage mental health problems can cause. Or are these language concerns the unnecessary obsessions of PC fanatics? In a booklet, *Shock Treatment*, the National Union of Journalists advises reporters to 'take a fresh look at their mental health coverage' and see 'people with mental health problems as an untapped source of stories and comment'.

HOW CAN COVERAGE OF DISABLED PEOPLE BE IMPROVED?

A survey by Peter White (2000), BBC's disability affairs correspondent, found up to 30 stories a day in national and local papers on disability. But he concluded: 'A close reading of the press leads me to believe that the disabled person as "newsworthy victim" is still alive and satisfyingly unwell.' Do not the media tend to assume their audiences are able-bodied? If people with disabilities are covered, the focus tends to be on the disability even when it is irrelevant. White expresses concern that in almost every newspaper story about actor Christopher Reeve (who had a freak riding accident) and 'pornographer' Larry Flynt (who was shot by a stranger) their disabilities will feature large. Yet he stresses that 'disability is a very minor factor in the way people behave compared with all the other quirks and oddities that are driving them'.

News about disability is usually represented by able-bodied 'experts'. As a booklet produced by the NUJ, *People First*, stresses: 'People with disabilities are the real experts on their own lives. The organised collective voice of people with disabilities is rarely consulted.' Damaging stereotypes often distort coverage. People with disabilities are presented as courageous, pathetic, helpless, victims, recipients of charity, eternally cheerful, grateful, constantly searching for miracle cures, asexual. How often is it acknowledged that they may be black, lesbian or gay? White also finds distinct advantages in being disabled. Of the war correspondent John Hockenberry, he says:

> We have both found that people talk to us more readily, trust us more quickly, identify with us more strongly. Both of us would admit to having used, and on occasion abused, the trust and identification to get a story. We are not necessarily proud of it but journalism is about publishing things some people don't want to be known. This is never going to be a clean business and eliciting information is what it's about.

HOW CAN COVERAGE OF PEOPLE WITH HIV/AIDS BE IMPROVED?

One in 100 people became infected with HIV in the decade between 1987 and 1997 and it killed 11 million people (compared to eight million people killed in World War One). By March 2000, around 20,000 people in Britain had been diagnosed with HIV, four-fifths of them men. In June 2000, the United Nations reported that 23.3 million Africans living south of the Sahara were infected with HIV – 70 per cent of the global total. But how much do these statistics blind us to the sufferings of the individuals behind them?

Originally AIDS was dubbed the 'gay plague'. For instance, *The Times* leader commented: 'AIDS horrifies not only because of the prognosis for its victims. The infection's origins and means of propagation excites repugnance, moral and physical, at promiscuous male homosexuality.' But since the over-sensationalised coverage in the mid-1980s, when a moral panic exploited and perpetuated fears of the fatal condition – and of sexuality in general – the issue has largely gone off the agenda in Britain (though Princess Diana constantly campaigned over AIDS and the *Sunday Times* ran a prominent and controversial campaign claiming HIV was not the principal cause). The AIDS 2000 conference in Durban gained substantial coverage with sensational comments and statistics emerging. For instance, the President of Botswana claimed his country faced extinction while scientists stated that AIDS represented the biggest infectious disease to befall humanity. But how much did this coverage reinforce negative stereotypes of Africa as a doom-laden continent? How dedicated were the media to campaign consistently for the revolution in spending priorities essentially needed to tackle the crisis?

Some style books highlight areas where special care is needed while covering AIDS-related stories. For instance, the Reuters style book says on reporting claims for an AIDS cure: 'If a story making dramatic claims for a cure for AIDS or cancer does not come from a reputable named source it must be checked with recognised medical experts before being issued (or spiked). If such a story is issued it should include whatever balancing or interpretative material is available from such authorities.'

According to a leaflet produced by the Health Education Authority and the NUJ, confidentiality about infection by either a child or adult should always be respected. When names and addresses have been supplied by the police, these should only be revealed with the consent of those concerned. Some stories perpetuate myths that AIDS can be spread through casual contact such as kissing. It can only be spread through intimate sexual contact, by the sharing of needles by drug addicts, by blood transfusion or from mother-to-infant in pregnancy. On the question of language, the NUJ suggests that instead of 'carrying AIDS', 'AIDS carrier' or 'AIDS positive' (which confuses the two phases of being infected with HIV and having AIDS) it suggests 'people with HIV'. Also, avoid using the term 'high-risk groups' since there is risk behaviour rather than risk groups. 'The fact of being classified a member of any particular group does not put anyone at greater risk, but what he or she does, regardless of groups, may do.' People with HIV often express concern over being represented as 'sufferers' and 'victims': many continue working after diagnosis. It is better to say 'person with AIDS'.

- The online site at http://www.aids.map.com has been developed by the National AIDS Manual, the British HIV Association and St Stephen's Aids Trust and carries a great deal of useful information.

DO THE MEDIA DISCRIMINATE AGAINST GAYS/LESBIANS?

The coverage of gays has improved significantly since 1990 when the PCC ruled against the use of the word 'poofters' to describe gays, at least according to activist Peter Tatchell (2000). He comments:

> Now gay people are more visible than ever before and public attitudes are moving towards greater acceptance. Positive gay images and characters abound on television. Politicians and entertainers are openly gay. The police are serious, at last, about tackling homophobic hate crimes. Gayness is no longer a sickness.

Other critics point to the underlying macho, aggressive heterosexuality of the mainstream media's culture which automatically marginalises other sexual orientations. Larry Gross (1998: 90–1) suggests that gays are always portrayed as controversial by the mass media:

> Being defined as controversial invariably limits the ways in which lesbians and gay men are depicted on the rare occasions that they appear, thereby shaping the effects of such depictions on the images held by society at large and by members of these minority groups.

Most of the sleaze coverage of the 1990s was premised on the reactionary notion of the 'normality' of heterosexual, family life and the consequent 'sinfulness' of variants, though right-wing commentators criticised it for highlighting a new permissiveness in media priorities and intrusiveness. Media commentator Roy Greenslade suggests that 'lots of people, including many of those who proclaim a lack of prejudice towards gays, find the actual acts involved in gay sex, especially between men, deeply repugnant'. And editors are quick to exploit those ambivalent feelings.

The most overt manifestations of discrimination can still appear in the red-top tabloids. For instance, the *Sun* has constantly vilified lesbians and gay men. Rupert Murdoch, its owner, is a born-again Christian, vocal in his denunciations of gays. So predictably, it attacked President Clinton's alleged obsession with hiring lesbians and gays and described Janet Reno, the US Attorney General, in this way: 'Her name is Janet Reno and she smokes a pipe. She is six foot tall, with a short shapeless hairdo and has never married.' The innuendo was clear (Page 1998: 134). A notorious example of anti-gay hysteria followed the hounding of Ron Davies MP after he claimed to have been mugged while on Clapham Common in November 1998. On the same day, *Times* columnist Matthew Parris mentioned on a TV programme that minister Peter Mandelson was gay. Soon afterwards the *News of the World* 'outed' Nick Brown, Agriculture Minister, and when the *Sun* followed it up with the headline: 'Tell us the truth Tony – is gay mafia running Britain?' the country appeared to be in the midst of an anti-gay 'moral panic'. The *Guardian* responded by publishing a poll which suggested a majority of voters regarded being gay as morally acceptable. And on 12 November, responding to the outrage its coverage had sparked, the *Sun* pledged it would no longer 'out' ministers.

But many Christians and politicians on the right argue that media toleration of gays is unacceptable. Significantly, the Pope condemned homosexuality in July 2000 as a 'moral disorder and an offence to Christian values'. The leader of Scotland's Catholics, Cardinal Thomas Welling, gave full support to the campaign against the repeal of the anti-gay Section 28 of the 1988 Local Government Act, describing homosexuality as a 'perversion'. And Scotland's biggest-selling newspaper, the *Daily Record*, launched a petition to keep Section 28, as Brian Souter, the multi-millionaire chief of the Stagecoach transport empire and member of the Christian fundamentalist sect, the Church of Nazarene, launched his own campaign against repeal and financed a private referendum on the legislation.

8
Battling for news: the dilemmas of war reporting (and not just on the frontline)

WHEN A GOVERNMENT WAGES WAR SHOULD JOURNALISTS AUTOMATICALLY GIVE IT THEIR SUPPORT?

Journalists tend to be more courageous in criticising the government when British forces are not engaged; when 'our boys' (and a few of 'our girls') are in action, most of the media tend to back it. But is this right? William Howard Russell's famous despatches for *The Times* from the Crimea chronicled the failings of the army and supposedly led to the resignation of Aberdeen's cabinet. But was he justified in sending his reports? Many commentators who stress the 'inevitable' adversarial relationship between the media and the military focus on Russell's reporting. Yet how much is this myth? Phillip Knightley (2000: 16), in his seminal history of war reporting, The First Casualty, says that while Russell exposed military failures he failed to understand their causes. And while he criticised the lot of the ordinary soldier, he never attacked the officers 'to whose class he belonged himself'. 'Above all, Russell made the mistake, common to many a war correspondent, of considering himself part of the military establishment.' Moreover, *The Times* played only a small role in the fall of the government. An important section of the elite was determined on Aberdeen's fall, irrespective of any views expressed in the press.

Were American journalists too outspoken in their coverage of US actions in Vietnam? For the US elite the defeat in Vietnam against a far less technologically sophisticated enemy – accompanied by assassinations, race and student upheavals at home – was a trauma of unprecedented proportions.

Many blamed the media. Long after the end of the conflict, it is argued, television images still dominate perceptions of it: a US Marine Zippo lighting a Vietnamese village, the execution of a Vietcong suspect in a Saigon street, a Vietnamese girl running naked and terrified down a road after a napalm attack. Images such as these, along with press criticism of the conduct of the war, are said to have eroded public support.

Yet how much of this is myth? Surveys showed that media consumption, in fact, promoted support for the war (Williams op. cit.: 305–28). And virtually every Vietnam reporter backed the war effort. A Gannett Foundation report commented (1991: 15): 'Throughout the war, in fact, journalists who criticised the military's performance did so out of a sense of frustration that military strategy and tactics were failing to accomplish the goal of decisively defeating the North Vietnamese forces.' Most commentators have seen a shift to more 'advocacy' reporting following the Vietcong Tet offensive of 1968. But such a shift occurred among the American elite with significant sections beginning to question the costs, effectiveness and overall moral/political justification for the war. The media followed the shift in the elite consensus rather than created it (Cummings 1992: 84; Hallin 1986: 21; Williams 1987: 250–4). Also, after 1968, many in the US military were concerned to show the difficulties and daily frustrations of the war to the American public and welcomed the press as potential allies in conveying this message.

The patriotic imperative lies at the heart of British journalists' culture. Not surprisingly this patriotic loyalty appears strongest during times of war. Both the BBC and ITN have identified themselves as guardians of national morale and national interest during wars. Significantly ITN's submission to a Commons select committee inquiry into handling of information during the Falklands War of 1982, opposed battlefield restrictions on journalists on these grounds: 'Great opportunities were missed for the positive projection of the single-minded energy and determination of the British people in their support of the task force.' Max Hastings, editor of the *London Evening Standard* but most famous for being the first journalist to march into Port Stanley at the end of the Falklands War, commented:

> I felt my function was simply to identify totally with the interests and feelings of that force [the task force] . . . when one was writing one's copy one thought: beyond telling everybody what the men around me were doing, what can one say that is likely to be most helpful in winning the war?

(Williams 1992: 156–7)

Other journalists argue that they have a permanent responsibility for bringing the authorities to account and that their dissident role is all the more important when lives are at stake. Censorship, they claim, is too often used to hide military incompetence and inefficiency resulting in the loss of service people's lives.

During the Gulf War of 1991, all Fleet Street significantly backed the 'allied' attacks on Iraq, though the *Guardian* maintained a certain scepticism throughout. Ron Spark, chief *Sun* leader writer, said journalists had a responsibility to support the cause uncritically: 'Newspapers are in the business of telling news and freedom of information is a precious part of our democracy. Yet when we are fighting men and women are in peril and we have no choice but to accept some limitations.' Max Hastings, in the *Telegraph* of 5 February 1991, remained 'unconvinced of the case for objectivity as between the US-led coalition forces and Saddam when even the most moral assessment . . . suggests he is an exceptionally evil man'. Robert Fisk, of the *Independent*, came in for particular criticism when on 23 January 1991, under the headline 'Bogged down in the desert', he described the complete breakdown of convoy discipline on the supply route and revealed details about medical preparations for casualties. Miles Hudson and John Stainer (1997: 235) comment: 'Such reporting was scarcely helpful to the families of those about to be launched into battle.' Should Fisk have exercised more self censorship in this case?

In 1999, the Fleet Street consensus again backed the US/UK attacks – this time on Yugoslavia (with the *Guardian* proving to be one of the most jingoistic) and called for a ground assault. Only the *Independent on Sunday* opposed the war, and its editor (Kim Fletcher) was sacked just days after the bombings ended. Some journalists, however, argue that while an editorial line may back a war, balance can be achieved in the coverage by presenting both sides. For instance, while the *Guardian* backed the Kosovo attacks, some of its prominent columnists opposed them and a large proportion of the letters took a similar 'balancing' line. Similarly, while the *Mail* backed the bombings, some of its most prominent columnists were given considerable space to express opposition.

Governments traditionally criticise media performances as being 'unpatriotic' during wars. During World War Two, Clem Attlee warned the Newspaper Proprietors' Association that if its editors were not restrained, the Government would bring in compulsory censorship. The *Daily Mirror* was close to being closed down after a cartoon by Donald Zec showed an exhausted sailor clinging to a life raft with the caption: 'The price of petrol has been increased by one penny.' In 1986, Norman Tebbit criticised the BBC's eminent war correspondent Kate Adie after the US/UK bombing of Libya. Similarly Alastair Campbell accused the media of being taken in by 'Serb lie machine' during the Kosovo War. The Government's attacks were specifically aimed at John Simpson, the BBC's man in Belgrade after he claimed in his *Daily Telegraph* column that the war 'wasn't working', and at John Humphrys who had said on Radio 4's *Today* programme that the war was 'a mess'. Minister Clare Short even attacked investigative reporter John Pilger in the Commons as a 'traitor' for using his columns in the *New Statesman* and *Guardian* to oppose the Kosovo War. But how much of this 'flak' is ritual serving to reinforce democratic myths of the adversarial media? Some journalists argue that, given the broadcasters' independence from government, conflict is inevitable during wars. John Simpson, the BBC's world affairs editor, for instance, criticised CNN during the Kosovo crisis for getting 'too close' to the US Government since senior journalists there knew about NATO's plans to bomb the Serb television station but had not warned them. 'The BBC has a difference of philosophy from CNN because we prefer not to get too close to the governments we are reporting on,' he said. He would have passed on the information: 'We're not just scribblers and recorders. We're human beings with consciences and souls' (Hodgson 1999).

Campbell also criticised Yugoslavia-based reporters for not taking risks to witness events with their own eyes. Not surprisingly, such views were swiftly condemned. Michael Williams, foreign correspondent for Radio 4's *Today* programme, commented:

> Every day we ran the risk of falling victim to NATO bombs or to the violent reaction of angry soldiers, policemen or ordinary Serbs. Two days after being expelled from Belgrade I returned to the country only to spend nine hours in the hands of enraged military policemen, screaming as they searched my bags and checked my notebooks, holding their guns to my head and threatening to shoot every time I failed to answer a question satisfactorily.

And Alex Thomson, chief correspondent of *Channel 4 News*, stressed: 'Like many, many others, I have been shot at, arrested, roughed up, shelled, abused and robbed by the Serb army through Vukovar, Srebrenica, Dubrovnik and sundry other war crime venues through the 90s. And yes, Alastair, we were telling the public about Serb fascism long before you were losing sleep over it.'

Many rank-and-file journalists certainly remain critical during wars, though their perspectives often differ and their activities gain little publicity. Some are concerned over media stereotyping and demonising of the enemy; some stress the journalist's constant need to challenge government/military propaganda and misinformation; others are concerned to highlight the ruthlessness of American capital's imperial ambitions (as, for instance, in the Middle East and in eastern Europe). Others are motivated by straight pacifist instincts. During the Cold War, Journalists Against Nuclear Extermination was formed by members of the NUJ to campaign for nuclear disarmament; during the Gulf War, Media Workers Against War was one of its most vociferous opponents, while during the Kosovo crisis journalists again came together at a packed London meeting to oppose the bombings. Significantly, no broadcasters or Fleet Street newspaper covered the event.

DID MAINSTREAM JOURNALISTS SUCCUMB TOO EASILY TO GOVERNMENT MEDIA AGENDA-SETTING AND MANIPULATION DURING THE GULF WAR?

Some journalists argued that government censorship ground-rules were inevitable and necessary during the Gulf conflict. The BBC's Kate Adie, who happily wore a military uniform, commented: 'I'm not just a reporter reporting independently, I'm actually with the army.' Yet many criticisms in 1991 focused on the use of the pools for US/UK journalists in Saudi Arabia to manipulate coverage. Journalists were the real prisoners of war, trapped behind the barbed wire of reporting curbs, according to William Boot (1991: 24). Alex Thomson, ITN *Channel 4 News* reporter during the conflict (1992: 82), used the same image: 'The pools were a prison.' Very few journalists were allowed to travel with the troops and very little actual combat was observed; most journalists were confined to hotels in Saudi Arabia. Those journalists who tried to evade these constraints were harassed by the authorities – and sometimes even by their colleagues.

Robert Fox, with the Seventh Armoured Corps for the *Daily Telegraph*, summed up the situation: 'Too few journalists were locked into the British armoured division for weeks on end with little to do.' David Beresford of the *Guardian* suggests that journalists were supposed to be eye-witnesses to history but added: 'Recent US Defense Department estimates that as many as 200,000 Iraqis may have died suggests that much witnessing was left undone.' The attacks were conducted from the air primarily but only one journalist, ABC's Forrest Sawyer, flew with a fighter jet. Pool reporters confined to ships saw virtually nothing. The pooling system was also used by the military to enforce delays in the transmission of news. Five of the six pool journalists in a 1991 International Press Institute survey complained of delays. Paul Majendie of Reuters, with the Americans, commented: 'At best the copy took 72 hours to get back to the pool. At worst it just vanished.' Almost 80 per cent of pool reports filed during the 'ground offensive' took more than 12 hours to reach Dhahran, by which time the news was often out of date.

Given these controls and constraints should journalists have co-operated with the pools? Some American journalists quit in protest at the manipulation; other journalists such as Peter Sharp, of ITN, and Robert Fisk, of the *Independent*, decided to work outside the official arrangements, being dubbed 'unilaterals', 'mavericks' or 'rovers'. They shared a mixed fate. They were tolerated (they clearly could have been kicked out at any time) but they were also closely watched and heavily intimidated. Many commentators have agreed with the conclusion of Phillip Knightley (1991: 5): 'The Gulf War is an important one in the history of censorship. It marks a deliberate attempt by the authorities to alter public perception of the nature of war itself, particularly the fact that civilians die in war.'

SHOULD JOURNALISTS ACCEPT RESTRICTIONS AND REPORT FROM 'ENEMY' COUNTRIES?

Journalists reporting from Berlin would have been unthinkable during World War Two. Yet during the undeclared Falklands, Gulf and Kosovo wars, British journalists sent despatches from 'enemy' territory, though not without sparking some major controversies. A number of prominent journalists (such as Peregrine Worsthorne in the *Sunday Telegraph*) and politicians argued in 1991 that journalists based in Baghdad would inevitably become pawns of the Iraqi dictatorship. Alexander Cockburn reported that the US attaché in Baghdad instructed all Americans to leave the capital just before the bombings began, while John Simpson revealed in his history of the conflict (1991: 277): 'President Bush himself telephoned various American editors to urge them to evacuate their teams. That frightened a lot of people.' CNN's Peter Arnett came in for particularly severe criticisms in the United States for his reporting. In Britain, anger at the BBC's presence in Baghdad boiled over after US jets attacked the al Ameriyya shelter, killing hundreds of women and children. Reporter Jeremy Bowen looked distinctly distressed as he consistently refused to be drawn by anchorman Michael Buerk to say the shelter appeared to have a dual military purpose, as the military and most of Fleet Street claimed the following day. *Today* said the broadcasters were 'a disgrace to their country'; the *Mail on Sunday* said the coverage, not the bombing, was 'truly disgusting' and 'deplorable'. As Steve Platt observed, the only occasion on which Fleet Street expressed 'outrage' during the war was over the

BBC's coverage of the shelter disaster. 'Outrage over BBC bias' headlined an edition of the *Express*. Central to the controversy is the belief that the 'enemy' issue propaganda (which goes on to 'infect' British journalists based in their capitals) while 'our side' reports the truth. But how true is this?

Moreover, the controversy, in focusing on the role of frontline reporters, tends to downplay the significance of journalists based 'at home'. In fact, some of the greatest war reporting has been done far from the battle zones. For instance, the exposure of the My Lai atrocity (in which 130 men, women and children were massacred on 16 March 1968) raised profound questions about the conduct of US soldiers in Vietnam. But it was exposed by freelance reporter Seymour Hersh, based in Washington. As Phillip Knightley comments (2000: 428):

> It was the racist nature of the fighting, the treating of the Vietnamese 'like animals' that led inevitably to My Lai and it was the reluctance of correspondents to report this racist and atrocious nature of the war that caused the My Lai story to be revealed, not by a war correspondent, but by an alert newspaper reporter back in the United States – a major indictment of the coverage of the war.

Many argue that the best reporting of the Iraq and Kosovo wars was done by John Pilger, again from his London base. Whatever your views on the merits of these reporters, it is clear that all journalists face ethical challenges during war (and peace time) to counter stereotypes, misinformation and lies.

DO MAINSTREAM MEDIA REPORTS SANITISE WAR?

On the one hand, journalists argue that the public simply has not the stomach for seeing horrific images of warfare: their self censorship is responding to these perceptions. As John Simpson commented: 'Television viewers no doubt want to be informed about the world but they do not enjoy being shocked.' On the other hand, the media are criticised for presenting a sanitised view of war. Anti-war campaigners argue that showing the 'brutal, horrific realities' will jolt people out of their apathy; others argue that journalists have a professional responsibility to show the 'truth', however unsettling it may be. And according to Miles Hudson and John Stainer (op. cit.: 315) modern mass media coverage of war has proved an 'enormous bonus to mankind': 'Could the carnage on the Somme, Passchendale or Verdun possibly have continued if it had been witnessed nightly in millions of European sitting rooms? The answer must be that it could not.'

Martin Bell, the white-suited BBC war correspondent turned Independent MP, has called for the 'journalism of attachment' arguing forcefully (1998: 21) that the media are increasingly failing in their representation of 'real-world violence'. Broadcasters were becoming more concerned with ratings than the truth:

> Some images of violence – as for instance most of the pictures of both the market place massacres in Sarajevo – are almost literally unviewable and cannot be inflicted on the public. But people have to be left with some sense of what happened, if only through the inclusion of pictures sufficiently powerful at least to hint at the horror of those excluded. To do otherwise is to present war as a relatively cost-free enterprise and an acceptable way of settling differences, a one-sided game that soldiers play in which they are seen shooting but never suffering. The camera shows the outgoing ordnance but seldom the incoming.

Veteran war correspondent and Middle East specialist Robert Fisk agrees. 'Pain, death, massacre are now all of "potential use to the enemy",' he comments. 'But war is not primarily about cynicism or defeat or victory or danger or blood. It is about pain and, ultimately, about death. Death, death, death. It's a word you don't often hear on CNN or Sky TV or BBC or even RTE. Having persuaded ourselves that we can go to war without casualties we don't believe in death any more.' Paradoxically, as media coverage portrays 'bloodless' wars, Hollywood recreates violence with ever increasing graphic 'realism'. Fisk adds: 'Saving Private Ryan was the final touch in this recreation. Why bother to visit wars when you can act them out in virtual reality? Why bother to smell the shit and blood – and those smells, unhappily, are exactly what you find in frontline hospitals – when you can watch wars without such distractions?'

Criticisms of the media's sanitising of wars have tended to focus on the coverage of the Gulf conflict. This was largely represented as a Nintendo-style, bloodless conflict fought by the 'heroic' allies with 'surgical', 'precise', super-modern weaponry. Shots from video cameras on missiles heading towards their targets (shown on television and reproduced in the press) meant viewers actually 'became' the weapons. These images, constantly repeated, came to dominate the representation of the Gulf conflict (and later the Kosovo War). As Kevin Robins and Les Levidow comment (1991: 325):

> It was the ultimate voyeurism: to see the target hit from the vantage point of the weapon. An inhumane perspective. Yet this remote-intimate kind of watching could sustain the moral detachment of earlier military technologies. Seeing was split off from feeling: the visible was separated

from the sense of pain. Through the long lens the enemy remained the faceless alien.

Also during the Kosovo War, many critics argued that the media failed to convey its real horror. According to Phillip Knightley (op. cit.: 505), between 10,000 and 15,000 civilians were killed, thousands were traumatised and left jobless and in terrible poverty. But these figures were rarely reported. When refugee convoys were bombed by NATO jets they were 'mistakes' (rather than moral outrages) or blamed on 'Milosevic'.

Kate Adie, however, prefers to stress the importance of the journalist's self censorship when covering scenes of appalling violence. 'I've seen things I would never put on the screen. It is immensely upsetting to see humans dead on-screen or alive being mistreated. A corpse is OK if it is not being interfered with. If it is kicked or bits are being removed, that is not acceptable.' She had once witnessed an infant crucifixion but would never screen it (Methven 1996). The issues are still further complicated since complex historical, political and ethical factors so often collide in the coverage of wars. The significance and power of images together with attitudes towards taste can change over time. For instance, John Taylor (1998: 22) highlights the way in which Eddie Adams' now famous picture of General Loan summarily executing a Vietcong suspect in a Saigon street on 1 February 1968 appeared when its moral and political dimension was acceptable to journalists:

> Harold Evans, a former editor of *The Times*, reports how in 1962 Dickey Chapelle photographed a Vietcong prisoner about to be executed by his captor, a South Vietnamese soldier with a drawn gun. But this picture was 'universally rejected and published only in an obscure little magazine', probably because in 1962 the war in Vietnam was too small or viewed too favourably for hostile coverage.

The decisions facing journalists are clearly never easy. To complicate the issue further for broadcasters, different criteria apply to programmes throughout the day's schedule. For instance, images following the horrific massacre in Bosnia at Amici were not shown during the day but later on *Channel 4 News* and *News at Ten*.

DOES NOT MEDIA COVERAGE OF WARS ALERT PUBLIC OPINION AND POLITICIANS TO HUMAN RIGHTS ABUSES AND HELP STOP THEM?

Here again, views amongst journalists are strikingly different. You may agree with Mark Lattimer, communications director of Amnesty International, who argues that media coverage of brutal rebel attacks in Freetown in April 2000 helped inspire government intervention. Or you may side with the *Independent*'s Robert Fisk who is more sceptical of the media's powers in halting the torturers: 'I have to question whether journalists really have the effect – long-term – of breaking open those prison doors, of tearing down the scaffolds and dismantling the torture equipment.'

One of the most famous instances of the media inspiring humanitarian intervention by the West occurred after images of fleeing Kurdish refugees filled our television screens soon after the end of the Gulf War in 1991. ITN's Nik Gowing wrote (1991: 9):

> [Six weeks after the end of the war] television further forced the hands of western politicians. Governments could not ignore the horror of the Kurdish catastrophe which unfolded on their TV screens. The pictures were politically uncomfortable and strategically inconvenient. But no government dare avoid them. Led by John Major, the British government had to jettison policy papers drawn up in the bureaucratic comfort of Whitehall. On an RAF jet flying to Luxembourg Britain's Prime Minister was forced to sketch out – on the back of an envelope – a concept for 'humanitarian' enclaves. As television showed the deepening catastrophe, George Bush had no option but to follow the British initiative. The US troops which he promised would never send back into Iraq's civil war, were sent back.

The media were representing the views of the compassionate, global community. As Martin Woollacott reported in the *Guardian*, the creation of the Kurdish safe haven was a job 'of which the whole world approved'. Similar conclusions were drawn in the States. Daniel Schorr commented in the *Columbia Journalism Review*: 'Within a two week period the president had been forced, under the impact of what Americans were seeing on television, to reconsider his hasty withdrawal of troops from Iraq.' How much of this was a myth? While the media represented Premier John Major (rather quaintly) as dreaming up the enclave idea on the spur of the moment, different political pressures probably had far more significance. In particular the Turkish leadership feared the mass of Kurds fleeing over their borders would aid support to the growing revolt of the Turkish Kurds spearheaded by the Marxist-oriented Partia Karkaris Kurdistan (PKK). Given their support during the allied attacks on Iraq, the Turks probably felt they had reason to expect some favours from the US. In fact, Turkish President Turgut Ozal first suggested the haven on 7 April; Major's proposal came the following day.

It was also argued that the West's intervention was far from altruistic. Bill Frelick commented: (1992: 27):

> Far from being a breakthrough for human rights and humanitarian assistance to displaced persons, the allied intervention on behalf of the Kurds of Iraq instead affirmed the power politics and hypocrisies that have long characterised the actions of states with respect to refugees and other victims of official torture.

The creation of the enclave in northern Iraq also served as a significant precedent for intervention by the US and UK elites into the affairs of foreign enemy states.

Significantly Gowing later modified his views about the power of the media to influence politicians. Commenting on the coverage of the Bosnian conflict, he wrote (1994):

> Certainly news pictures can shock policy-makers just as they do the rest of us . . . But television's new power should not be misread. It can highlight problems and help to put them on the agenda but when governments are determined to keep to minimalist, low-risk, low-cost strategies, television reporting does not force them to become more engaged.

You may also consider the saturation coverage of the terrible plight of the Kosovo refugees fleeing the Serb terror helped inspire and legitimise NATO's 'humanitarian' bombing in 1991. Ethnic cleansing on such a mammoth scale (with accompanying stories of massacres and mass rapes) was totally unprecedented in Europe and demanded massive global coverage, according to those who backed the bombing. When NATO forces entered Kosovo at the end of the bombing campaign they were accompanied by 2,700 media personnel (compared to just 500 war correspondents in Vietnam at its peak). But you may join those critics who accused the mainstream media of meekly following the agenda of the US/UK elites who were determined to draw Yugoslavia into the capitalist bloc alongside other east European countries. Significantly, the worst human rights crisis throughout the 1990s occurred in Colombia where thousands of lawyers, teachers, journalists, trade unionists and teachers have been assassinated. In addition, as Noam Chomsky stresses (1999: 49) the civil war between the government and left-wing guerrillas had created well over 1 million internal refugees, far more than in Kosovo. In Turkey, as a result of the civil war between government forces and Kurdish rebels, up to 3 million refugees have been created. In both these cases, the media have remained silent over the refugees' plight. Is not the fact that the US/UK support the appallingly repressive governments of Colombia and Turkey with massive military aid packages significant?

BECAUSE IT'S SO HARD TO DEFINE PRECISELY WHAT IS WAR TODAY AREN'T THE ETHICAL ISSUES EVEN MORE DIFFICULT TO DEFINE?

Historians and journalists conventionally focus on a few major, post-1945 wars. So the main spotlight tends to fall on Vietnam, the Falklands, the Gulf War of 1991 and the NATO attacks on Yugoslavia of 1999. Yet these conflicts constitute only a tiny fraction of US/UK military activities. Some critics point to the fact that the focus on the few major wars serves to represent Britain as primarily at peace, only turning to war in defence against unforeseen threats (from the 'Argies' in 1982; 'mad monster, new Hitler Saddam Hussein' in 1991 and 'evil Milosevic' in 1999). Most significantly, the dominant perspective obscures the offensive elements of US/UK military strategies. In fact, Britain and the US have deployed military forces every year since 1945 – on many occasions in secret and away from the gaze of the prying media. Do not ethical and political issues become even more problematic in the face of this growth of secret warfare (known in the jargon as Low Intensity Conflict)? (Collins 1991)

Moreover, the ending of the Cold War – with the collapse of the Berlin Wall and the old Soviet Union – has meant that the military/industrial complex has had to look elsewhere for 'enemies'. Some critics have suggested that major overt wars today are essentially 'manufactured'. The threats posed by the 'enemy' are grossly exaggerated; in the end US/UK jets are left (as in Libya in 1986, Panama in 1989, Iraq from 1991 to the present and Yugoslavia in 1999) attacking defenceless 'targets'. This is certainly not warfare as generally understood. In this new era of manufactured, 'humanitarian', short wars, when Britain's national security is hardly at stake (but when weapons are 'clean' and 'precise' and soldiers are all pacifists at heart) propaganda becomes an even more crucial arm of the military. As Tony Blair's press secretary Alastair Campbell said on *Panorama*'s 'Moral Combat' on 12 March 2000 (looking back on the Kosovo War): 'It wasn't just a military campaign it was also a propaganda campaign and we had to take our public opinion with us.'

James Combs identifies the emergence of a distinctly new kind of warfare with the UK's Falklands campaign and the US invasion of Grenada in 1983. He argues (1993: 277):

It is a new kind of war, war as performance. It is a war in which the attention of its *auteurs* is not only the conduct of the war but also the communication of the war. With their political and military power to command, coerce and co-opt the mass media the national security elite can make the military event go according to script, omit bad scenes and discouraging words and bring about a military performance that is both spectacular and satisfying.

The shift to volunteer forces and nuclear 'deterrent' signalled in both the US and UK a growing separation of the state and military establishment from the public. According to some critics, the populist press, closely allied to the state, serves to create the illusion of participatory citizenship. As *The Times* editorial trumpeted during the Falklands crisis: 'We are all Falklanders now.' How justified are these criticisms?

9
Constraints on journalists

GIVEN THE MANY CONSTRAINTS ON JOURNALISTS, HOW CAN WE TALK OF THE FREE MEDIA?

Murder

The ultimate constraint on journalists is said to be imposed through murder. The killing of Veronica Guerin, crime reporter of the *Sunday Independent*, in Dublin on 26 June 1996, highlighted starkly the dangers posed to intrepid investigative journalists. Yet her death raised serious questions about journalists' training for dangerous assignments and newspapers' cultivation of their star reporters' personalities as a deliberate marketing ploy. In her biography of Guerin, Emily O'Reilly (1998) quotes Ben Bradlee, editor of the *Washington Post*: 'Although it has become increasingly difficult for this newspaper and for the press generally to do since Watergate, reporters should make every effort to remain in the audience, to stay off the stage, to report history, not to make history.' According to O'Reilly, the *Sunday Independent* broke the Bradlee rule – and Guerin paid a terrible price.

Fortunately, in Britain and Ireland murder remains an extremely rare threat to journalists (though correspondents on foreign assignments can be killed, beaten up and intimidated). Not so in many other countries. Each year the Paris-based group, Reporters Without Borders, and the US-based Committee to Protect Journalists (accessible at www.cpj.org) issue reports documenting the numbers of journalists killed in action or jailed. They make for grim reading. In 1999, according to the CPJ, 34 journalists were killed, up from 24 the previous year. Controversially, this figure did not include the 16 employees of Radio and Television of Serbia killed in a NATO attack in April. But even in Britain, journalists are coming under increasing threats covering demonstrations, while investigative journalists constantly face intimidation. For instance, after writing a story about a Brazilian illegal immigrant for the *London Evening Standard* in 1997, Jo-Ann Goodwin faced death threats, anonymous phone calls and open hostility. Clearly managements have a responsibility to invest more in the training in risk awareness for all their staff, while journalists on dangerous assignments should always be encouraged to work in pairs or threes.

Legal constraints

Many laws exist in Britain restraining the media. In 1992, the White Paper, *Open Government*, identified 251 laws outlawing information disclosure. Two years later the Guild of Editors listed 46 directly relating to journalists. They included the Children and Young Persons Act 1993 and the Trade Union Reform and Employment Rights Act 1993 which imposed reporting restrictions on industrial tribunals involving sexual harassment. The Criminal Procedures and Investigations Act 1998 gave the courts further powers to impose reporting restrictions. Reporters have found restrictions imposed under Section 39 of the Children Act – even in cases where the identity of minors is known. Andrew Johnson (1997a) comments: 'In many cases the kneejerk response is to impose restrictions and overturn them only when challenged.'

In addition, the laws of libel, contempt, defamation, on obscenity and blasphemy, and 'gagging' injunctions to stop alleged breaches of confidence all act as restraints on the media. More recent controversies have focused on the police's attempts to use the 1997 Protection from Harassment Act against photographers such as Chris Eades of *Kent News and Pictures* after he tried to take shots of John Major's son James and partner Emma Noble at their new house in Kent in April 1999. Concerns also grew that the Youth Justice and Criminal Evidence Act 1999 would ban identification of child witnesses. But then after a Government compromise, only the naming of alleged perpetrators of crime was banned if they were under 18.

The Public Record Office officially operates a 30-year rule before releasing official documents. As John Willis comments (1991: 34): 'but as anyone knows who has worked in this area, most papers relating to secret events or other sensitive matters are exempt from this and "closed" to public access for much longer – sometimes as much as 100 years.' This is allowed under the 1958 Public Records Act with the permission of the Lord Chancellor, who does not appear to object very often. In the case of the secret services, nothing ever enters the PRO. As a result of the US Freedom of Information

Act, a researcher in Britain can usually find out more about the UK secret services in the US because of their links with the CIA.

The Prevention of Terrorism Act is, in reality, used for intelligence gathering rather than securing prosecutions, since only a very small percentage of those held are charged with terrorist offences. It has also been used by the state in an attempt to intimidate journalists into revealing confidential sources. Thus, in 1988, the BBC was forced to hand over footage of the mobbing of two soldiers who ran into a funeral procession in Belfast. Following a *Dispatches* programme by the independent company, Box Productions, in 1991, alleging collusion between Loyalist death squads and members of the security forces in Northern Ireland, Channel 4 was committed for contempt for refusing to reveal its source and fined £75,000.

Government plans in 2000 for a new anti-terrorism legislation also provoked serious concerns amongst civil rights campaigners and journalists. The bill, introduced into the Commons on 2 December 1999, radically extended the definition of terrorism to mean: 'The use of serious violence against persons or property or the threat to use such violence, to intimidate or coerce a government, the public or any section of the public for political, religious or ideological ends.' Journalists covering direct action could be caught by Clause 18, carrying a five-year sentence for failure to report information received professionally which could lead to a terrorist act (Zobel 2000). In 2000, concerns also mounted that the Regulation Investigatory Powers Act would provide a 'Big Brother's charter' (Naughton 2000), since it would allow the police and security services wide-ranging powers to intercept e-mail and other electronic communications – and could lead to people facing criminal charges if they could not decode files on their computers, even if they did not create them. In response, Home Secretary Jack Straw stressed that intrusive surveillance was to be used only in accordance with human rights principles.

Advertisers

Sometimes pressures from advertisers can be overt as when they seek to influence editorial policy or withdraw support after critical coverage. But some critics suggest that more often the pressure operates more subtly: Curran and Seaton (1991: 38) argue that the emergence of an advertisement-based, mass-selling newspaper industry in the latter half of the nineteenth century helped stifle the development of a radical, trade union-based press. 'The crucial element of the new control system was the strategic role acquired by advertisers after the repeal of the advertisement duty in 1853.' Newspapers' focus shifted from overt political propaganda to a more subtle, entertainment-based propaganda. Thus today, you may consider advertisers are best seen as promoting the values of materialism and consumerism as well as a conservative respect for the status quo. Or you may consider them as the bulwark of the free press, freeing it from any dependency on the state for funding.

Pressure from proprietors: is this inevitable or a serious threat to democracy?

Over the years, newspaper journalists have also faced considerable pressures from their proprietors. Men like Northcliffe, Beaverbrook, Rothermere, Rowland, Murdoch and Maxwell have all gained reputations of being eccentric, egocentric, super-powerful, super-rich – and constantly interfering in the operations of their newspapers. Editorials have been re-written, layouts have been changed; editors have been sacked and favoured hacks have been promoted. Robert Maxwell, owner of the *Mirror* until his mysterious drowning in 1991, even paid £40,000 to have his offices bugged so that he could keep a close watch on critical journalists. Moreover, as Anthony Bevins (1990: 15) argues, dissident reporters who do not follow the proprietor's line suffer professional death. Most recently Rupert Murdoch, owner of vast media interests world-wide, has been described as 'a highly politicised proprietor who perceives himself to be fighting a global battle on behalf of capitalism, the free market and Christian values' (McNair 2000: 20). Despite being a stout defender of media freedoms, Murdoch shows little hesitation in censoring writers who cross his path. For instance, Doug Gay's religious *Credo* column in *The Times*, was abruptly ended after he criticised the proprietor in 1998. A row erupted after Murdoch, owner of the publishing company, HarperCollins, intervened to ban a book by former governor Chris Patten about Hong Kong and critical of China (where he holds significant media interests). And in July 2000 an unauthorised biography of Murdoch by Michael Crick, due to be published by Fourth Estate, was suddenly dropped after the company was purchased by HarperCollins.

In particular, the integration of the proprietors' empires into the world of global finance has given rise to concerns that a vast range of no-go areas has been created for the media. Not surprisingly, proprietors are not keen to have reporters probing into their more murky activities. Maxwell managed to keep the scandal of his pension fund rip-off secret during his lifetime through a merciless use of the libel laws, intimidation and a clever exploitation of journalists' desire for the quiet life (Greenslade 1992). The moguls have also tended to promote their own financial interests through their own media. Tiny Rowland campaigned in the *Observer* against the Al Fayeds following their purchase of Harrods (Bower 1993), Maxwell constantly publicised his many 'charities' and political activities, while Murdoch's media interests take every opportunity to attack the BBC and ITV and promote his own Sky channels.

Investigative reporter John Pilger puts special blame for the *Sun*'s trashy tabloid style on its proprietor, Murdoch. He writes (1998: 449):

> Labour politician Tony Benn is not a hyprocrite, but his principles are anathema to Murdoch. Benn was declared 'insane' in a malicious *Sun* story whose 'authority', an American psychologist, described the false quotations attributed to him as 'absurd'. The Thatcher government's campaign against 'loony' London councils, which probably helped turn the Labour Party in on itself and away from progressive policies, was based substantially on a long-running series of inventions and distortions in the *Sun*. The person ultimately responsible for this is Rupert Murdoch.

But Reiner Luyken, of the German newspaper *Die Zeit*, stresses: 'The most striking effect of Murdoch is self-censorship. Self-censorship is now so commonplace in the British media that journalists admit to it without blushing.'

Nick Cohen (1999: 128–9) comments on the role of press magnates:

> Freedom of the press means the freedom for these gentlemen to do what they want. They, and their counterparts in television, have changed journalism from a trade that encouraged reporters to develop specialist knowledge to a kind of feudal system with a few over-paid managers, columnists and newscasters at the top and a mass of casual, pressured and often ignorant serfs underneath.

Perhaps more inspiration should be drawn from countries such as Sweden, France, Norway, Finland and the Netherlands where selective subsidy systems have countered monopolising trends and helped preserve vigorous minority political media (Curran 2000: 46). Many journalists, however, argue that the ownership structures in the media are an inevitable product of a profit-based economic system within an advanced capitalist society. The media may have their many faults, but at least there is no Orwellian thought control like that which strangled free expression in the old Soviet Union.

New pressures from the police?

Concerns were mounting in 2000 that police interpretation of data protection legislation had seriously restricted the reporting of crimes over the previous two years. Nearly two-thirds of regional journalists surveyed by *Press Gazette* (14 July 2000) believed it had become more difficult to report crimes accurately as a result of media policies adopted by police forces around the country. Many journalists commented that it was not just details of road traffic accident victims or victims of crime which were being withheld but information about serious crimes – including rape, murder and assault. Harry Blackwood, editor of the *Hartlepool Mail*, commented:

> Many police officers don't want newspapers to report crime as they say it increases the fear of crime. Maybe they'd like to consider how the victims feel when their house is burgled and they feel their whole world has collapsed. The victims then discover that the crime wasn't serious enough to merit a couple of paragraphs in the local paper.

In response to journalists' pressure, the Association of Chief Police Officers, in July 2000, said it would advise its members to encourage people to allow their names and other details to be given to the press.

DOES THE SECRET STATE IMPINGE ON THE WORK OF JOURNALISTS?

Richard Thurlow (1994: 399) talks of the 'insidious growth of the secret state throughout the 20th century' creating another vast no-go area for journalists. And *Independent* journalist Paul Vallely comments: 'That power corrupts is now a truism. But it does not just apply to the dictators of Africa. It applies to the elective dictatorship which has taken root in Britain since the war whereby governments exercise power largely unchecked by parliament.' According to Clive Ponting (1990: 16): 'In Britain, absolute secrecy has been the policy of all post-war governments.' Today an estimated £750m is spent annually on MI5 (domestic security), MI6 (overseas intelligence) and GCHQ (surveillance headquarters). Yet some argue that the growth of the secret services is an inevitable and necessary process in an era of political extremism, global terrorism and drug-running – and in the face of threats from such unpredictable 'rogue' states as Iraq, Libya and North Korea. Journalists must simply accept the consequences. What do you think?

The secret state is protected from probing media by a series of laws. The 1989 Security Service Act (actually drafted by MI5 lawyers) placed the service on a statutory basis for the first time and provided it with legal powers to tap phones, bug and burgle houses and intercept mail. The *UK Press Gazette* commented (6 September 1993): 'The greatest invasion of privacy is carried out every day by the security services, with no control, no democractic authorisation and the most horrifying consequences for people's employment and lives. By comparison with them the press is a poodle' (see Urban 1996: 53). The Intelligence Services Act of 1993 created the Intelligence and Security Committee which meets in secret to overview services' activities, reporting to the Prime Minister and not Parliament. Following the 1996 Security Service Act, MI5's functions were extended to 'act in support of the prevention and detection of crime'. The in-coming Labour Government then moved to extend the powers allowing the intelligence services and other government agencies to conduct covert surveillance including bugging phones and property.

In 1989, a new Official Secrets Act (OSA) replaced the 1911 OSA which had proved notoriously cumbersome, particularly after civil servant Sarah Tisdall was jailed in 1983 for leaking to the *Guardian* government plans for the timing of the arrival of cruise missles in England. Then followed the acquittal of top civil servant Clive Ponting charged under Section 2 (1) of the OSA after he leaked information showing the Government had misled the House of Commons over the sinking of the Argentinian ship, the *Belgrano*, during the Falklands conflict of 1982. The 1989 Act covered five main areas: law enforcement, information supplied in confidence by foreign governments, international relations, defence, and security and intelligence. The publishing of leaks on any of these subjects was banned. Journalists were also denied a public interest defence. Nor could they claim in defence no harm had resulted to national security through their disclosures.

The system of Defence Advisory Notices (better known as D Notices) also serves to restrain the media in their coverage of sensitive security issues. Once a notice is issued by the secretary of the defence, press and broadcasting advisory committee, editors are asked to censor reporting. The system, introduced in 1912 to prevent breaches in security by German spies, is entirely voluntary (see its website at www.dnotice.org.uk). There are six notices in all: covering the operations, plans and capabilities of the UK armed forces, the nuclear industry, emergency underground oil reserves, and so on (Sheldon 1999). Around 800 media professionals have a copy of the official list (though it is available on the Web at www.btinternet.com/~d.a.notices). Rear Admiral David Pulvertaft said that during his six years in the post of D Notices secretary, there had been a remarkably high level of co-operation with the media. In July 2000, the new secretary, Rear Admiral Nick Wilkinson, said the sytem was 'not allowed to stifle debate about politically sensitive matters'.

Yet should journalists always co-operate? Some critics argued in 1999 that the harassment of former *Sunday Times* defence correspondent Tony Geraghty after he refused to submit his book, *The Irish War*, for clearance exposed the myth of the 'voluntary' system. Geraghty became the first journalist charged under the new Official Secrets Act after he revealed the extent of the army's surveillance operations and MI5 dirty tricks in Northern Ireland. The charges were eventually dropped but one of his alleged contacts, Col. Nigel Wylde, faced the prospect of a criminal trial. The *Sunday Times* Northern Ireland editor, Liam Clarke, was also summoned by the police special squad after his newspaper was prevented by an injunction from publishing allegations of further dirty tricks by the army's force research unit – a clandestine cell set up to handle informants in the IRA and Loyalist paramilitary groups (Norton-Taylor 2000).

Even at the European level, sweeping new controls on information were agreed by EU governments in August 2000. Drawn up in secret by Javier Solana, the EU security supremo, the blanket secrecy rules will cover plans to set up a 5,000 strong EU paramilitary police force and a rapid reaction force as well as all EU discussions on criminal justice, border controls and trade policy.

HOW SHOULD JOURNALISTS RESPOND IF THEIR SERVICES ARE SOUGHT BY THE SECRET SERVICES?

According to Ann Rogers (1997: 64):

> Journalists, critics and scholars have focused on the legal–rational processes mandated by the OSA and by doing so have amplified a liberal model of adversarial state–media relations. However, an examination of the record of official secrecy cases involving the press suggests that this focus obscures the extent to which the media have actually supported and colluded with the secret state. The media have been more likely to contribute to, rather than mitigate, secrecy in Britain.

Indeed, David Leigh (2000) records a series of instances in which the secret services manipulated prominent journalists. He says reporters are routinely approached by intelligence agents: 'I think the cause of honest journalism is best served by candour. We all ought to come clean about these approaches and devise some ethics to deal with them. In our vanity, we imagine that we control these sources. But the truth is that they are very deliberately seeking to control us.'

John Simpson, BBC world affairs editor (1999: 296–7), describes in his autobiography how he was once approached by a 'man from MI5'. 'At some point they might make me broadcast something favourable to them. Or they might just ask me to carry a message to someone. You never knew,' he said. But Simpson adds: 'It doesn't do journalists any good to play footsie with MI5 or the Secret Intelligence Service; they get a bad reputation.' *Observer* foreign correspondent Mark Frankland talks in his autobiography of his time in SIS in the late 1950s and comments (1999: 92): 'Journalists working abroad were natural candidates for agents and particularly useful in places such as Africa where British intelligence was hurrying to establish itself.'

The hard evidence of journalists' links with the secret services is inevitably limited, but it can be striking. Take, for instance, the spy novelist John le Carré who worked for MI6 between 1960 and 1964. He has stated that the British secret service then controlled large parts of the press – just as they may do today (Dorril 1993: 281). David Leigh (1989: 113), in his seminal study of the way in which the secret service smeared and destabilised the government of Harold Wilson before his sudden resignation in 1976, quotes an MI5 officer: 'We have somebody in every office in Fleet Street.' Investigative reporter Phillip Knightley, author of a seminal study of the secret services, argues that today not only do they have representatives in all the major publishing houses but also at their printing works.

In 1975, following Senate hearings on the CIA which highlighted the extent of agency recruitment of both American and British journalists, sources revealed that half the foreign staff of a British daily were on the MI6 payroll. Jonathan Bloch and Patrick Fitzgerald (1983: 134–41), in their study of British intelligence and covert action, report the 'editor of one of Britain's most distinguished journals' as believing that more than half its foreign correspondents were on the MI6 payroll. And Roy Greenslade, former editor of the *Mirror*, has commented: 'Most tabloid newspapers – or even newspapers in general – are playthings of MI5. You are recipients of the sting' (Milne 1994: 262). Also, in 1991, Richard Norton-Taylor revealed in the *Guardian* that 500 prominent Britons had been paid by the CIA and now defunct Bank of Commerce and Credit International, including 90 journalists (Pilger 1998: 496).

Just before his mysterious death in 1991, *Mirror* proprietor Robert Maxwell was accused by the American investigative journalist Seymour Hersh (1991) of acting for Mossad, the Israeli secret service, though Dorril (2000: 141) suggests his links with MI6 were equally strong. Following the resignation from the *Guardian* of Richard Gott, its literary editor, in December 1994 in the wake of allegations that he was a 'paid agent' of the KGB, the role of journalists as spies suddenly came under the media spotlight – and many of the leaks were fascinating. For instance, according to *The Times* editorial of 16 December 1994: 'Many British journalists benefited from CIA or MI6 largesse during the Cold War.'

The release of Public Record Office documents on 17 August 1995 about some of the operations of the MI6-financed propaganda unit, the Information Research Department of the Foreign Office, threw new light on this secret body which even George Orwell aided by sending them a list of 'crypto-communists' (Saunders 1999: 298–301). Set up by the Labour Government in 1948, it 'ran' dozens of Fleet Street journalists until it was closed down by Foreign Secretary David Owen in 1977. According to John Pilger, 'in the anti-colonial struggles in Kenya, Malaya and Cyprus, IRD was so successful that the journalism served up as a record of those episodes was a cocktail of the distorted and false in which the real aims and often atrocious behaviour of the British were suppressed'. Dorril later claimed that, despite IRD's closure, some of its elements 'lingered on'. Some journalists work for foreign secret services. Kim Philby had worked as foreign correspondent for the *Observer* as a cover for his work as a Soviet spy; another *Observer* journalist Farzad Bazoft (hanged in Baghdad in March 1990) was, according to Gordon Thomas (2000: 167–74), a spy for Mossad, Israel's secret service.

HOW MIGHT JOURNALISTS RESPOND TO THESE CHALLENGES, TEMPTATIONS AND THREATS?

Journalists have adopted a variety of strategies for evading these constraints. For instance, after dissident MI5 official David Shayler alleged MI6 had been involved in an unsuccessful plot to assassinate Colonel Gaddafi, of Libya, the *Guardian* published details, claiming they had entered the public domain through publication in the *New York Times*. When Shayler and the *Mail on Sunday* were sued by the Government for breaches of confidence and of contract in February 2000, and he sent names to the media of two intelligence officers involved in the Gaddafi plot, newspapers obeyed instructions not to publish. But later when the Labour Government threatened to send reporters on the *Observer* and *Guardian* to jail over their contacts with Shayler, 150 fellow journalists signed up to a half-page advertisement in *The Times* on 3 May 2000 protesting at the threat to press freedom. Then, on 23 July, Lord Justice Igor Judge ruled that the newspapers were right to resist police pressure to hand over documents. Lawyers for the newspapers claimed the police action was clearly in breach of Article 10 of the European Convention on Human Rights (due to become part of British law on 2 October 2000) and of Article 6 which guarantees the rights of suspects not to incriminate themselves. The ruling was said to be 'the most ringing defence of freedom of expression heard in Britain for years' by the *Guardian*.

The media sometimes campaign against specific constraints. For instance, the *Guardian*'s campaign against EU secrecy gained a major success in October 1995 after the European Court in Luxembourg upheld a claim that it was unlawfully denied the minutes of ministers' private debates. Moreover, following the *Guardian*'s 'Open Up' campaign for freedom of information, on 15 March 2000 it was reported that the minutes of the Welsh Assembly Cabinet were to be put on the Internet within six weeks of the meeting. In Britain, in contrast, the Home Secretary was insisting that much government information would remain a state secret for 30 years.

Whistle-blowers are often used by the media to expose corruption in high places and break through the constraints on coverage. For instance, Cathy Massiter, an MI5 F Branch officer, bravely revealed to Channel 4's *20/20* how surveillance of Campaign for Nuclear Disarmament activists had been stepped up in the early 1980s. Peter Wright, a retired MI5 officer, is the whistle-blower *par excellence*. After he revealed a series of security service dirty tricks in his largely unreadable memoirs, *Spycatcher*, the Thatcher Government began a long, drawn-out and ultimately futile attempt to prevent publication. In June 1986, the *Observer* and *Guardian*, which had published some of Wright's allegations ahead of publication, were served with injunctions. Then the short-lived *News on Sunday*, the *Sunday Times* and the *Independent* were each fined £50,000 for having intended to prejudice legal proceedings in the original case through publishing extracts from the book. Eventually these fines were set aside on appeal, as were the injunctions, after the Law Lords ruled that, in view of the world-wide publicity, national security could not be damaged by publication in the UK.

Controversy has also flared over Labour's Freedom of Information (FoI) legislation which many critics argue does more to reinforce the culture of secrecy. A well-researched, hard-hitting campaign by the *Nottingham Evening Post* against the FoI legislation tackled an important national issue by focusing on strong local angles. Thus it highlighted the police's refusal to say how many Nottinghamshire officers had registered membership of the Freemasons and how hygiene reports on city restaurants had been kept secret. It called for clause 28 to be amended since it would prevent the public learning which Nottinghamshire hospitals or care homes were being investigated for allegedly withholding food and drink from elderly patients. Clause 34 would deny the public the right to see scientific advice about hazards such as BSE while clause 41 would conceal information about firms lobbying the Government to promote GM foods.

Protests have also grown over Labour's local government legislation allowing councils to set up secret cabinet-style meetings. A campaign by the *Evening Chronicle*, Newcastle, forced the city council to back down in April 2000. In November 1999 the *Evening Echo*, covering Southend and Basildon, forced its local authority to back down while the *Uxbridge Gazette* in 1999 ran a hard-hitting campaign against the introduction of cabinet-style government to the London borough of Hillingdon. The *Evening Echo*, covering Southend and Basildon, and the *Nottingham Evening Post* also ran campaigns for open local government. Only scepticism greeted the announcement by the Government in July 2000 that meetings on 'key decisions' would be open to the public.

The media across the country have also consistently challenged Section 39 'gagging' orders – with some success. *Keighley News* overturned a court order issued to protect a schoolboy – even though he was not part of the judicial proceedings. A Norwich judge's ruling that a defendant accused of indecent offences against a young girl should not be named was successfully opposed by the *Evening News*, while reporter Alex Hannaford of the *Advertiser and Times* series successfully challenged a New Forest magistrates court ban on naming a young girl attacked by a dog. And an intervention by a PA News trainee to stop a court order banning identification of a two-year-old attacked by his mother was even praised by the barrister who had sought the ban.

A campaign by two resourceful journalists over journalists' right to visit prisoners and write about their cases also ended in a notable victory. Bob Woffinden, an investigative journalist, and Karen Voisey, a BBC Wales producer, had earlier refused to sign undertakings not to publish material obtained during visits to two prisoners whose life sentences for murder they were investigating as possible cases of miscarriages of justice. On 20 December 1996, the High Court ruled that a blanket ban by the Government a year earlier on journalists interviewing prison inmates was illegal and an unjustified restriction of freedom of speech. The appeal court renewed the ban. But this decision was finally over-ruled by the Law Lords on 8 July 1999.

The magazine *Index on Censorship* and the campaigning body Article 19 have consistently fought for the rights of writers and journalists world-wide.

Lobster magazine takes a close, critical watch on the activities of the security services in Britain while *Covert Action Quarterly* does the same in the United States. Both are invaluable resources for journalists. *State Research, Socialist Worker*, monitored and infiltrated by MI5 F7 section, according to Stephen Dorril (1993: 8), and the US *Z Magazine* and the investigative *Mother Jones* are all worth watching. *Project Censored* published each year by Sonoma University highlights major stories censored by the mainstream media in the US.

HOW DO YOU THINK JOURNALISTS SHOULD RESPOND WHEN THE POLICE DEMAND CAMERA FOOTAGE OF RIOTS AND DEMONSTRATIONS?

Following the Police and Criminal Evidence Act (PACE) 1984, police investigating a 'serious offence' can obtain an order requiring the journalist to hand over evidence considered useful to the court. This can include unpublished notes and photographs. Very few other countries provide the police with such powers. In France, *juges d'instruction* have powers to search and seize reporters' notebooks and film rushes but they must go in person to examine the material. No interference in the free flow of information is allowed. They must leave copies of material seized so that the broadcast or publication can go ahead. In the US, the First Amendment guarantees freedom of speech. Police and prosecutors can apply for access to notebooks and rushes but the presumption is that press freedom is paramount. Press freedom is enshrined in German law, being protected from state interference ever since *Der Speigel* was raided on the order of Defence Minister Franz-Joseph Strauss (Graef 1993).

In Britain, then, journalists are faced with a difficult dilemma: on the one hand, they may consider their first responsibility is to uphold the law; on the other hand, they may feel their independence is best preserved by rejecting the dictate of the state. The first major controversy emerged just eight months after PACE passed into law. The *Bristol Evening News* refused to hand over film following a drug bust, lost the case and had the police take away 264 pictures and negatives. After violent demonstrations at Rupert Murdoch's News International offices in Wapping, east London, in early 1987, the *Independent, Mail on Sunday* and *Observer*, two television companies and four freelance photographers appealed against an order requiring them to hand over pictures. On 23 May 1988, Mr Justice Alliot ruled that the pictures should be surrendered since this would not undermine the freedom and independence of the press. All complied except the four freelance photographers who had earlier taken the unprecedented step of sending their materials, via the NUJ, to the International Federation of Journalists in Brussels. In October 1988, the contempt charges against the freelances were thrown out because they were considered to be no longer owners of the material or to possess it.

Following the poll tax riots of 31 March 1990, the police applied under PACE for access to 'all transmitted, published and/or unpublished cine film, video tape, still photographs and negatives of the demonstration and subsequent disturbances which was obtained with a view to being of a newsworthy interest'. Some national newspapers complied. Again, the NUJ moved fast, sending prints and negatives out of the country. And an attempt by the police to force the media to hand over photographs and journalists' notes taken during the riots in the City of London in June 1999 was thrown out by a judge on 2 July 1999.

10
The ethical challenge: how you may respond

In the face of the vastness and complexities of the ethical dilemmas thrown up by the modern media, how is the journalist to react? What precisely is good journalism? What are the models for 'good' practice? How can the bad, the ugly and the unacceptable be eliminated? Journalists often focus on skills when describing a 'good journalist'. Thus, 'having a nose for a story', being able to take a reliable note and handle the computer technology confidently, writing accurately and colourfully are amongst the attributes commonly stressed. However, most journalists, if pressed to identify the strictly ethical aspects of 'good journalism', are likely to display ambivalent, contradictory and confused attitudes. To clarify the issue, it might be useful to identify a few prominent positions.

THE CYNICAL APPROACH

You may be tempted to adopt the cynical, amoral approach. This was summed up by a national newspaper editor, invited to a London journalism school to give a talk on ethics. 'Efficks – wot's that?' he asked, bemused. And so he simply proceeded to tell the gathered throng of students about his life and (highly successful) times in the industry. It is an attitude based on the conviction that ethical issues have little relevance for journalists. There is not enough time for them, and journalists have little power to influence them anyway. Profits are at the root of all journalism, so why bother with such idealistic fancies as ethics? Or cynicism may be linked to a philosophical, existential position which regards all human experience as essentially amoral. Ethical egotism takes a cynical view of the altruism behind moral conduct, suggesting that all actions (however much they are clothed in the rhetoric of morality) are essentially motivated by self interest.

unselfish
concern for
others

Often accompanying this stance, paradoxically, is a belief in the market. In other words, people get what they want and deserve. If the masses want trashy TV, then why should middle-class, snooty journalists with their highfalutin' ethical concerns, deny them that? The cynical approach has been evident in widespread criticisms by mainstream journalists of media training courses which are increasingly incorporating courses on ethics. Consequently, media studies have, in the national media, acquired the demonised status held by sociology in the 1960s and peace studies in the 1980s. A leader in the *Independent* of 31 October 1996 summed up this view bluntly saying 'this paper regards a degree in media studies as a disqualification for a career of journalism'.

THE STRESS ON INDIVIDUAL CONSCIENCE

Some journalists prefer to adopt *ad hoc* responses to specific ethical challenges rather than follow some broadly defined ethical system. Such an approach can be accompanied by an ethical relativism according to which moral judgements are viewed as varying across historical periods and cultures. Thus all moral systems can be considered equally good, even if they are antithetical. Formal codes of ethics are viewed with scepticism. As American media theorist John C. Merrill argues: 'Journalists must seek ethical guidance from within themselves not from codes of organisations, commissions or councils.' Bob Norris, former *Times* correspondent and associate director of PressWise, the media ethics body, says on codes: (2000: 325): '. . . they all have one thing in common: they are not worth the paper they are written on.' He continues: 'Every story is different and every reporter is driven by the compulsion to get the story and get it first. To imagine that he or she is going to consult the union's code of ethics while struggling to meet a deadline is to live in cloud-cuckoo land.'

But he stresses he lives by his personal code of ethics (ibid.: 329); 'I will not wear a uniform, carry a gun or act as a spy for my own government or any other. Yet I have known reporters who will do any or all of these things and regard them as perfectly ethical.' He describes how, when working for *The Times*, he was asked to spy for his country by the Military Attaché at the British High Commission in Lagos. He turned down the offer. 'I later learned that his offer had been taken up by one of my colleagues on a rival paper.' Former assistant editor of the *Observer* David Randall (1996: 93) takes a similar approach: 'So these journalistic ethics are either the codification of prevailing behaviour and culture or an irrelevant exhortation to standards of behaviour that are doomed to be unmet. Either way, there is not a great deal of point to them.'

This emphasis on personal conscience is often linked by journalists with an idiosyncratic, maverick stance according to which it becomes the responsibility of the virtuous journalist to question authority and, where necessary, break rules. As Klaidman and Beauchamp argue (1987: 138): 'Persons seeking wholeness and maturity rise above the implicit utilitarianism of rule-keeping to develop the conscience of virtuous persons. To follow rules blindly is to surrender moral impulse.'

THE STRESS ON PROFESSIONALISM

As a journalist you may be inclined to claim a professional commitment to journalistic standards. Such an approach can be driven by a religious or humanistic value system. Underlying this approach are a range of closely interlinked notions, listed below.

The free press

The free press is a central feature of the dominant value system of Western, capitalist democracy, distinguishing it clearly from, say, military or Islamic dictatorships where state-controlled propaganda enjoys total control. According to the theory, the free press, independent of the state and free from any direct funding by political parties, mediates between the rulers and the ruled, providing the necessary political, financial and social information to the electorate which they can use to form rational voting decisions. As John O'Neill says (1992: 15): 'A free market brings with it a free press that supplies the diversity of opinion and access to information that a citizenry requires in order to act in a democratic, responsible manner. The free market, journalism and democracy form an interdependent trinity of institutions in an open society.' Charles Moore (1997), editor of the *Daily Telegraph*, summed up this view when he described the general election of 1997 as 'the sacred moment in a democracy'. He continued: 'The people's choice is what validates the whole process. Newspapers must try to give their readers all the material they need to make that choice.'

The free press notion essentially emerged from the Reformation's stress on the liberty of religious expression. This became part of a broader assertion and defence of freedom of expression in general, with the media carrying special responsibilities to guard the public's 'right to know' – such as later enshrined in Article 19 of the Universal Declaration of Human Rights (Bromley 2000: 113–14). According to Brian Winston (1998: 44) John Milton's assertion of '[T]he liberty to know, to utter and to argue freely according to conscience, above all' marked the beginnings of a powerful dissenting tradition in our political life. Yet until the recent legislation incorporating the European Convention on Human Rights into British law, there were no legal guarantees of freedom of expression or of the press such as that contained in the First Amendment to the American constitution.

The concept of the free individual is also critical here. Emerging during the Renaissance and achieving maturity in the Enlightenment, this concept was developed by the French philospher Jean-Jacques Rousseau who promoted the notion of the self-determination of the personality as the highest good (Klaidman and Beauchamp op. cit.: 59). Thus, you may wish to argue, journalists, operating freely, are able to pursue the highest professional standards. Or they can serve as agenda setters, alerting their audience to the significance of an issue, and encouraging them to place it on their personal agendas of important issues (McNair 1996: 18).

The press/media as Fourth Estate

The notion of the press/media as the Fourth Estate is closely linked to the free press concept. First propounded by the historian Thomas Babington Macaulay (1800–59), for whom the first three estates of the realm were the Lords temporal, Lords spiritual and the Commons, it stresses the watchdog role of the media in providing checks on abuses of power by both government and professionals. In this spirit, mainstream journalists often say: 'The best stories are those that afflict the comfortable and comfort the afflicted, the ones that the people of power do not want told,' as, indeed, Peter Beaumont and John Sweeney (2000) wrote in their *Observer* tribute to two colleagues, killed covering the fighting in Sierra Leone. Accordingly, journalists assume the role of the 'public's guardians' protecting them against the moral failures of the authorities. This role is perhaps best reflected in the many campaigns local and national media run (complete with appropriate logos) bringing authorities to account. To name but a few:

- In September 1997, the *Independent on Sunday* launched a campaign to decriminalise cannabis, inspiring 16,000 people to march in support in March 1998.

- In 1998, freelance Updesh Kapur launched an Internet campaign for an investigation into the death of his wife in a hit-and-run crash in India which ultimately led to an arrest.

- In May 1998, the *Guardian* joined the Jubilee 2000 campaign and launched its own 'The new slavery' campaign aiming to relieve the poorest countries of their debt burden.

- The *Citizen*, in Gloucester, ran a campaign to win Government support for a £31 million re-building programme for a local hospital.

- In November 1998, the *Evening Chronicle*, Newcastle, forced the local council to think again about charging for Sunday parking in the city centre.

- Early in 1999, the *Lancashire Evening Post* launched a campaign to persuade the Queen to make Preston a city.

- During the NATO attacks on Yugoslavia in 1999, many newspapers raised money for Kosovo refugees (though did any collect for the Chechen refugees when the Russians began attacking them soon afterwards?).

- In February 2000, a campaign by the *Oxford Mail* to create an offence of corporate killing, following the Paddington rail disaster of October 1999, was backed by an all-party group of MPs.

- In March 2000, the *Manchester Evening News* celebrated victory in its 'Metrolink for the Millennium' campaign after Deputy Prime Minister John Prescott announced plans to spend nearly £300m extending the city's tram system.

- In the same month, Cardiff's *South Wales Echo* claimed victory after a three-month campaign against a massive rise in local councillor's allowances.

- In April 2000, the *Huddersfield Daily Examiner* won a victory in its campaign to save a local maternity unit after 10,000 people signed a petition.

Interestingly, such ideals of campaigning/muckraking journalism can coexist in an often ambiguous relationship with the ideology of objective journalism. But Tim Burrowes, editor of *Hospital Doctor*, was frank when he said of his award-winning, 2000 campaigns on airline emergency medical facilities: 'Well, readership rose 15 per cent during the campaigns. In the end, that's the only thing that counts.'

The Fourth Estate concept is often linked to support for a liberal model of adversarial state–media relations. The Watergate investigation by the two *Washington Post* journalists, Bob Woodward and Carl Bernstein, is seen as the most famous example of this 'adversarialism' since their reports ultimately led to the resignation of US President Richard Nixon in 1974. This adversarial model also appears prominently during wars. As Derrik Mercer commented in a major study of the Falklands War coverage (1987: 3): 'The clash of interests between media and government has always been fundamental and frequently acrimonious. In a democracy this is inevitable and many would say desirable.'

Objectivity, neutrality, detachment and balance

These concepts were first used by journalists in the latter part of the nineteenth century in the United States and Britain, alongside notions of professionalism (McNair 1998: 64–77). As newspapers gradually lost their party affiliations, journalists worked to establish their independence as searchers after objective truth. And news became a commodity which acquired its market value on account of its accuracy. Over time, these concepts were modified to mean not so much the quest for absolute truth, rather more an assertion of the need to strive for truth in the face of subjective anarchy and propagandist bias. Matthew Kieran (1998: 23) argues that 'it has become increasingly fashionable, within cultural, media and even journalistic studies, to dismiss claims concerning objectivity'. Bad journalism, he says, is 'truth-indifferent and fails to respect truth-promoting practices'. And he concludes (ibid.: 35): 'Honesty, discipline and impartiality are required to be a good journalist.'

Similarly, John Wilson, former editorial policy controller for the BBC, comments (1996: 44):

> For the normal run of programme making and newspaper reporting, balanced treatment means being even-handed, not giving one side of an argument unreasonable attention to its advantage or disadvantage. It means exploring issues in an uncommitted way so that viewers, listeners and readers appreciate all the important arguments, including the weight of support they enjoy.

Veteran Scots journalist Sinclair Dunnett (1996: 38) said the good journalist should be 'interested in everything, cultivate an accurate memory and be able to detach himself from his prejudices and his passions'. Moreover, as Denis McQuail points out (1987: 130) the rise of television has helped promote the concept of objectivity: 'Most European public broadcasting systems either legally require or expect news and information to be neutral (non-evaluative and factual) or balanced, according to various criteria, depending on the particular society.' In Britain, broadcasters' legal responsibility to be impartial was reaffirmed in the 1996 Broadcasting Act. The BBC's commitment to truth-seeking is continually stressed throughout the *Producer Guidelines*. On issues relating to taste, for instance, it says:

'The basic pillars of decency rest on telling the truth about human experience, including its darker side.' Significantly, in describing his July 2000 'behind the scenes' film on Tony Blair's press secretary Alastair Campbell, *News from No 10*, reporter Michael Cockerell described it as looking 'objectively at the state of relations between Number 10 and the media' (though investigative reporter John Pilger dismissed it as 'an incestuous and trivial documentary about what a nice man the Prime Minister's public relations manager really is').

Linked to the notion of objectivity is the belief that journalists should remain detached from the events they cover. As Gill Swain comments (2000): 'It is one of the fundamental rules of journalism: don't get emotionally involved.' Textbooks on interviewing skills tend to stress the need for the reporter to remain detached, listening carefully and simply asking pertinent questions.

Fairness and accuracy

There is a strong ethical commitment amongst many journalists towards fairness in reporting and accuracy. These values are stressed in codes of conduct throughout the world. Despite all the pressures facing the media (from proprietors, advertisers, politicians), the special freedoms allowed by the market economy are said to make these values attainable. Significantly, a survey by the Independent Television Commission in July 2000 found that the majority of viewers found TV channels fair and unbiased.

Social responsibility and the public interest

You may be attracted to the notion that journalists have a social responsibility to work ultimately in the interests of the public. While it is usually acknowledged that the media operate according to the demands of a profit-oriented economy, it is still stressed that the market can function benignly, not just in the interests of shareholders but of all the people. This notion is particularly applied to the public service operations of the terrestrial television channels, though this is seen as coming under threat from mounting commercial pressures and privately-owned channels. Yet there remains a strong belief that the public service responsibility of the BBC has tended to protect it from the worst excesses of commercialisation (see Bell 1998: 17).

In recent years in the United States, many journalists have updated the social responsibility theory by promoting the concept of civic journalism. In the face of mass voter apathy in the States, journalists have opted to drop their detachment and intervene in the political process deliberately to increase knowledge and encourage participation. But as Michael Bromley points out, this concept has, intriguingly, found few promoters in Britain (2000: 114).

The social responsibility theory was famously highlighted in the report of the 1947 Commission on the Freedom of the Press, chaired by Robert M. Hutchins, of the University of Chicago (Jaehnig 1998). Denis McQuail sums it up this way (1987: 116–17):

> It can be seen that social responsibility theory has to try to reconcile three somewhat divergent principles: of individual freedom and choice, of media freedom and of media obligation to society. There can be no single way of resolving the potential inconsistencies but the theory has favoured two main kinds of solution. One is the development of public, but independent institutions for the management of broadcasting. The second is the further development of professionalism as a means of achieving higher standards of performance.

The promotion of pluralism: media as the mirror of society

You may consider that the media are crucial in promoting political and cultural pluralism. Along with this attitude generally goes the view that the media bear the responsibility of reflecting society in all its complexity: with as many (legal) viewpoints as possible covered; and the different perspectives – of the old and young, working class and middle class, black and white, women and men, gay and heterosexual and so on – acknowledged.

Codes of Conduct/Practice

Professionalism is usually linked to the promotion of codes of conduct. Accordingly, individual journalists unite with others to acknowledge common standards of behaviour with various practices recognised as being the best to which they should all aspire. Ethical codes, in effect, serve to create a collective conscience of a profession. That's the theory at least. Some even argue that journalists, given their social and political responsibilities, should be considered on a par with doctors and lawyers and thus those who violated its professional code would suffer the penalty of being removed from the 'professional register'.

The need for training

Linked to notions of professionalism comes the emphasis on the need for training to impart standards. Not surprisingly, journalism textbooks tend to promote professionalism unproblematically (e.g. Dick 1998: 139–45). And in his seminal work on broadcasting training, Ivor Yorke reproduces dominant notions of neutrality and objective truth. He writes (1987: ii): 'Our job is to present fact and truth with clarity, dispassion and neutrality however inconvenient or dismaying much of that information is.'

CRITICAL RESPONSES

There are a number of critical responses to the dominant professional perspective. A liberal critique would challenge one or a few of these basic 'pillars' of the professional stance. Accordingly, you may choose to reject the notion of objectivity or argue that training is useless compared to learning through 'on-the-job' experience. But the other central 'pillars' remain untouched. A radical critique would tend to adopt most if not all of the following attitudes.

The political perspective

The more radical response to the ethical dilemmas facing journalists comes largely from the political left, being based on a politically-rooted value system. Thus, you may be inclined to stress journalism's function as one of social reproduction in the interests not of the whole of society but of dominant groups and classes. Accordingly, all the central concepts highlighted above (the free press, democracy, the public interest, objectivity, neutrality) are exposed as myths. Strict Marxists go further and argue that the media are best viewed as 'tools of the ruling class' (Coxall and Robins: 1998: 194).

The myths of objectivity and impartiality

On the myth of objectivity, Brian McNair comments: (1994: 33): 'News is never a mere recording or reporting of the world "out there" but a synthetic, value-laden account which carries within it dominant assumptions and ideas of the society within which it is produced.' Accordingly, objectivity becomes part of a strategic ritual for journalists to legitimise their activities which are, at root, serving the interests of the economic and political elite. Chris Frost (2000: 40) even argues that the very act of attempting to be impartial carries dangers, leading 'some journalists to limit independent thinking for fear that using unusual sources or contacts would be seen as abandoning impartiality. How can a journalist use creative intellect to advance a story, make unusual connections or talk to different people to widen their reader's view of a topic and still remain objective?' According to freelance environment journalist Hugh Warwick: 'Journalism should be about making people aware of what is going on and encouraging them to take action. When you've got issues as big and all-encompassing as the environment or war, any debate about impartiality is simply hindering the opportunities for positive change' (Walsey 2000).

Critics of objectivity also point to the many great writers/journalists (such as William Cobbett, William Hazlitt, Albert Camus, Jean-Paul Sartre, Simone de Beauvoir, Nawal El Saadawi, George Orwell, Martha Gelhorn, James Cameron, John Pilger, Paul Foot, Seymour Hersh) who have been outspoken and far from impartial on the great issues of their day. And many reporters, inevitably as sensitive human beings, become emotionally involved with the people they meet. ITN reporter Mike Nicholson discovered young Natasha Mihaljcic caught up in the war in Sarajevo and ended up taking her to live with his family. And Bronwen Jones, a freelance, met the appallingly scarred young Dorah Mokoena in South Africa. She ended up bringing Dorah back to England with her mother for operations and launching the charity, Children of Fire, for burns victims. Photographer Chris Steele-Perkins met Haron, a 14-year-old Somalian suffering from TB, and tried to get him treatment – but failed. And Small World is a campaigning television production company that provides footage of environment and peace protests mainstream stations will not touch.

Some journalists are even outspoken advocates of 'subjectivity'. James Cameron, the first Western journalist to visit Hanoi during the Vietnam War, dared to show the North Vietnamese as human rather than communist monsters. He commented: 'It never occurred to me, in such a situation to be other than subjective. I have always tended to argue that objectivity was of less importance than the truth.'

The myth of professionalism

Similarly, the promotion of professionalism is seen as a sophisticated rhetorical strategy aiming to hide journalism's inherent pro-systemic bias. As Daniel Hallin comments (1986: 10):

> The 'profession' of journalism has not one but many sets of standards and procedures, each applied in different kinds of political situations. In situations where political consensus seems to prevail journalists tend to act as 'responsible' members of the political establishment, upholding the dominant political perspective and passing on more or less at face value the views of authorities assumed to represent the nation as a whole. In situations of political conflict, they become more detached or even adversarial though this normally will stay well within the bounds of debate going on within the political 'establishment'.

Moreover, many dissenting journalists prefer to see journalism, not as a profession but as a trade. One such was James Cameron who wrote in his 1967 autobiography about the insecurity journalists felt about their status. He continued: 'It is fatuous, however, to compensate for our insecurity by calling ourselves members of a profession; it is both pretentious and disabling; we are at best craftsmen [sic], and that is by no means an ignoble thing to be.'

Critique of the notion that fact and opinion are separate

Opinion and fact are so closely interlinked, you may consider it is impossible to separate them. Notions of objectivity and balance, moreover, become highly problematised when it is seen that a subjective process of selectivity governs the reporting of 'facts'. As mainstream media commentator Roy Greenslade (2000) argues: 'The concept of the separation of facts and opinion does not exist and never has in most of Britain's press. It is partisan and it does not hide that fact except, of course, from readers.'

Critique of BBC claims to 'impartiality'

Even the BBC's claims to impartiality, supposedly enshrined in law, have come under attack from critical media sociologists. The Glasgow University Media Group (1976; 1980; 1982; 1985; 1993), in studying coverage of industrial disputes and the peace movement of the early 1980s, argued controversially how even television news reflected the interests of the British establishment against those of organised labour and the peace movement. For instance, in its 1976 study, *Bad News*, the group found that while employers were given studio interviews and asked deferential questions, trade unionists were either ignored or made to appear unreasonable, being interviewed in the street and asked intimidating questions. Formed in 1922, the BBC, it is argued, has been an integral part of the British state at least since 1926 when it refused striking miners or representatives of the Labour opposition access to the airwaves. Significantly, from 1948 to 1985 all BBC applications were vetted by MI5. As investigative journalist John Pilger argues (1998: 489):

> Perhaps in no other country does broadcasting hold such a privileged position as opinion leader as in Britain. When 'information' is conveyed on the BBC with such professional gravitas, it is more likely to be believed. Possessing highly professional talent, the illusion of impartiality and an essentially liberal ethos, Britain's 'public service broadcasting' has become a finely crafted and infinitely adaptable instrument of state propaganda and censorship.

Propaganda and the critique of the notion of pluralism

Contrary to the notion of pluralism, some journalists highlight the consen-sual news value system operating throughout the mainstream media, with only a limited range of opinions permitted, particularly at times of crisis. This view stresses the collusion between propagandist dominant media and the national security state in the manufacture of consent to the status quo. Traditional theorists see propaganda as being a useful conceptual tool to apply to media products of totalitarian dictatorships while applicable to the media of Western democracies only in exceptional periods – such as during overt wars. In their classic study, *Four Theories of the Press*, Siebert, Peter-son and Schramm (1963) apply the libertarian and social responsibility systems to the Western free press and relate notions of propaganda and indoctrination to the Soviet communist and authoritarian systems. Chomsky and Herman (1988: xi), in contrast, argue that the propaganda function is a permanent feature of Western media systems with the power-ful elite 'able to fix the premises of discourse, to decide what the general populace is allowed to see, hear and think about and to manage public opinion by regular propaganda campaigns'.

In a modified form, Douglas Kellner draws on the theories of Antonio Gramsci (1971) in stressing that the dominant ideology is not all-powerful but can be contested. News organisations, accordingly, can be seen to play a crucial role in the hegemonic struggle for ideological domination. There is a consensus but it can be shifted by dissenting voices. This position, Kellner argues (1990: 73), more aptly portrays the formidable antagonisms of a social order governed by class divisions and often contradictory imper-atives of capitalism and democracy.

With reference to radio, Peter Wilby and Andy Conroy take issue with the notion of the media reflecting reality. They comment (1994: 183): 'The codes through which listeners interpret radio's portrayal of the "real" world are journalistic. The audio text overall purports to reflect the world but in fact applies codes to construct a representation of the world within the terms of the radio experience.' And according to John Pilger (op. cit.: 488): 'Far from the independent "Fourth Estate" envisaged by Lord Macaulay, much of serious journalism in Britain, dominated by television, serves as a parallel arm of government, testing or "floating" establishment planning, restricting political debate to the "main centres of power"' and 'promoting western power in the wider world'.

The economic roots of media practice – and ethics

Critics of the dominant media myths often focus on the economic roots of journalistic practices and bureaucratic structures. As the media consensus has narrowed, so the monopoly ownership structures have intensified. Critics who highlight the monopoly structures in media industries often refocus the ethical debate away from the individual journalist to the employer. As media commentator and journalism lecturer Michael Foley argues (2000: 49–50):

> For too long it has been assumed that unethical behaviour is the prerogative of the individual journalist . . . Much that passes for unethical behaviour takes place because too few journalists are taking too many decisions quickly and without time to reflect. This is because proprietors have not invested in journalism. It is difficult for journalists to refuse to write particular stories or take certain decisions when a proprietor sees increased circulation or readership potential. Journalists have to know that if tickets or freebies are refused that the employer will pay for it.

The democratic façade

Some critics even challenge the very notion of democracy which under-pins all the activities and ethical claims of the mainstream media, arguing it is a myth serving to legitimise the rule of the few over the many. Daniel Hellinger and Dennis Judd (1991: 9–10) suggest there are three major arenas used by the elites for creating a popular sense of legitimacy: the educational institutions which inculcate in each new generation a polit-ical ideology that legitimates the state; the mass media which are 'pivotal for socializing mass publics into accepting sanctioned versions of political and economic reality'; and, finally, the electoral process which 'provides ritualised opportunities for people to participate, as individuals and as members of a collective citizenry, in the political process. When people vote, they reaffirm their belief that the political system listens to their voice'.

With specific reference to radio, Wilby and Conroy (op. cit.: 33) highlight its capacity to 'propagate an illusion of public participation and create a mythologised listening "community"'. They continue: 'Presenters fre-quently play the role of devil's advocate when conducting interviews or hosting phone-in discussions, reinforcing radio's cultural role of stimulating discussion, providing a forum of debate and maintaining a neutral position within "consensual" and ideological boundaries of acceptability and non-deviance'.

Critique of campaigning journalism

Critics argue that even journalists' exalted claims to be working as the noble Fourth Estate, safeguarding the interests of the public, are mere rhetoric. In essence, media practices do not reflect a genuine public spiritness but rather a concern to boost sales or improve ratings. As Magnus Linklater (2000) said of the *Daily Record*'s campaign against the repeal of Section 28 (which forbids the promotion of homosexuality in schools): 'They have detected a populist issue on which to build much-needed circulation and demonstrate their credentials as a red-blooded, red top paper – a combination of the *Mail* and *Sun*, though, without the charm of either. In pursuit of that, anything goes.'

The need for political action

The increasing media emphasis on infotainment has accompanied (and even helped promote) the depoliticising of civil society. In contrast to this trend, dissenting journalists are more likely to focus on the need for political action (through trade unions/political parties/campaigning groups) to improve ethical standards in the media. Such journalists may choose to work critically within mainstream media or for alternative media (trade union, political, human rights, environmental campaigning, gay or feminist). A similar dissident response is possible, of course, based on religious principles: the journalist may decide to work critically within mainstream media or within religious alternative media. These dissident responses to the ethical challenges are becoming all the more difficult to adopt given the growth of a globalised infotainment media, the increasing power of proprietors, the decline in alternative media and power of trade unions. But is not the challenge worth taking up?

DEALING WITH THE DILEMMAS: FOUR JOURNALISTS UNDER THE SPOTLIGHT

Phillip Knightley was an investigative journalist with the *Sunday Times* for 20 years where he won many awards. His books include *The Second Oldest Profession: The Spy as Patriot, Bureaucrat, Fantasist and Whore* and *The First Casualty*, a seminal study of war reporting.

What do you think are the three most important ethical issues facing journalists today in Britain?
1. Finding the courage to resist executive pressure to push stories further than the facts justify, often by the use of anonymous quotes. 2. Finding

the determination to distinguish what is important and what is froth.
3. Finding the energy to return journalism to its public service function.

*You have written and spoken about the 'death' of war reporting, given the
government and military controls over the media. What can journalists do to
reverse these trends?*
They could put aside their commercial and professional rivalry to form a
united front against the military and the government.

*Given the control of the pools during the Gulf War, do you think there is a case
for journalists refusing to participate in such arrangements?*
Yes, but see 2. Their ambition and rivalry probably means that there will
always be enough willing to accept pools.

*Some journalists have promoted the notion of a more responsible 'peace journal-
ism'. How viable is this for mainstream journalists? Will commitment be
inevitably tokenistic?*
I'm afraid that both the public and journalists themselves think that peace
journalism is not sexy. Unfortunately war sells papers.

*Which is the most impressive individual example of war reporting that young jour-
nalists could look to as providing models of good practice?*
Nick Tomalin in Vietnam (*The General Goes Zapping Charlie Cong*). Robert
Fisk in Kosovo (all his stories there).

*Noam Chomsky accuses the mainstream media of being the propaganda arm of
the state – in periods of both peace and war. How would you respond?*
Certainly in wartime, frequently in peace time. The commercial interests of
newspapers are usually best served by supporting the government of the day
(maybe the realm is a better word), especially in times of national crisis.
Sure, they appear to be attacking the Government at every opportunity but
a lot of that is froth. They quickly fall in line when the national interest
appears to demand it.

How do you rate the performance of alternative, leftist journals (such as Socialist Worker, Living Marxism/deceased, New Left Review, Morning Star) *in
the coverage of wars?*
A frequently valuable alternative view of what is happening as long as you
keep in mind that they have agendas of their own. Certainly a corrective to
the official view put out by most of the media.

War correspondents are likely to be approached at some time by the security services and asked to provide assistance. In your experience, how do journalists respond? What do you feel is the correct response?

More likely by intelligence services rather than by security services, but both apply. How do they respond? Depends on the approach. A friend who was a *Newsweek* war correspondent says he was approached by the Saigon CIA chief with the suggestion that they collaborate. 'You've been up on the Plain of Jars. I haven't. I've been in town. You tell me what's going on up there and I'll give you my slant on what's been happening here.' My friend thought it over and agreed. But he made the mental reservation that he would tell the CIA guy nothing more than what he planned to write for *Newsweek* that week. True, he was telling him two days before it appeared in the magazine. The collaboration worked very well. My friend got the CIA slant on what was happening in Vietnam. The CIA guy got herograms from Langley on the lines of 'Great report on Plain of Jars situation. It's now confirmed by *Newsweek*'s current issue. Well done.' This is the only case I know of where it has worked. There is, of course, still the risk that if the opposition discovers that one journalist is (or has) helped an intelligence service, then it is entitled to assume that all journalists are doing the same thing and treat the lot of them as spies (as frequently happens).

If during a war you were leaked information which, if released, could seriously damage the country's war effort and morale at home would you still publish?

Depends on the war. In a war of national survival I would probably not publish, although even here it is a tricky decision. Someone published an article about British shell shortages in WWI. Certainly damaging to the war effort. But it led to reforms that ended the shortage. But in a war that was not one of national survival (the Gulf, Falklands, Kosovo) I would publish.

There is a lot of talk about the 'dumbing down' of the media. Can this notion be applied in any way to the coverage of wars?

Yes. There were lots of stories from Kosovo about mass graves, rape camps, bombing missions, missile strikes, but not a lot of analysis, historical background, reflection and stories expressing honest doubt. Understandable when the chief propagandist for NATO says he ran the NATO information campaign on the lines of a soap opera because that is what the public wanted.

Tessa Mayes is an investigative TV reporter and writer. She has worked for BBC's *Panorama*, ITV's *The Cook Report*, Carlton TV's *The Investigators*,

Sky News and BBC Radio Foyle (Northern Ireland) and written for national newspapers and magazines.

What do you consider are the most important ethical challenges facing journalists in Britain today?
It depends on the type of journalism being referred to. For example in news reporting, attempting to report new facts in an objective way is a challenge in an era when news reporters are judged as being 'too forensic' (as Kate Adie was during her news reporting of the Dunblane tragedy) if they try and do so. The implication is that news reporters are less humane or fail to empathise with victims of tragedies if they attempt to be forensic in gathering the news. Sadly, news reporters are more likely to be judged on their personal morals and what they feel about an event, rather than on the qualities of factual accuracy and analysis. News reporters are supposed to adopt a therapeutic approach to news rather than a scientific one these days.

To show they are ethical, journalists are supposed to identify with a 'goodie' and villify the 'baddie' in a situation. The reporting of the war in former Yugoslavia is a good example of this. A complicated civil war was reduced to a simplified moral tale of good and evil by some journalists. The only ethic a journalist should adhere to is a rigorous pursuit of the truth based on explanations which consider a wide not narrow-ranging set of influences on events. War reporting is entering a new Dark Age; journalists need to resist the trend to present human conflict in the language of a kindergarten morality play.

Can you identify an assignment where you faced particularly difficult ethical decisions?
Following the death of Jamie Bulger, I was reporting on how children rent videos underage from local shops. I didn't know anyone who had children aged 10–14 years who could appear on the programme. I asked a taxi driver one night if he knew any kids late one night, and he said his son would be willing to appear. His son turned out to be one of the most articulate, mature boys I have ever met. The boy was black, and two other young interviewees were white. This wasn't of any significance to me until I showed my producer the rushes. She gasped in horror. The audience will think all black kids are criminal types who rent underage videos, she claimed. It seemed she was inferring that I (a white person) was unconsciously presenting a black boy as criminal which only she (an Asian person) had seen the significance of. I pointed out that two other interviewees talking about the same subject were white, that the voice-over

would clearly state that the video shop owners were acting illegally (by renting out videos to those underage) and not the kids themselves, and that to assume a TV audience would be racist was to have a dim view of audiences. I resolved the matter by including the boy's interview where he explained that kids generally don't carry out copycat violence after watching videos. This showed that far from conforming to stereotypes of black people as delinquents and criminals (as the producer feared), the black interviewee came across as what he was, an extremely eloquent and thoughtful young teenager on a controversial subject.

As an investigative journalist you used subterfuge to gain a story. Did any broadcasting guideline/code help you resolve the ethical issues involved? If not, what special considerations came into play?
BBC and ITC guidelines as well as discussions with editors and lawyers are a normal part of how decisions are made with TV reporters concerning subterfuge. In the last few years, guidelines have had additional rules introduced concerning harassment, especially the harassment of those said to be most vulnerable such as children and grieving relatives of those involved in tragedies. Criticism of the use of hidden cameras has rightly focused on the over-use of surveillance footage as a lazy way of implying the reporter is unearthing something of great significance simply because they've got such footage. What is important is to give the viewer a context in which the subterfuge is being used i.e. a description of the significance of the events being shown. Employing a description of how an event fits in to the Big Picture is as important as the use of a mini cam, and often this is missed out. As a result, events shown in grainy footage become just another wobbly, camera shot suggesting how brave the reporter is. Thus the viewer only receives a diminished explanation of why something is happening.

What lessons should journalists draw from the killing of Veronica Guerin?
Some journalists quip that 'it's only TV' and colleagues shouldn't risk their lives for a story. But there are occasions when journalists do risk their safety whether it's exposing drug dealers or reporting from war zones, and they make personal judgements constantly as a story unfolds about how far they are willing to go. Some employers now fund training courses on personal safety for journalists, but this is normally for staff only. Not all productions provide insurance and even if they do, journalists are potentially subject to attacks long after a TV programme has aired. But if we all lived in fear of such problems, many stories would never get shown. It's a risk you decide to take and accept the consequences, or not.

Journalists are accused of relying too much on elite sources. How have you managed to expand the range (ethnic, gender, age, etc.) of your sources?
What's wrong with elite sources? Are we to ignore those with political power, those who have shown expertise in a subject such as science or art? The point is that elites should have their views challenged by a range of opinions, but journalists are often encouraged to ignore elite views altogether. The fact that the elites may not be offering anything inspirational or interesting is a different matter and needs challenging, rather than ignoring those opinions altogether. It is a useful thing to include a diversity of opinion but not all opinions are equal: some are more incisive than others.

I don't judge my sources according to their ethnic background or sexuality but according to their expertise, depth of opinion, closeness to a story, experience and relevance to an issue. The issues I tackle often focus on those in society who are subject to the rules and legislation enforced by elites. But the reason I am interested in their stories is because I wish to explore the nature of power and the effects of policy on people. I do not wish to be answerable to some kind of official, politically correct quota system concerning sources. For example, I investigated the case of the M25 Three (the three black men jailed for life following a series of brutal attacks and robberies in the M25 region who have recently been released) for several years. The criminalisation of black people was an important concern for me and no doubt for many black people, especially the way the media reported the story at the start. But so too was the fact that any person – whatever their ethnic origin – could be subject to the rules governing non-disclosure of evidence (as happened in their case). This case, I would argue, was of concern to everyone because it highlighted the problems of getting a fair trial in Britain.

Jon Grubb has been deputy editor of the *Nottingham Evening Post* for three years. He started at the *Post* in 1995 as head of content. The paper won *Press Gazette* Newspaper of the Year award in 1999 and was a runner-up the following year. He previously worked at the *Gloucester Citizen* and the *Buckinghamshire Advertiser*.

What do you consider are the major issues confronting journalists in Britain today?
Firstly privacy v. freedom of information – this presents a huge dilemma for newspapers, not least because they need the public's support if they are to successfully lobby the Government for greater freedom of information. The

main problem is that, on some issues, newspapers have lost complete touch with their readers. Newspapers may be deeply involved in debates over the release of the names and addresses of accident victims but do we really believe that is what the public want? Do we really think that the average man in the street is happy to have his identity splashed across the news pages because somebody drove into him? If newspapers lose sight of reality and fight tooth and nail for freedoms their own readers don't want them to have we will have a problem.

Growing commercialisation of editorial departments. This is a particular problem for regional newspapers whose budgets do not have room for luxuries. Most editors accept that a campaigning edge is necessary for a newspaper to be successful but very few are provided with a budget to do so. To cover costs many get sponsorship from a private company. This area is fraught with dangers, such as conflict of interest, accusations of 'buying' editorial. An acceptable line can be trod but it is difficult.

Finally, diversity. For too long newspaper editorial departments have been dominated by white, middle-class staff. If newspapers want to truly connect with the community they must strive to better reflect the multi-cultural nature of their audience. This issue is not just about colour. We need more journalists with working-class roots. Until papers can understand the problems, hopes, aspirations and fears of all sections of the community they will find it difficult to win their hearts and minds.

You have undertaken at the Post *a prominent campaign against new Freedom of Information legislation. Do you think the majority of your readers are seriously interested in these sorts of issues? How do you make it relevant? What sort of a response have you received?*
If you took a straw poll in the high street of any British town on a Monday lunchtime about the Freedom of Information Act you won't get a good response. Most people do not understand the issue and fewer still care about it. After all, the vast majority of people already think the press has too much freedom. But they are also naturally suspicious about politicians, organisations, councils and the Government. Secrecy is something they expect. I think newspapers can make the FoI debate relevant to readers by talking about how this secrecy can affect their everyday lives through Council Tax spending, health service priorities, crime and punishment and education. At Nottingham, we concentrated on how readers' lives may be changed by the new laws and the implementation of existing ones, such as Data Protection. We have received support from our readers and not one single dissenting voice.

What efforts have your editorial staff made to develop contacts with the black community?

The writers at the *Post* are constantly making contacts with a whole variety of people in the community, whatever their racial or cultural background. Inevitably, as part of that process, we have made contacts with people from the black communities. However we recognise that we must be more proactive in this area. We have now appointed a training company from the black community to give all our editorial staff a crash course in understanding the different cultures and religions in our city. The acceptable terms and language will form part of that course. We hope it will dispel some of the inhibitions that may exist and encourage our reporters to seek out people with confidence.

This is not, however, seen as a substitute for creating a multi-cultural, diverse newsroom. The *Post* is the first regional newspaper to sign up to the plans of the Creative Collective, supported by the Freedom Forum, to introduce a UK version of the Chips Quinn Scholarship providing paid work experience for an ethnic minority trainee, and it is hoped this will provide a starting place for recruiting more ethnic minorities. We have discovered, while visiting schools and colleges, that ethnic minority teenagers in Nottingham show little enthusiasm for newspapers and, consequently, we have struggled to encourage applicants. We want to address the problem by trying to give ethnic minority communities a taste of newspapers and have signed up to a new project with a local charity. The scheme aims to provide a newsletter written, researched and produced *by* the community *for* the community. It will be launched in an inner-city area where the concentration of ethnic minority population is high. The *Post* will be providing a great deal of support via expert help and teaching for those working on the newsletter. It is hoped we can plant the seeds of interest which will bear fruit in the coming years.

What story did your newspaper handle recently which provided special ethical dilemmas?

One that springs to mind centres on a paedophile. Information was given to the *Post* about a paedophile living locally who had been seen near a city school. We made some inquiries and discovered that both the school and police were concerned about his presence but could do nothing to prevent it.

We had a story and a picture of the suspect. Should we publish or not? The team spent a considerable amount of time discussing this issue and the balance between public interest and the safety of the individual we would be identifying. In the end we did publish the full story and the picture. The stance we took was clear. We did not publish simply because he was a paedophile, a decision we would have found unacceptable. We published because there was evidence from both the police and the school that his behaviour was indicating he would offend again. We informed all the appropriate agencies before publication so they could move him if it was deemed necessary. It was felt a warning to parents using that school was appropriate. There was no vigilante reaction. In the event the man did offend again, was charged and convicted.

Penny Wrout has worked for 12 years as a journalist for the BBC. For the last three-and-a-half years she has been home affairs correspondent at BBC South East, reporting on crime, policing, prisons, civil rights, immigration and race relations.

Can you identify an assignment where you faced particularly difficult ethical decisions?
I did a lot of work on the allegations of malpractice by officers at Wormwood Scrubs in 1999. Some 27 warders were charged with assaulting inmates and, as I speak, court cases are still on-going. This was a long way from a neat 'goodies and baddies' picture that journalists prefer. For a start, the victims were by definition also villains. It's far easier to justify using slightly devious or non-straightforward journalistic methods to uncover wrong-doing against an 'innocent' than a murderer.

That said, there's clearly a huge public interest in having our penal system properly managed and run humanely. Once that dimension is considered, big political questions also come into play about the power of the Prison Officers' Association, the effectiveness of management inside the Prison Service, the possible complicity of some managers and the ineffectiveness of the various watchdog bodies. Each potential journalistic source had a vested interest, which wasn't necessarily obvious, so it became harder to judge whether a source was telling the truth or trying to plant a line. In a very information-hungry climate, with most of my sources also conducting their own investigations, I had to swap knowledge to gain any useful information, knowing full well that an error in my judgement could alter the future outcome of the story or see myself cited in court (a journalist's nightmare).

Although my enquiries were generating regular short news stories, I tried to keep my mind on the longer-term picture. Thinking about the broader good enabled me to behave in a fairly two-faced way on occasion and also at the back of my mind, the BBC's guidelines, while restrictive, also helped to clarify in my mind where the straight and narrow lies.

Some critics suggest that specialist correspondents get too close to their sources. How would you respond?
It depends what you mean by too close. If the relationship becomes corrupt (with articles placed in exchange for money, goods, services, etc.) then clearly it's wrong. If by close you mean the journalist developing a personal interest in a story so they're prepared to use their position to, in effect, campaign, then I think inevitably this will happen on occasion. It's the editor/producer's job to keep an eye open for this and make sure a counter-balance is put in place if needed. On the positive side, some of the best journalism emerges precisely because a journalist has got the bit between their teeth and is prepared to push harder than normal. Equally, the best exclusives often come because a relationship of trust has developed between a journo and their contacts (with the exception of the more polit-ical arenas, where stories are much more likely to be 'placed').

I personally find it hard to develop a relationship of trust without becoming 'close', i.e. revealing something of myself as an individual rather than simply as a journalist. When it comes to not reporting negative stories about those you need to keep in with, I think most journalists have it in their blood to find a way of getting a story out if it's a decent tale. Some-times it may mean you don't break the story yourself, but whomever you give it to will owe you one for the future!

Have you had to take special steps to develop contacts in the black community?
Not really, other than to listen a bit harder and put in some effort attend-ing meetings and talking to people when there's no immediate story in prospect. I am probably a little more reticent than usual voicing my own opinion on race matters with black people – I hope because I've enough humility to recognise my view lacks the vital ingredient of direct experience. I find too that many black people don't want to discuss racism very readily. For us it's an interesting 'issue' (albeit one we care about) where for them it's about delving into their personal lives – which they're understandably reluctant to share with a stranger. Overall though I find the black community is extremely responsive to journalists they believe will give a fair crack of the whip to their point of view, regardless of the journo's colour. Sadly I think black people in Britain are used to a norm where journos barge in at sensitive (newsworthy) moments with a set of assumptions which it's impossible to challenge in the heat of an intensive media bushfire.

11
And finally: more useful websites

- **amnesty.org.uk/journos** is a site devoted to campaigning for journalists jailed worldwide

- **www.uta.fi/ethicnet:** University of Tampere, Finland, provides the texts of many European codes of conduct

- **www.poynter.org:** Poynter Institute, of St Peterburg, United States, provides links to sites devoted to journalism ethics

- **www.cjr.org:** *Columbia Journalism Review*

- Alternative Press Centre's site at **www.altpress.org**

- Claude-Jean Bertrand's journalism ethics site at **www.paris2.fr/ifp/ deontologie** provides links to a wide range of useful sites

- **www.cpj.com** US-based Committee for the Protection of Journalists campaigning on behalf of harassed/killed journalists worldwide

- Mike Holderness' site (with lots of sound advice for journalists on using the Internet as a source) at **poptel.org.uk/nuj/mike/lecture.htm**

- **www.pressgazette.co.uk**, the trade magazine's important news and comment site

- Randy Reddick's site also providing advice to journalists: **facsnet.org/ogi-bin/new/facs/18**

- **www.holdthefrontpage.co.uk:** news from and about the UK's daily regional papers. Who's Who listing of more than 2,500 journalists, legal updates, story ideas and advice on how to get into journalism

Bibliography

Aitchison, James (1988) *Writing for the Press*, London, Hutchinson

Alford, Dawn (2000) 'Would You Care If I Had a Beard?', the *Guardian*, 31 May

Alibhai-Brown, Yasmin (2000) 'Goodness Gracious Me! The BBC is Still a White, Middle Class Ghetto', the *Independent*, 25 July

Allan, Stuart (1999) *News Culture*, Buckingham, Open University Press

Bagdikian, Ben H. (1992 orig 1983) *The Media Monopoly*, Boston, Massachusetts, the Beacon Press

Baistow, Tom (1985) *Fourth-Rate Estate*, London, Comedia

Beaman, Jim (2000) *Interviewing for Radio*, London, Routledge

Beaumont, Peter and Sweeney, John (2000) 'The Price of Telling the Awful Truth', the *Observer*, 28 May

Bell, Martin (1998) 'The Journalism of Attachment', *Media Ethics*, Kieran, Matthew (ed.) London, Routledge, pp. 15–22

Belsey, Andrew and Chadwick, Ruth (1992) *Ethical Issues in Journalism and the Media*, London, Routledge

Bernstein, Carl (1992) 'The Idiot Culture', *New Republic*, 8 June, pp. 22–8

Bertrand, Claude-Jean (2000) *Media Ethics and Accountability Systems*, Piçcataway (NJ) and London, Transaction

Bertrand, Claude-Jean (2001) *Arsenal for Democracy*, Creeskill (NJ), Hampton Books

Bertrand, Claude-Jean (1999) *La Déontologies des Médias*, Paris, PUF

Bevins, Anthony (1990) 'The Crippling of the Scribes', *British Journalism Review*, 1.2, pp. 13–17

Bloch, Jonathan and Fitzgerald, Patrick (1983) *British Intelligence and Covert Action*, London, Junction Books

Boorstin, Daniel (1962) *The Image*, New York, Basic Books

Boot, William (1991) 'The Press Stands Alone', *Columbia Journalism Review*, March/April, pp. 23–4

Bourdieu, Pierre (1998) *On Television and Journalism*, London, Pluto

Bower, Tom (1993) *Tiny Rowland: Rebel Tycoon*, London, Heinemann

Bromley, Michael (1994) *Teach Yourself Journalism*, London, Hodder and Stoughton

Bromley, Michael (1998) 'The "Tabloiding" of Britain: "Quality" Newspapers in the 1990s', *Sex, Lies and Democracy: The Press and the Public*, Stephenson, Hugh and Bromley, Michael (eds) London/New York, Longman, pp. 25–38

Bromley, Michael (2000) 'The Manufacture of News: Fast Moving Consumer Goods

Production or Public Service?', *Ethics and Media Culture: Practices and Representations*, Berry, David (ed.) Oxford, Focal Press, pp. 111–31

Bromley, Michael and O'Malley, Tom (1997) *A Journalism Reader*, London, Routledge

Brown, Gerry (1995) *Exposed! Sensational True Story of Fleet St Reporter*, London, Virgin Books

Browne, Christopher (1996) *The Prying Game: the Sex, Sleaze and Scandals of Fleet Street and the Media Mafia*, London, Robson Books

Burgh, Hugo de (ed.) (2000) *Investigative Journalism: Context and Practice*, London, Routledge

Burke, P. (1988) *Popular Culture in Early Modern Europe*, Hants, Wildwood

Campbell, Duncan (2000) 'I spy an Ally', the *Guardian*, 15 March

Carter, Cynthia and Allan, Stuart (2000) '"If it Bleeds, it Leads": Ethical Questions about Popular Journalism', *Ethics and Media Culture: Practices and Representations*, Berry, David (ed.) Oxford, Focal Press, pp. 132–53

Carter, Meg (1999) 'Hey, Good Looking', the *Guardian*, 29 November

Chilton, Paul (ed.) (1985) *Language and the Nuclear Arms Debate: Nukespeak Today*, London, Frances Pinter

Chippendale, Peter and Horrie, Chris (1988) *Disaster*, London, Sphere

Chomsky, Noam (1999) *The New Military Humanism: Lessons from Kosovo*, London, Pluto Press

Chomsky, Noam and Herman, Edward (1988) *Manufacturing Consent: The Political Economy of Mass Media*, New York, Pantheon Books (reissued 1994, Vintage Books, London)

Christmas, Linda (1997) *Chaps of Both Sexes? Women Decision-Makers in Newspapers: Do They Make a Difference?*, Wiltshire, Women in Journalism in association with the BT Forum

Cockerell, Michael, Hennessy, Peter and Walker, David (1984) *Sources Close to the Prime Minister: Inside the Hidden World of the News Manipulators*, London, Macmillan

Cohen, Nick (1999) *Cruel Britannia*, London/New York, Verso

Collins, John M. (1991) *America's Small Wars*, Washington/London, Brasseys (US)

Combs, James (1993) 'From the Great War to the Gulf War: Popular Entertainment and the Legitimation of Warfare', *The Media and the Persian Gulf War*, Denton, Robert (ed.) Westport CT, Praeger, pp. 257–84

Cottle, Simon (1993) *TV News, Urban Conflict and the Inner City*, Leicester, Leicester University Press

Cottle, Simon (1999) 'Ethnic Minorities and the British News Media: Explaining (Mis)-representation', *The Media in Britain: Current Debates and Developments*, Stokes, Jane and Reading, Anna (eds) Basingstoke, Hampshire, Macmillan, pp. 191–200

Coward, Ros (1999) 'Women Are the New Men', the *Guardian*, 1 July

Coxall, Bill and Robins, Lynton (1998) *Contemporary British Politics*, London, Macmillan (third edition)

Crooks, Tim (1998) 'An Ocean Apart on Freedom', *Press Gazette*, 13 February

Cummings, Bruce (1992) *War and Television*, London, Verso

Curran, James (2000) 'Press Reformism 1918–98: A Study in Failure', *Media Power, Professionals and Policies*, Tumber, Howard (ed.) London, Routledge, pp. 35–55

Curran, James and Seaton, Jean (1991) *Power Without Responsibility: the Press and Broadcasting in Britain*, London, Routledge, fourth edn.

Curtis, Liz (1994) 'Hands Off!', the *Journalist*, February/March

Delano, Anthony and Henningham, John (1995) *The News Breed: British Journalism in the 1990s*, London, London Institute

Devenport, Mark (2000) *Flash Frames: Twelve Years Reporting Belfast*, Belfast, the Blackstaff Press

Dick, Jill (1998) *Freelance Writing for Newspapers*, London, A. and C. Black, second edition

Donovan, Paul (1999) 'Are We Being Too Reckless with the Issue of Race?', *Press Gazette*, 15 January

Dorril, Stephen (1993) *The Silent Conspiracy: Inside the Intelligence Services in the 1990s*, London, Heinemann

Dorril, Stephen (2000) *MI6: Fifty Years of Special Operations*, London, Fourth Estate

Dorril, Stephen and Ramsey, Robin (1991) *Smear! Wilson and the Secret State*, London, Fourth Estate

Dunnett, Sinclair (1996) 'Advice to a Young Journalist', *The Journalists' Handbook*, October, No. 17, pp. 38–9

Ellis, Carolyne (1998) '*Out Go the Suit, In Come the Skirts*', the *Guardian*, 24 August

Engel, Matthew (1996) *Tickle the Public: One Hundred Years of the Popular Press*, London, Victor Gollanz

Evans, Harold (1999) 'Freedom of Information: Why Britain Must Learn From America', the *Guardian*, 31 May

Fisk, Robert (2000) 'War is Not Primarily about Cynicism or Defeat . . .', *Press Gazette*, 21 April

Foley, Michael (2000) 'Press Regulation', *Administration*, Vol. 48, No. 1, pp. 40–51

Foot, Paul (1991) 'Strenuous liberty . . . a nervous revival', *British Journalism Review*, 2 (4), pp. 5–8

Foot, Paul (1999): 'The Slow Death of Investigative Journalism', *Secrets of the Press: Journalists on Journalism*, Glover, Stephen (ed.) London, Allen Lane/the Penguin Press, pp. 79–89

Frankland, Mark (1999) *Child of My Time*, London, Chatto and Windus

Franklin, Bob (1997) *Newszak and New Media*, Arnold, London

Franklin, Bob and Murphy, David (1991) *What News?: The Market, Politics and the Local Press*, London, Routledge

Franklin, Bob and Murphy, David (eds) (1998) *Local Journalism in Context*, London, Routledge

Frelick, Bill (1992) 'The False Promise of Operation Provide Comfort: Protecting Refugees or Protecting State Power', *Merip*, May/June, pp. 22–7

Frost, Chris (2000) *Media Ethics and Self-Regulation*, Harlow, Essex, Longman Education

Gall, Gregor (1993) 'The Employers' Offensive in the Provincial Newspaper Industry', *British Journal of Industrial Relations*, 31.4, pp. 615–24

Galtung, Johan and Ruge, Mari (orig 1973) 'Structuring and Selecting News', *The Manufacture of News: Deviance, Social Problems and the Mass Media*, Cohen, Stanley and Young, Jock (eds) London, Constable, pp. 52–63

Gannett Foundation (1991) *The Media at War: The Press and the Persian Gulf Conflict*, Columbia University, New York City, the Freedom Forum

Gatton, Adrian (2000) 'Get Your Kit Off', the *Big Issue*, 4–10 September

Glasgow University Media Group (1976) *Bad News*, London, Routledge and Kegan Paul

Glasgow University Media Group (1980) *More Bad News*, London, Routledge and Kegan Paul

Glasgow University Media Group (1982) *Really Bad News*, London, Writers and Readers

Glasgow University Media Group (1985) *War and Peace News*, Milton Keynes/Philadelphia, Open University Press

Glasgow University Media Group (1993) *Getting the Message*, Eldridge, John (ed.) London, Routledge

Glover, Stephen (1999) 'What Columnists Are Good For', *Secrets of the Press: Journalists on Journalism*, Glover, Stephen (ed.) London, Allen Lane/Penguin Press, pp. 289–98

Goodwin, Eugene (1994) *Groping for Ethics*, Iowa, Iowa State University Press

Gowing, Nik (1991) 'Dictating the Global Agenda', *Spectrum*, Independent Television Commission, summer, pp. 7–9

Gowing, Nik (1994) 'Instant Pictures, Instant Policies?' *Independent on Sunday*, 8 July

Graef, Roger (1993) 'Can Justice be Seen to be Done?', *The Times*, 27 October

Graef, Roger (1998) 'Friend of the Family', the *Guardian*, 6 April

Graef, Roger (2000) 'Garbage In, Garbage Out', *New Statesman*, 28 August

Gramsci, Antonio (1971) *Prison Notebooks: Selections*, London, Lawrence and Wishart

Greenslade, Roy (1992) *Maxwell's Fall*, London, Simon & Schuster

Greenslade, Roy (2000) 'Reaping the Whirlwind', the *Guardian*, 6 March

Grevisse, Benoit (1999) 'Chartres et Codes de Déontologie Journalistique: Une Approche Internationale Comparée', *L'Arsenal de la Democratie: Media, deontologie et MARS*, Claude-Jean Bertrand (ed.) Paris, Economica, pp. 54–70

Gripsrud, Jostein (1992) 'The Aesthetics and Politics of Melodrama', *Journalism and Popular Culture*, Dahlgren, Peter and Sparks, Colin (eds) London, Sage, pp. 84–95

Gross, Larry (1998) 'Minorities, Majorities and the Media', *Media, Ritual and Identity*, Liebes, Tamar and Curran, James (eds) London, Routledge, pp. 87–102

Hall, Phil (2000) 'You Couldn't Make it Up!', *The Times*, 20 July

Hall, Stuart (1995) 'The Whites of their Eyes: Racist Ideologies and the Media', *Gender, Race and Class: A Text Reader*, Dines, Gail and Humez, Jean M. (eds) Thousand Oaks/London/New Delhi, Sage, pp. 18–22

Hall, Stuart, *et al.* (1978) *Policing the Crisis*, London, Macmillan

Hallin, Daniel (1986) *The Uncensored War*, Oxford, Oxford University Press

Hanlin, Bruce (1992) 'Owners, Editors and Journalists', *Ethical Issues in Journalism and the Media*, Belsey, Andrew and Chadwick, Ruth (eds) London, Routledge, pp. 33–48

Hanna, Mark and Epworth, Jennifer (1998) 'Media Payments to Witnesses: The Press Faces the First Breach of its Post-Calcutt Defences', *Self Regulation and the Media*, papers for annual conference of the Association for Journalism Education, London, pp. 5–18

Harris, Nigel (1992) 'Codes of Conduct for Journalists', *Ethical Issues in Journalism and the Media*, Belsey, Andrew and Chadwick, Ruth (eds) London, Routledge, pp. 62–76

Harris, Robert (1990) *Good and Faithful Servant*, London, Faber

Harrison, Bridget (1997) 'Thousands Die, but is Diana Flying Out?', the *Independent*, 15 January

Heller, Zoë (1999) 'Girl Columns', *Secrets of the Press: Journalists on Journalism*, Glover, Stephen (ed.) London, Allen Lane/Penguin Press, pp. 10–17

Hellinger, Daniel and Judd, Dennis (1991) *The Democratic Façade*, Belmont, California, Wadsworth

Hencke, David (2000) 'A Little Mole Told Me – Honest', the *Guardian*, 24 July

Hersh, Seymour (1991) *The Samson Option: Israel, America and the Bomb*, London, Faber and Faber

Hodgson, Jessica (1999) 'CNN Get "Too Close" To US Government', *Press Gazette*, 12 November

Hogan, Dan (1998) 'Sobriety in the Last Chance Saloon', *Self Regulation and the Media*, papers for the annual conference of the Association of Journalism Education, pp. 26–9

Holland, Patricia (1998) 'The Politics of the Smile: "Soft News" and the Sexualisation of the Press', *News, Gender and Power*, Carter, Cynthia, Branson, Gill and Allan, Stuart (eds) London, Routledge, pp. 17–32

Hollingsworth, Mark (1990) *The Press and Political Dissent*, London, Pluto Press

Hollingsworth, Mark (2000) 'Secrets, Lies and David Shayler', the *Guardian*, 17 March

Hollingsworth, Mark and Fielding, Nick (1999) *Defending the Realm: MI5 and the Shayler Affair*, London, André Deutsche

Hudson, Miles and Stanier, John (1997) *War and the Media*, Stroud, Gloucestershire, Sutton Publishing

Huntingdon, Samuel P. (1997) *The Clash of Civilisations and the Remaking of World Order*, London, Touchstone Books

Jack, Ian (1999) 'Gandhi's Luck to Miss the Spiteful Press', the *Independent*, 6 February

Jaehnig, Walter (1998): 'Kith and Sin: Press Accountability in the USA', *Sex, Lies and Democracy: The Press and the Public*, Stephenson, Hugh and Bromley, Michael (eds) London/New York, Longman, pp. 97–110

James, Oliver (2000) 'Playing on Parents' Fears', the *Guardian*, 20 July

Johnson, Andrew (1997) 'Taking More Care Over Mental Health Coverage', *Press Gazette*, 8 August

Johnson, Andrew (1997a) 'The Rising Tide of Shutdown Culture', *Press Gazette*, 15 November

Jones, Nicholas (1996) *Soundbites and Spin Doctors: How Politicians Manipulate the Media – and Vice Versa*, London, Indigo

Jones, Sylvia (1998) *Disclosure: Media Freedom and the Privacy Debate after Diana*, Mayes, Tessa (ed.) London, London International Research Exchange Media Group

Kabani, Rana (1994) *Imperial Fictions: Europe's Myths of the Orient*, London, Pandora

Karpf, Anne (2000) 'Net Stations? We've Got Thousands of 'em', the *Guardian*, 27 May

Katz, Jon (1997) *Media Rants: Postpolitics in the Digital Nation*, San Francisco, Hardwired

Keeble, R. (1997) *Secret State, Silent Press: New Militarism, the Gulf and the Modern Image of Warfare*, Luton, John Libbey Media

Keeble, R. (1998) 'The Politics of Sleaze Reporting', *Recherches en Communication*, Catholic University of Louvain, pp. 71–81

Kellner, Douglas (1990) *Television and the Crisis of Democracy*, Boulder/San Francisco/Oxford, Westview Press

Kellner, Douglas (1995) *Media Culture: Cultural Studies, Identity and Politics Between the Modern and the Postmodern*, London, Routledge

Kerbel, Matthew Robert (1995) *Media Politics in a Cynical Age*, Boulder, Westview

Kieran, Matthew (1998) 'Objectivity, Impartiality and Good Journalism', *Media Ethics*, Kieran, Matthew (ed.) London, Routledge, pp. 23–36

Kieran, Matthew (2000) 'The Regulatory and Ethical Framework', *Investigative Journalism: Context and Practice*, de Burgh, Hugo (ed.) London, Routledge, pp. 156–76

Kiley, Robert (1999) 'Easy as Falling Off a Log', the *Guardian*, 12 January

Killick, Mark (1994) *The Sultan of Sleaze: The Story of David Sullivan's Sex and Media Empire*, London, Penguin

Klaidman, Stephen and Beauchamp, Tom L. (1987) *The Virtuous Journalist*, Oxford, Oxford University Press

Knightley, Philip (1991) 'Here is the Patriotically Censored News', *Index on Censorship*, London, pp. 4–5

Knightley, Philip (1998) *A Hack's Progress*, London, Vintage

Knightley, Philip (2000) *The First Casualty: The War Correspondent as Hero and Myth Maker from the Crimea to Kosovo*, London, Prion, second edition

Kurtz, Howard (1993) *Media Circus: The Trouble with America's Newspapers*, New York, Random House

Laitila, Tiina (1993) 'Codes of Ethics in Europe', *Reports on Media Ethics in Europe*, Nordenstreng, Kaarle (ed.) Tampere, University of Tampere Department of Journalism and Mass Communication, pp. 23–79

Lashmar, David (2000) 'Character Assassination by Committee', the *Independent*, 6 June

Lashmar, Paul and Oliver, James (1998) *Britain's Secret Propaganda War 1948–1977*, Stroud, Gloucestershire, Sutton Publishing

Leigh, David (1989) *The Wilson Plot: The Intelligence Services and the Discrediting of a Prime Minister*, London, Heinemann

Leigh, David and Vulliamy, Ed (1997) *Sleaze: The Corruption of Parliament*, London, Arnold

Liebes, Tamar (1998) 'Television's Disaster Marathons', *Media, Ritual and Indentity*, Liebes, Tamar and Curran, James (eds) London, Routledge, pp. 71–84

Linklater, Magnus (2000) 'A Bunfight in Scotland', *The Times*, 17 March

Lodge, David (2000) 'Public Property', *The Times*, 7 July

McCue, Andy (2000) 'Is it cos i is black?', *xcity*, City University Journalism Department, pp. 20–1

MacDowall, Ian (ed.) (1992) *Reuters Handbook for Journalists*, Oxford, Butterworth-Heinemann

McGowan, Eve (2000) 'Let's Talk About Sex Baby', *xcity*, City University Journalism Department, pp. 26–7

McNair, Brian (1996) *News and Journalism in the UK*, London, Routledge, second edition

McNair, Brian (1998) *The Sociology of Journalism*, London, Routledge

McNair, Brian (2000) *Journalism and Democracy: An Evaluation of the Political Public Sphere*, London, Routledge

McQuail, Denis (1987) *Mass Communication Theory: An Introduction*, London/Newbury Parl, Sage, second edition

McQuail, Denis (1992) *Media Performance: Mass Communications and the Public Interest*, London, Sage

Malcolm, Janet (1991) *The Journalist and the Murderer*, London, Bloomsbury

Marks, Naomi (2000) 'Money Can Boost Your Circulation', the *Independent*, 14 March

Marr, Andrew (1999) 'The Lying Game', the *Observer*, 24 October

Martinson, Jane (2000) 'Spider in the Web', the *Guardian*, 3 May

Mayes, Ian (2000) 'My Word', the *Guardian*, 1 July

Mayes, Tessa (ed.) (1998) *Disclosure: Media Freedom and the Privacy Debate after Diana*, London, London International Research Exchange Media Group

Melin-Higgins, Margareta (1997) *The Social Construction of Journalist Ideals: Gender in Journalism Education*, paper presented at Journalists for the New Century conference, London College of Printing, 24 April

Mercer, Derrik (ed.) (1987) *The Fog of War*, London, Heinemann

Merrill, John C. (1996 orig 1977) *Existential Journalism*, Iowa, Iowa University Press

Methven, Nicola (1996) 'Gruesome TV News Reports Should Be Cut, Says Kate Adie', *Press Gazette*, 11 October
Metzler, Ken (1997) *Creative Interviewing*, Boston, Allyn and Bacon
Meyer, Philip (1987) *Ethical Journalism: A Guide for Students, Practitioners and Consumers*, Lanham, University Press of America
Milne, Seamus (1994) *The Enemy Within: The Secret War Against the Miners*, London, Pan
Moore, Alison (1999) 'Articles of Faith', *Press Gazette*, 5 February
Moore, Charles (1997) 'The Right Way to Tell It', the *Guardian*, 14 April
Morgan, Peter (2000) 'Can We Stop Global Capital?', *Socialist Review*, July/August
Mosley, Ivo (2000) *Dumbing Down: Culture, Politics and the Mass Media*, London, Imprint Academic
Mosynski, Peter (2000) 'Mumbo Gumbo', *Index on Censorship*, No. 5, p. 24
Naughton, John (2000) 'Your Privacy Ends Here', the *Observer*, 4 June
Newman, Jay (1992) 'Some Reservations about Multiperspectival News', *Philosophical Issues in Journalism*, Cohen, Elliot D. (ed.) New York/London, pp. 205–17
Nordenstreng, Kaarle (ed.) (1997) *Reports on Media Ethics in Europe*, Tampere, University of Tampere Department of Journalism and Mass Communication
Norman, M. E. (1999) 'A Shotgun Wedding', *Press Gazette*, 12 December
Norris, Bill (2000) 'Media Ethics at the Sharp End', *Ethics and Media Culture: Practices and Representations*, Berry, David (ed.) Oxford, Focal Press, pp. 325-38
Northmore, David (1990) *Freedom of Information Handbook*, London, Bloomsbury
Northmore, David (1994) 'Probe shock: Investigative Journalism', *The Newspapers Handbook*, Keeble, Richard (ed.) London, Routledge, pp. 319–36
Norton-Taylor, Richard (2000) 'Secrets and Spies', the *Guardian*, 18 May
Oborne, Peter (1999) *Alastair Campbell: New Labour and the Rise of the Media Class*, London, Aurum Press
O'Neill, John (1992) 'Journalism in the Market Place', *Ethical Issues in Journalism and the Media*, Belsey, Andrew and Chadwick, Ruth (eds) London, Routledge, pp. 15–32
O'Reilly, Emily (1998) *Veronica Guerin: The Life and Death of a Crime Reporter*, London, Vintage
O'Sullivan, Sally (1999) 'Change is Good for Your Figures', the *Independent*, 16 February
Page, Adrian (1998) 'Interpreting Codes of Conduct', *Sex, Lies and Democracy: The Press and the Public*, Stephenson, Hugh and Bromley, Michael (eds) London/New York, Longman, pp. 127–35
Palast, Greg (2000) 'Corporate Criminals', *Socialist Review*, July/August (recorded by Pete Ainsley and Sonia Carroll)
Peak, Steve and Fisher, Paul (eds) (2000) *The Media Guide, 2000*, London, Fourth Estate
Petley, Julian (1999) 'The Regulation of Media Content', *The Media in Britain: Current Debates and Developments*, Stokes, Jane and Reading, Anna (eds) Basingstoke, Hampshire, Macmillan, pp. 143–57
Pierce, Andrew (2000) 'Whispers in the Corridors of Power', *The Times*, 7 July
Pilger, John (1996) 'The Hidden Power of the Media', *Socialist Review*, September
Pilger, John (1998) *Hidden Agendas*, London, Vintage
Platell, Amanda (1999) 'Institutionalised Sexism', *Secrets of the Press: Journalists on Journalism*, Glover, Stephen (ed.) London, Allen Lane/Penguin Press, pp. 140-7
Platt, Steve (1998) 'The Barbarous Coast', the *Independent*, 15 December
Ponting, Clive (1990) *Secrecy in Britain*, Oxford, Basil Blackwell

Porter, Bernard (1991) 'How Difficult is it for Today's Historians to Uncover Secret Histories?', *History Today*, November, pp. 33–5

Postman, Neil (1985) *Amusing Ourselves to Death*, London, William Heinemann

Prince, Stephen (1993) 'Celluloid Heroes and Smart Bombs: Hollywood at War in the Middle East', *The Media and the Persian Gulf War*, Denton, Robert (ed.) Westport CT, Praeger, pp. 235–56

Randall, David (1996) *The Universal Journalist*, London, Pluto Press

Reading, Anna (1999) 'Campaigns to Change the Media', *The Media in Britain: Current Debates and Developments*, Stokes, Jane and Reading, Anna (eds) Basingstoke, Hampshire, Macmillan, pp. 170–83

Reddick, Randy and King, Elliot (1997) *The Online Journalist: Using the Internet and Other Online Resources*, Fort Worth, Harcourt Brace College Publishers, second edition

Reeves, Ian (2000) 'We have been watching . . .', *Press Gazette*, 2 June

Richstad, Jim (1999) 'Le Droit de Communiquer a l'Age de l'Internet', *L'Arsenal de la Démocratie: Médias, Deontologie et MARS*, Bertrand, Claude-Jean (ed.) Paris, Economica, pp. 31–41

Robertson, Geoffrey (1993) *Freedom, the Individual and the Law*, London, Penguin

Robins, Kevin and Levidow, Les (1991) 'The Eye of the Storm', *Screen*, Vol. 32, No. 3, autumn, pp. 324–8

Rogers, Ann (1997) *Secrecy and Power in the British State: A History of the Official Secrets Act*, London, Pluto

Rowe, David (1999) *Sport, Culture and the Media*, Buckingham, Open University Press

Said, Edward (1981) *Covering Islam: How the Media and Experts Determine How We See the Rest of the World*, London, Routledge

Saunders, Frances Stonor (1999) *Who Paid the Piper? The CIA and the Cultural Cold War*, London, Granta Books

Schesinger, Philip (1978) *Putting Reality Together*, London, Methuen

Schiller, Dan (1981) *Objectivity in the News*, Philadephia, University of Pennsylvania Press

Schudson, Michael (1978) *Discovering News*, New York, Basic Books

Sebba, Anne (1994) *Battling for News: The Rise of the Woman Reporter*, London, Hodder and Stoughton

Sheldon, Ed (1999) 'Public Exposure', *Press Gazette*, 5 May

Siebert, Fred, Peterson, Theodore and Schramm, Wilbur (1963) *Four Theories of the Press*, Urbana, University of Illinois Press

Simpson, John (1991) *From the House of War*, London, Arrow

Simpson, John (1999) *Strange Places, Questionable People*, London, Pan Books

Snoddy, Raymond (1993) *The Good, the Bad and the Unacceptable*, London, Faber and Faber, second edition

Spark, David (2000) *Investigative Reporting: A Study in Technique*, Oxford, Focal Press

Sparks, Colin (1999) 'The Press', *The Media in Britain: Current Debates and Developments*, Stokes, Jane and Reading, Anna (eds) Basingstoke, Hampshire, Macmillan, pp. 41–60

Stephen, Jaci (1997) 'The Trouble With Women', the *Guardian*, 7 July

Stephenson, Hugh (1998) 'Tickle the Public: Consumerism Rules', *Sex, Lies and Democracy: The Press and the Public*, Bromley, Michael and Stephenson, Hugh (eds) Harlow, Essex, Addison Wesley Longman pp. 13–24

Steyn, Mark (1998) 'All Venusians Now: Sentimentality in the Media', *Faking It: The Sentimentalisation of Modern Society*, London, Penguin Books, pp. 163–79

Stone, Elizabeth (1999) 'Using Children as Sources', *Columbia Journalism Review*, September/October, pp. 32–4

Swain, Gill (2000) 'I Can't Just Choose to Walk Away', the *Independent*, 6 June

Tait, Richard (1999) 'This Man is About to be Murdered', the *Guardian*, 20 December

Tatchell, Peter (2000) 'It's Now OK To Be Gay But What's Next?', the *Observer*, 2 July

Taylor, John (1998) *Body Horror: Photojournalism, Catastrophe and War*, Manchester, Manchester University Press

Thomas, Gordon (2000) *Gideon's Spies: Mossad's Secret Warriors*, London, Pan Books

Thomas, Rosamund M. (1991) *Espionage and Secrecy: The Official Secrets Acts 1911–1989*, London, Routledge

Thomson, Alex (1992) *Smokescreen: The Media, Censors and the Gulf*, Tunbridge Wells, Laburnham Books

Thurlow, Richard (1994) *The Secret State: British Internal Security in the Twentieth Century*, Oxford, Blackwell

Tiffen, Rodney (1989) *News and Power*, London, Unwin Hyman

Tracey, Michael (2000) 'Death of a Dream', *New Statesman*, 24 July

Travis, Alan (1999) 'One in Three Britons Online, But the Net Shows Big Gaps', the *Guardian*, 20 December

Tulloch, John (1998) 'Managing the Press in a Medium-Sized European Power', *Sex, Lies and Democracy: The Press and the Public*, Stephenson, Hugh and Bromley, Michael (eds) London/New York, Longman, pp. 63–83

Tusa, John (2000) 'Miserable Small-Mindedness', *New Statesman*, 24 July

Urban, Mark (1996) *UK Eyes Alpha: The Inside Story of British Intelligence*, London, Faber

Walsey, Andrew (2000) 'Peace Offerings', *Press Gazette*, 31 March

Wells, Matt (2000) 'BBC "Tries to Bury" Inquiry on Equality', the *Guardian*, 28 April

Whale, John (1977) *The Politics of the Media*, London, Fontana

White, Peter (1999) 'A Blind Bit of Difference', *Press Gazette*, 5 February

White, Peter (2000) 'Different . . . But Equal', *Press Gazette*, 10 March

Wilby, Peter and Conroy, Andy (1994) *The Radio Handbook*, London, Routledge

Williams, Hywel (2000) 'Politics: Showbusiness for Ugly People', the *Observer*, 28 May

Williams, Kevin (1987) 'Vietnam: The First Living Room War', *The Fog of War*, Mercer, Derrik (ed.) London, Heinemann, pp. 213–60

Williams, Kevin (1992) 'Something More Important than Truth: Ethical Issues in War Reporting', *Ethical Issues in Journalism and the Media*, Belsey, Andrew and Chadwick, Ruth (eds) London, Routledge, pp. 154–70

Williams, Kevin (1998) *Get Me a Murder a Day! A History of Mass Communciation In Britain*, London, Routledge

Wilson, John (1996) *Understanding Journalism*, London, Routledge

Winston, Brian (1998) '8 v 10: The British Press and the ECHR', *Self Regulation in the Media*, papers from the annual conference of the Association for Journalism Education, pp. 43–7

Wittstock, Melinda (2000) 'How TV Crossed the Taste Barrier', the *Observer*, 5 March

Worsthorne, Peregrine (1999) 'Dumbing Up', *Secrets of the Press: Journalists on Journalism*, Glover, Stephen (ed) London, Allen Lane/the Penguin Press, pp. 115–24

Yorke, Ivor (1987) *The Techniques of Television News*, London, Focal Press, second edition

Zadeh, Somaye (2000) 'Double Standards for Bosses', *Socialist Review*, July/August

Zobel, Gibby (2000) 'Rights Mess', the *Guardian*, 3 May

Index

ABC 101
accuracy 14, 17, 20, 120
Action Aid 23
Adie, Kate 100, 101, 105, 140
advertising 2, 8, 112–13; advertorials 10
agenda setters 9
AIDS 75, 93–4
Aitchison, James 32
Aitken, Jonathan 41, 52
Aitken, Victoria 41
Alford, Dawn 85
Alford, John 57
Alibhai-Brown, Yasmin 73
Allan, Stuart 72, 85
Allwood, Mandy 40
alternative media 11
Alternative Press Centre 147
American Society of Newspaper Editors 81
Amnesty International 72, 105, 147
anarchists 5
Andrew, Prince 51
Anglia 6
Annan committee 18
Arnett, Peter 102
Article 19 121
Ashley, Mark 64
Asian Times 82
Association of British Editors 52
Association of Chief Officers of Probation
  38
Association of Chief Police Officers 115
Association of Investigative Journalists 69
athletics 3
'attack journalism' 4

'back to basics' 3, 48

Bacon, Richard 57
bad news 63–5
BBC 7, 18, 19, 29, 36, 42, 43, 45, 49, 57, 62,
  64, 65, 67, 68, 73, 76, 81, 82, 84, 85, 98,
  102, 112, 114, 118, 129, 130, 139;
  Broadcasting Research 82; digital
  channels 8; impartiality 134; as state
  propagandist 8; World Service 7, 73;
  producers guidelines 20, 129, 141, 145;
  governors 20; BBC1 20; The World This
  Weekend 24; Radio 5 Live 88; Radio
  Leicester 82 BBC Wales 121; BBC Radio
  Foyle 140; BBC South East 145
Baig, Anila 81
Bailey, Ian 59
Bain, Deborah 73
Baird, Rachel 31
Baistom, Tom 9
Baker, Sue 92
Barnett, Steve 62–3
Bastone, William 68
Bazoft, Farzad 119
Beaman, Jim 37
Beauchamp, Tom L. 126, 127
Beaverbrook, Lord 112
BECTU 73
Being John Malkovich 7
Bell, Emily 35
Bell, Martin 104, 130
Bell, Mary 41
Belsey, Andrew 3
Beresford, David 101
Bernstein, Carl 128
Bertelsmann 11
Bertrand, Claude-Jean 24, 147
Bevins, Anthony 113

Big Brother 7
Big Issue 3, 35
Big Story 68
Birt, John 7, 73
Black, Guy 13
BlackBritain 82
Blacknet 82
Blackwood, Harry 115
blasphemy 111
Blair, Euan 37
Blair, Leo 37
Blair, Professor Thom 73, 81
Blair, Tony 3, 5, 32, 37, 43, 53, 54, 57, 108, 130
Bliss 22
Bloch, Jonathan 118
body language 26
Böll, Heinrich 5
'bonk journalism' 4, 48
Booker award 4
Boorstin, Daniel 5
Boot, William 101
Bottomley, Virginia 53
Bourdieu, Pierre 5
Bower, Michelle 85
Bower, Tom 114
Box Productions 30, 112
Boycott, Rosie 85
Bradford Telegraph and Argus 81
Bradlee, Benjamin C. 58, 110
Brass Eye 70
Brennan, Justice William J. 54–5
Brindle, David 92
Bristol Evening Post 74, 122
Brittain, Victoria 23
British American Tobacco 69
British Guild of Travel Writers 42
British HIV Association 94
British Medical Association 5
British National Party 75
British Social Attitudes 3
Broadcasting Act (1990) 7, 8, 9, 18; (1996) 9, 18, 129
Broadcasting Complaints Commission 18
Broadcasting Cultural Diversity Network 81
broadcasting on the Web 1; producers 1; uniformity 6, 9
Broadcasting Standards Commission (BSC) 18, 19, 37, 53, 55, 66, 74
Broadcasting Standards Council 18
Bromley, Michael 5, 24, 64, 131
Brown, Allison 41
Brown, Gordon 28

Brown, James 10
Brown, Nick 95
Browne, Christopher 52
Browne, John 50
Buckinghamshire Advertiser 142
Buerk, Michael 102
bugging 51
Buitenen, Paul Van 31
Burgh, Hugo de 67–8
Burke, P 48
Burrowes, Tim 128
Bush, President George 3, 79, 102
'buy-outs' *see* journalism, chequebook

Calcutt, David 16, 51; Calcutt Committee of Inquiry into Privacy and Related Matters 50
Cambridge Evening News 62
Cameron, James 133, 134
Campaign against Racism and Fascism 82
Campaign for Nuclear Disarmament 120
Campaign for Press and Broadcasting Freedom 23, 24
Campbell, Alastair 5, 100, 108, 129
Campbell, Nicky 43
Camus, Albert 133
Canal-Plus 9
Carlton 8, 65, 66, 70, 139
Carter, Meg 89
Castaway 7
Castro, President Fidel 66
CBS 3, 32
censorship 14, 22, 45, 99, 102; self-censorship 114
Chadwick, Ruth 3
Channel 4, 30, 65, 66, 67, 70, 74, 76, 81, 112, 120; *News* 49, 76, 85, 96, 100, 101, 105
Channel 5 76
Chapman, Patsy 88
Checkpoint 56
Chicago Sun-Times 58
children 18 *see* reporting
Children Act 36
Children and Young Persons Act 36, 111
Children of Fire 133
Chippendale, Peter 11
Chips Quinn 81, 144
Choice FM 82
Chomsky, Noam 107, 138
Christian Aid 23
Christmas, Linda 85, 86, 87
Chronicle 73, 81

Central News 19
CIA 118, 139
Citizen, Gloucester 128
City Slickers 42
City University 49, 81, 82, 86
Cinven 11
civic/public journalism 130
Clarke, Liam 117
Classic FM 9
Clifford, Max 5, 39
Clinton, President 48, 68, 95
CNN 37, 100, 102
Cobbett, William 133
Cockburn, Alexander 102
Cockerell, Michael 31, 130
codes of conduct/practice 13, 131; and
    professionalisation 13; as rhetorical
    devices 13; NUJ 14, 15, 42, Broadcasting
    Standards Commission 18, 55; ITC 19,
    55, 141 *see* PCC
Cohen, Nick 4, 34, 62, 114
Cold War 3, 47, 48, 108, 119
Cole, John 64
Collins, John M. 108
Columbia Journalism Review 106, 147
columnists 4
Combs, James 108–9
comment pieces 4
Commission on the Freedom of the Press
    (1947) 131
Committee to Protect Journalists 110, 147
competition 2, 10, 48
Condé Nast 84
Condé Nast Traveller 41
confidentiality 14, 16, 22, 29–31
conflict of interests 14
Connection, The 6, 65
Conroy, Andy 135, 136
consensus 10
Conservative Party 8, 68
constraints on journalists 2, 110–23
Consumers' Association 11
Contempt of Court Act 1981 29, 30, 40, 46,
    111
Cook, Roger 56; *Cook Report* 69, 70, 139
Cooke, Sidney 38
Cottle, Simon 74, 80
Countdown 66
Counterpunch 69
Countryside Undercover 68
Covert Action Quarterly 69, 122
Coward, Ros 87, 89
Coxall, Bill 132

Creative Collective 81, 144
Crick, Michael 113
Criminal Evidence and Youth Justice Act
    36
Criminal Justice Act 36
Criminal Procedures and Investigations Act
    111
Crooks, Tim 55
Cummings, Bruce 98
Curran, James 10, 17, 34, 112, 114
Curtis, Liz 84
Cutting Edge 66, 68

Dacre, Paul 80
Daily Express 15, 31, 41, 85, 102
Daily Herald 34
Daily Mail 29, 41, 60, 71, 72, 80, 137
Daily Record 96, 137
Daily Sketch 29, 34
Daily Sport 9
Daily Star 40, 61, 91
Daily Telegraph 41, 72, 99, 100, 101, 126
Dallaglio, Lawrence 57
DarkerthanBlue.com 82
Davies, Anne Marie 40
Davies, Ron 95
Day, Sir Robin 43
'deathknocks' 59–60
defamation 20, 45, 111
Defence Advisory Notices (D Notices) 116
Delano, Anthony 72–3
democracy 4
Demon Internet 45
demonisation 5
Department of International Development
    77
depoliticisation 5
Derby Trader 34
Der Speigel 122
deskilling 5
Devenport, Mark 6
Diana, Princess of Wales 5, 16, 47, 49, 50,
    51, 52, 53, 91, 94
Dimbleby, David 43
Dimbleby, Jonathan 19, 75
discrimination, avoiding 14, 17
Dispatches 74, 112
Diss Express 85
Donovan, Paul 72
doorstepping 18, 38–9
Dorril, Stephen 31, 118, 119, 122
Dougary, Ginny 85
Dover Express 72

Driving School 65
Drudge, Matt 48, 68
Duchess of York ('Fergie') 51
'dumbing down' 3, 61–70, 75–8, 139
'dumbing up' 61–70
Dunblane massacre 60, 140
Dunnett, Sinclair 129
Dyke, Greg 73

Eades, Chris 111
Eapen, Matthew 41
Early Evening News 19
Eastern Daily Press 30
Eastern Eye 82
Economist 31
editorial independence 20
editors 14, 24
Ellis, Carolyne 96
Ellison, Chris 22
email 12, 44, 46, 112
EMAP 11
Engineer 29
English, Pat 85
environmental activists 5
Epworth, Jennifer 40
Esther 66
European Commission 31
European Commision of Human Rights 30
European Convention on Human Rights 54, 120, 127
European Court of Human Rights 30, 120
Evans, Harold 69
Evening Chronicle, Newcastle 121, 128
Evening Echo 121
Evening Standard, London 98, 111
Evening News, Norwich 121
Express see Daily Express
Express Newspaper Group 61

Face the Facts 68
fairness 14, 20, 130
fakes 6
Falk, Bernard 29
Falklands conflict 43, 139
Fallows, James 4
family values 7, 48
Farming Today 68
Fawcett Society 85, 86
features 4, 6
feminists 5, 11
FHM 9, 17
Fight Racism Fight Imperialism 82
File on Four 68

Financial Times 18, 64
Fisk, Robert 78, 99, 102, 106
'fly-on-the-wall' documentaries 7
Fitzgerald, Patrick 118
Fleet Street 9, 10, 11, 48, 79, 85, 87, 102
Fletcher, Robin 64
Follett, Ken 32
Foley, Michael 136
Food Programme, The 68
Foot, Paul 10, 68, 133
Foster, Reginald 29
fourth estate *see* media
Fourth Estate (publishing company) 2, 113
Fowler, Neil 17
Fox, Robert 101
Fox, Samantha 88
Fox Television 68
Frankland, Mark 118
Franklin, Bob 3, 5, 9, 33, 85
Franzen, Peter 30
Free Press 23
freebies (or junkets when they involve travel) 41–2
Freedom Forum 81, 144
freedom of expression 14, 120
Freedom of Information Act (US) 111–12
freedom of the press 2, 114, 122, 126–7
freelancing/freelances 1, 22
Freelick, Bill 107
freesheets 9; free magazines 11
Frost, Chris 15, 33, 35, 132

Gaddafi, Colonel 69, 78, 119
Gale, Roger 37
Galtung, Johan 33
Galvin, Adrian 30
Gannett Foundation 98
Garavelli, Dani 30
Gatton, Adrian 88
Gay, Doug 113
Gelhorn, Martha 133
General Council of the Press 15
Geraghty, Tony 117
Gilbey, James
Gill A.A. 86
Glasgow University Media Group 34, 43, 65, 77, 134
Glitter, Gary 41
globalisation 1, 2, 5, 11
Gloucester Citizen 142
Glover, Stephen 4
GMTV 73
Godfrey, Lawrence 45

Goodman, Clive 53
Goodwin, Bill 29, 30
Goodwin, Jo-Ann 111
Gopsill, Tim 15, 18
gossip 4
Gott, Richard 119
Gowing, Nik 106, 107
GQ 10
Graef, Roger 7, 36, 67
Gramsci, Antonio 135
Granada 8, 65
Green, Daniel 68
Green, Michael 6
Greenslade, Roy 10, 53, 54, 79, 95, 114,
    118, 134
Grevisse, Benoit 14
Grierson, John 67
gross indecency 45
Gross, Larry 95
Grubb, Jon 63, 142–5
Guardian, the 4, 10, 15, 18, 22, 24, 27, 28,
    29, 31, 38, 41, 44, 52, 53, 54, 62, 64, 65,
    68, 69, 73, 74, 75, 81, 92, 96, 101, 106,
    116, 118, 119, 120, 127
Guerin, Veronica 110, 141
Guild of British Editors 52, 111
Gulf War 5, 99, 102, 106, 138, 139
Guns on the Street 66

Hague, William 72
Haines, Joe 31
Hall, Douglas 57
Hall, Phil 3, 41
Hall, Stuart 79
Hall, Tony 62
Hallin, Daniel 98, 133
'hard' news 6
harassment 16, 17, 50
Hamilton, Ben 30
Hamilton, Neil 49, 68
Hamilton, Thomas 60
Hanna, Mark 40
Hannaford, Alex 121
Hardwicke, Earl of 57
Hardy, Rebecca 85
HarperCollins 113
Harris, Nigel 14
Harris, Robert 32
Harrison, Bridget 77
Hartlepool Mail 115
Hastings, Max 98, 99
Health Education Authority 91, 94
Heller, Zoë 4

Hellinger, Daniel 136
Hencke, David 27
Hennessy, Peter 31
Henningham, John 72–3
Henley Centre for Forecasting 6
Here and Now 68
Hersh, Seymour 102, 118, 133
Higgins, Stuart 16
High Court 121
Hizbollah 78
Hilsum, Lindsey 86
Hilton, Tessa 4
Hockenberry, John 93
Hodgson, Jessica 100
Hodgson, Patricia 19
Hogan, Dan 46, 49
Holderness, Mike 147
Holland, Patricia 88
Hollick, Lord 8
Hollingsworth, Mark 71
Hollywood 2, 3, 7, 78
Holmes, Alex 57
Horrie, Chris 11
Howe, Lady Elspeth 18
HTML 1
HTV 8
Huddersfield Daily Examiner 128
Huddersfield FM 21
Hudson, Miles 99, 102
'human interest' 4, 48
Humphrys, John 6, 42, 43, 64, 85, 100
Huntingdon, Samuel P. 78
Hussein, Saddam 3, 79, 99
Hutchins, Robert M. 131
Hutton, Will 62, 78
Hyman, Judge Michael 30

IBA 19, 21
impartiality 20
Independent The, 15, 23, 29, 31, 62, 78, 84,
    106, 115, 120, 122, 125
Independent on Sunday 47, 85, 99, 127
Independent Traveller 41
Index on Censorship 121
Information Research Department of the
    Foreign Office 119
information revolution 4
information overload 12
Ingham, Bernard 31
INLA 8
Insider, The 3
Institute of Journalists 15
Intelligence Services Act 116

International Broadcasting Trust 23, 76
International Consortium of Investigative
    Journalists 68
International Federation of Journalists 22,
    123
International Press Institute 52, 101
Internet 5, 7, 11–12, 43–4, 48, 63, 69, 78,
    127; discussion groups 44–5
Internet Freedom 22
Internet Watch Foundation (IWF) 22
interviewing 20, 50; ambush 38; off-the-
    record 26, 27; on-the-record 26, 27; over-
    confrontational 6, 42–3;
    unattributed/background 26, 27, 28
Investigators, The 70
IPC 11
IRA 8, 75, 117; Provisional 29
Iraq 10
Irvine, Lord 15, 40, 53
ITC (Independent Television Commission)
    19, 65, 70, 130 *see* codes
ITN 6, 19, 43, 55, 98, 102, 133
ITV 8, 65, 76, 85, 114

Jack, Ian 3
Jaehnig, Walter 131
James, Oliver 38
Jennings, Humphrey 67
Jerry Springer 66
Jewish Chronicle 82
John, Sir Elton 31
Johnson, Andrew 111
Johnson, Samuel 61
Jones, Bronwen 133
Jones, Nicholas 22
Jones, Sylvia 34
Joulson, Mr Justice 54
journalism, chequebook 4, 16, 17, 28,
    39–41; show business 4; scoop 10
Journal, Newcastle 30
Journalist, The 24
journalists 6: rights 1; conformism 6; culture
    1; deprofessionalisation 12; fear 2, 6;
    financial 14; salaries 11; stresses 5;
    political 14; working practices 2;
    professionalism 35, 44, 71, 126, 129, 131,
    132; myth of professionalism 133–4;
    autonomy 35; sharing contacts and quotes
    39; social responsibility 130–1; training 2,
    131–2
Journalists Against Nuclear Extermination
    (JANE) 101
Judd, Dennis 136

Kabani, Rana 79
Kapur, Updesh 127
Karpf, Anne 1
Katz, Jon 44
Kaufman, Gerald 40
Keane, Fergal 82
Keeble, R 48, 79
Keeler, Christine 61
Keighley News 121
Kellner, Douglas 78, 135
Keneally, Thomas 77–8
Kennedy, President 48
Kent News and Pictures 111
KGB 119
Kidd, Jodie 5
Kieran, Matthew 49, 67, 129
Kiley, Robert 45
Killick, Mark 9
Kilroy 66
King, Elliott 44
Klaidman, Stephen 126, 127
Knight, Sarah 34
Knightley, Phillip 42, 69, 97, 102, 105, 118,
    137–9
Kournikova, Anna 88, 89
Kurtz, Howard 57

Labour Party 53, 54
Laden Osama bin 78
laddish culture 9
Laitila, T, 14
Lancashire Evening Post 128
Lange, David 54
Lashmar, Paul 30
Latimer, Mark 105
Law, Asylum and Media Group 83
Law Lords 121
Lawrence, Stephen 80
Late Night Live 66
Lee-Potter, Lynda 89
Leicester Mercury 81
Leigh, David 31, 43, 52, 117, 118
lesbians 5
letters to the editor 24
Levidow, Les 104
Levy, Lord 54, 57
Lewinsky, Monica 48, 49, 68
Lewis, Denise 88
Lewis, Martyn 63–4, 65, 75
libel 23, 45, 54–5, 111
Liebes, Tamar 6
Linklater, Magnus 137
LM 55, 138

LWT 73
Loaded 9
lobby (parliamentary) 31–2
Lobster 122
Local Government Act 96
Lodge, David 7
London College of Printing 26, 55
Longford, Lord 87
Luff, Peter 10
Luyken, Reiner 114

MacArthur, Brian 37
Macaulay, Thomas Babington 127, 135
Macey, Paul 74
MacIntyre. Donal 56–7, 69
Mackay, Lord 51
MacKenzie, Kelvin 4, 24, 88
Macpherson report 80
Mahmood, Mazher 57
Mail on Sunday 35, 102, 122
Majendie, Paul 101
Major, John 3, 41, 47, 48, 51, 52, 106, 111
Malcolm, Janet 36
Manchester Evening News 128
Mandelson, Peter 68
Mann, Michael 3
Margaret, Princess 15
Marr, Andrew 4
Massiter, Cathy 120
Mawhinney, Brian 8
Maxwell, Robert 47, 113, 114, 118
Mayes, Ian 23, 44
Mayes, Tessa 69–70, 139–42
McCue, Andy 72
McDonald, Trevor 43
MacDowall, Ian 79
McEwan, Ian 4
McGowan, Eve 21
McGregor, Lord 18, 50
McGregor, Sue 85
McLaughlan, Lucille 41
McNair, Brian 9, 43, 48, 63, 113. 127, 129, 132
McQuail, Denis 129, 131
media: monopoly ownership 2, 8, 18, 136; culture of abuse 4; management 1, 5, 6; as fourth estate 43, 48, 126, 127–9, 135, 137; as propaganda 135; as public service 136
Media Education 23
Media Workers Against War in the Gulf 101
Med-TV 19

Melin-Higgins, Margareta 84
Mellor, David 51
Merchant, Piers 49
Mental Health Foundation 90–1
Mercer, Derrik 128–9
Meridian 8
Merrill, John C 125
Metzler, Ken 78
Methven, Nicola 105
Meyer, Philip 58
MI5 23, 115, 116, 117, 118, 119, 120, 122, 134
MI6 (SIS) 115, 118, 119
militarism 2. 8, 10
Milne, Seamus 69, 118
Mirror (Daily) 15, 34, 41, 46, 51, 61, 66, 69, 78, 79, 84, 85, 89, 99, 118
Molloy, Mike 34
Moloney, Ed 30
Montgomery, Helen 62
Moore, Charles 126
Moore, Mike 78
Moore, Pat 85
moral panic 3–12
Morgan, Peter 11
Morgan, Piers 42, 52, 84
Morning Star/Daily Worker 33, 138
Morris, Bill 82
Morris, Chris 70
Morton, Andrew 50
Moss, Kate 5
Mossad 52, 118, 119
Mother Jones 122
multi-skilling 1, 5, 12
Mulholland, Brendan 29
Murdoch, Rupert 10, 11, 52, 61, 68, 87, 95, 113, 114, 122
Muslim News 82
Murphy, David 33
My Lai 103
Myler, Colin 51

National Assembly Against Racism 74
National Association of Norwegian Newspapers 23
National Front 75
National Heritage Committee 40
National Union of Journalists (NUJ) 8, 16, 18, 30, 72, 73, 82, 86, 92, 93, 94, 123; guidelines on covering race, disability 22, 75, 80; Equality Style Guide 90; *see also* codes
National Union of Mineworkers 69

National Viewers and Listeners Association 7

Nato 139

Naughtie, James 85

Naughton, John 45, 112

Network First 65

Newman, Jay 33

New Nation 82

News at Ten 6, 19, 105

New Statesman 100

News International Corporation 11

New Left Review 82, 138

News of the World 3, 4, 38, 39, 40, 41, 52, 53, 57, 61, 85, 88, 95

News on Sunday 11, 120

newspapers: free press concept 132; watchdog role 2; circulations 2; proprietors 2; monopoly ownership 10, 11

Newspaper Proprietors' Association 99

Newspaper Publishers' Association 16

Newsweek 139

'new world order' 3, 77, 79

New York Times 54, 119

Nicholson, Mike 133

Nixon, President Richard 128

nme.com 12

Nolan, Lord 52

Nordenstreng, Kaarle 13

Norris, Bob 125

Northampton Chronicle and Echo 64

Northcliffe, Lord 113

Northern Ireland 30, 43

Northmore, David 69

Norton-Taylor, Richard 117, 118

Norwegian Editors' Association 23

Nottingham Evening Post 63, 81, 147; campaign on freedom of information 120–1, 142–3

Nottingham Trent University 67, 69

Oborne, Peter 5, 32

obscenity 111

objectivity 129, 132,

Observer, The 11, 15, 28, 35, 45, 51, 56, 62, 71, 114, 119, 120, 122, 125, 127

Office of Telecommunications 18

Official Secrets Acts 31, 116, 117

O'Malley, Tom 5

O'Neill, John 126

O'Reilly, Emily 110

Organisation for Economic Co-operation and Development 35

Orwell, George 119, 133

O'Sullivan, Sally 10

Outcast 45

Oxfam 23

Oxford Mail 128

Page, Adrian 95

Page 3 girl 61, 87–8

Palast, Gregory 56, 76

PA News 121

Panorama 37, 49, 53, 70, 108, 139

paparazzi 16, 17

Parris, Matthew 66, 95

Parry, Deborah 40–1

Paul, Nora 44

Paxman, Jeremy 6, 42, 64

payment for information *see* journalism, chequebook

peace campaigners/movement 5, 11

peace journalism 138

Peace News 82

Pell, Benjamin 28

People, The 51, 87

Persaud, Dr Raj 7

Peterson, Theodore 135

Petley, Julian 17

Philby, Kim 119

Phillips, Trevor 73, 80

Philo, Greg 43

photojournalism 16, 17

Pierce, Andrew 32

Pilger, John 19, 24, 25, 27, 68, 70, 78, 100, 102, 114, 118, 119, 130, 133, 134, 135

Pines, Jim 73

Pinker, Professor Robert 51, 52

Pirie, Jacqueline 53–4

PKK (Kurdish Workers Party) 19, 106

plagiarism 44

Platell, Amanda 84, 85

Platt, Steve 72, 102

Playboy 12, 88

pluralism 131

police 39

Police and Criminal Evidence (PACE) Act 1984 29, 30, 122, 123

'political correctness' (PC) 1–2, 71, 79, 92

Pollard, Eve 89

Ponting, Clive 115

pools 39

pornography/porn 7, 11–12; child 22, 41

Postman, Neil 3

Poynter Institute 37, 147

PR (Public Relations) 10, 34, 35

'precision journalism' 45

Presley, Elvis 9
Press Complaints Commission (PCC) 13, 16, 17, 19, 37, 40, 41, 42, 50, 51, 52, 53, 55, 58, 59, 91, 95
press conferences 39
Press Council (UK) 15, 16, 17, 50
Press Gazette 25, 67, 70, 115, 116, 147
PressWise 23, 39, 82–3, 125
Preston, Peter 52
Prevention of Terrorism Act 30, 112
Prince, Stephen 78
Prior, Joanna 2
Prison Officers' Association 145
privacy 17, 18, 20, 53; invasions of 4, 7, 16; law 4, 10, 16, 46, 49–55; rights to 14, 54
Private Eye 38
Project Censored 122
Protection from Harassment Act 70, 111
pseudo events 5
Public Interest Disclosure Act 31
public opinion 3; polls 10
Public Records Act 111
public service broadcasting 7
punditocracy 4
Pulvertaft, Rear Admiral David 116

Q News 82

racism/anti-racism 2, 8, 10, 22, 71–83, 143–4, 146
Radio 5 66
Radio Authority 21
Radio Clyde 9
Radio Joint Audience Research Unit 6
Rahn, Stephanie 87
Rambo 78
Ramsay, Robin 31
Randall, David 125
ratings 7
Reading Chronicle 55
Reagan, President 69, 78
'reality TV' 7
reconstructions 67
Reddick, Randy 44, 147
Rees, Maureen 65
Reeves, Ian 46
Regulation of Investigatory Powers Act 45–6, 112
religion 3, 14
Reno, Janet 95
Reporters Without Borders 110
reporting 1; investigative 6, 10, 39, 55–8, 67–70; of children 11, 20, 36–8, 50;

children in sex cases 16; of crime 20; of current affairs 3; disabled people 22, 92–3; of disasters 6, 18; election campaigns 21; of financial affairs 16; foreign affairs 5; gays 5, 95–6; of health 5; mental health issues 90–2; parliament 22 personalities 3; of politics 4, 20; refugees 71; rich 35; royals 15, 17, 49; sex 18, 21, 61–3; stories involving grief or shock 16, 17; of victims of sexual assault 16, violence 21; wars 97–109, 137–8; working class 34; paedophiles 144–5
Reuters 79, 94, 101
reviewing 1
Richstad, Jim 12
Ricki Lake 66
Riddick, Graham 52
right/opportunity to reply 16, 17
Robertson, Geoffrey 17, 21
Robertson, Lord 42
Robins, Kevin 102
Robins, Lynton 132
Rogers, Ann 117
Rousseau, Jean-Jacques 127
Rowe, Bridget 85, 87
Rowe, David 88
Rowland, Tiny 113, 114
Royal Commissions 15, 17, 49
Royal Ulster Constabulary 30
Ruge, Mari 33
Runnymede Trust 74; *Runnymede Bulletin* 82
Rusbridger, Alan 22, 28, 54, 62
Russell, William Howard 97

Sabras Sound 82
Said, Edward 79
St. Stephen's Aids Trust 94
Sanders, Lesley 55
Santos, John Phillip 72
Saunders, Frances Stonor 119
Save the Children 23
Sawyer, Forrest 101
Scargill, Arthur 69
Schlesinger, Philip 33
Schorr, Daniel 106
Schramm, Wilbur 135
Scotsman 31, 85
Scottish Daily Record 89
Scruton, Roger 7
Secret History 68
security, national 20, 47
Security Service Acts 115, 116
sensationalism 3, 49

Seagram 9
Seaton, Jean 34, 112
Sebba, Anne 84
Secret Intelligence Service (SIS) *see* MI6
secret state 115–20
'sentimentalisation' 4
Serbia 3, 10
Sereny, Gitta 41
sex 4, 5, 10
sexism/anti-sexism 2, 8, 10, 22, 84–90
Sharma, Vijay 82
Sharp, Peter 102
Shayler, David 119
Sheldon, Ed 116
Shepherd, Freddie 57
Shevington Courier 64
Short, Clare 75, 87, 100
Siebert, Fred 135
Sieghart, Mary Ann 88–9
Simpson, John 64, 100, 102, 118
Sinn Fein 8
Sissons, Peter 64
Sky TV 102; News 140
sleaze 4, 47–9
Small World 133
Smith, Martin 72
Smith, Tim 49
Snow, Jon 76
Social Affairs Unit 10
Socialist Worker 72, 82, 122, 138
'soft' news 6
Soley, Clive 18
sources, primary and secondary 32–3;
    Internet 43–6; elite 142
Souter, Brian 96
South Wales Echo 128
Spark, David 56, 57
Spark, Ron 99
Sparks, Colin 2, 9
Spectrum International 82
speculation 4
Spencer, Countess 52; Earl 52, 54
spin doctors 4, 10, 25
Spinner.com 21
sport 5
Stainer, John 99, 102
Standish Courier 64
Stannard, Stephen 24
State Research 122
Steele-Perkins, Chris 133
Stephen, Jaci 87
Stephenson, Professor Hugh 49, 61
stereotyping 22

Stewart, Allan 49
Steyn, Mark 4
'stings' 55
Stoke Sentinel 59
Stolen Goods 66
Stone, I.F. 27
Stone, Jennie 76
Straw, Jack 70, 85, 112
Street Legal 68
Stuff 9
style book 26, 90
subterfuge 18, 55–8
Sullivan, David 9
Sunday Sport 9
Sunrise Radio 82
suppression of information 14
surveillance 51
sub editing 1
Sun, the 4, 16, 17, 24, 51, 60, 61, 71, 72, 88,
    89, 95, 96, 99, 114, 137
Sunday Express 38, 85
Sunday Graphic 34
Sunday Mirror 4, 35, 51, 85
Sunday People 47
Sunday Sport 50
Sunday Telegraph 2, 57, 62, 102
Sunday Times 10, 30, 41, 50, 52, 54, 57, 69,
    86, 94, 117, 120, 137
Sunday Tribune 30
Supreme Court, US 45, 54
Swain, Gill 130
Sweeney, Jon 127

tabloids 3, 4
'tabloidisation' 3
Talk Radio 9
talk shows 7
TalkSport 4
taste 18, 20
Tatchell, Peter 95
Taylor, John 60, 77, 105
Teenage Magazine Advisory Panel (TMAP)
    21
Telecommunications Act 1984 45
television 4; deregulation 7;
    'reconstructions' 7; soaps 2
Thatcher, Margaret 8, 16, 31, 32, 43, 50,
    114, 120
TheSmokingGun 68
Thomas, Gordon 52, 119
Thomas, Mark 70
Thomson, Alex 100, 101
Thornton, Anthony 12

Thorpe, Jeremy 40
Thurlow, Richard 115
Tiffen, Rodney 27
Tisdall, Sarah 116
Times, The 10, 28, 37, 41, 85, 93, 95, 97, 108, 113, 119, 125
Time Warner-AOL 9
Tisdall, Sarah 29
Today 102
Today Programme 68, 85, 100
Tomalin, Nick 138
Tompkins, Al 37
Tonight with Trevor McDonald 19
Total Sport 88
Toynbee, Polly 71
Tracey, Professor Michael 7
Trade Union Reform and Employment Rights Act 111
Travis, Alan 11
Tredinnick, David 52
trivia 3
Truman Show, The 7
truth 3, 14
Tulloch, John 72
Tusa, John 8

UCAS 74
UDA 8
United News and Media 8
unions, derecognition of 6
Urban, Mark 116

Vallely, Paul 115
Vanessa Show 66, 67
Vidal, John 75
Video Recordings Act 70
Vietnam 97–8, 105, 108
Village Voice 68
violence 18
Virgin Aitlines 41
Virgin Radio 9
Vivendi 9
VNU 11
Voice 74
Voluntary Service Overseas 23
Voisey, Karen 121
voyeurism 7
Vulliamy, Ed 43, 52

Wade, Rebekah 38, 85
Wakeham, Lord 16, 18, 52, 53, 58
Walden, Brian 43

Walker, David 31
Walker, Johnnie 57
Walsey, Andrew 133
Warner, Jeremy 29
Warwick, Hugh 132
Washington Post 58, 81, 110, 128
Watchdog 55
Watergate 128
Wazir, Burhan 56
Web *see* Internet
Wells, Matt 73
Welsh, Tom 37
West, Rosemary 40
Western Mail 17, 85
Westminster, University of 72, 82
Which? 11
whistleblowers 31
White, Peter 92
Whitehouse, Mary 7
Who Wants to Marry a Millionaire? 68
Wigan Courier 64
Wilby, Peter 135, 136
Wilkinson, Rear Admiral Nick 117
William, Prince 17, 47
Williams, Hywel 48
Williams, Kevin 9, 98
Williams, Michael 100
Willis, John 111
Wilson, Giles 45
Wilson, Harold 31, 118
Wilson, John 29, 42, 79–80, 129
Winston, Brian 126
Witness 68
Witt, Katarina 88
Wittstock, Melinda 68
Woffinden, Bob 121
women, representations of 5
Women in Journalism 85, 86
women's magazines 10
Women's Sport Foundation 88
Worsthorne, Peregrine 62, 102
Woodward, Bob 126
Woodward, Louise 41
Woollacott, Martin 106
World Association for Christian Communication 23
World Bank 76
World in Action 55, 56
World this Weekend 68
Wright, Peter 120
Wrout, Penny 145–6
WWF 23
Wylde, Col. Nigel 117

Yahoo! 12, 43
Yelland, David 17
Yentob, Alan 66–7
Yorke, Ivor 132
Yorkshire Ripper 40
Yorkshire Television 19
Younge, Gary 74
Younger Committee on Privacy 50

Youth Justice and Criminal Evidence Act
111

Zadeh, Somaye 73
Zec, Donald 99
ZMag 69, 122
Zobel, Gibby 112